Praise for *The Groom Will Keep His Name*

"Matt Ortile's ardent and precocious collection sets the page aflame with its explosive mixture of passion and politics, cultural analysis and self-examination. Cruising through virtual and nocturnal circuits, Ortile riffs like a guitar savant on what it means to be a young wanderer in the city today, with astute carnality and endearing candor. *The Groom Will Keep His Name* is a daring brown and queer manifesto that proclaims to everyone making our way in the world: never bow to the false gods of whiteness and normalcy."

 —Meredith Talusan, author of *Fairest*

"Matt Ortile writes with precision and power, and his work overflows with probing insight both inward and outward facing. Ortile's essays deftly navigate the complicated intersection of race, sex, history, family, and self. Propelled by bracing candor and impeccable skill, *The Groom Will Keep His Name* rushes straight to the reader's eyeballs, demanding to be read."

 —Josh Gondelman, author of *Nice Try*

"Matt Ortile writes this book as a kind of open invitation to readers, exploring themes of family (chosen and otherwise), relationships, race and identity with refreshing wit and vulnerability. Some of his essays might remind you of favorite conversations you've had with your sharpest, smartest friends—if you're very lucky, that is, and happen to have friends as thoughtful and brilliant as he is. Wry, funny, and poignant by turns, *The Groom Will Keep His Name* is an honest and moving account of a young immigrant's evolving understanding of himself, as well as the two countries he's called home."

 —Nicole Chung, author of *All You Can Ever Know*

THE GROOM WILL KEEP HIS NAME

And Other Vows I've Made About Race, Resistance, and Romance

MATT ORTILE

BOLD TYPE BOOKS

New York

Bold Type Books
116 East 16th Street, 8th Floor, New York, NY 10003
www.boldtypebooks.org
@BoldTypeBooks

Printed in the United States of America

First Edition: June 2020

Published by Bold Type Books, an imprint of Perseus Books, LLC, a subsidiary of Hachette Book Group, Inc. Bold Type Books is a copublishing venture of Type Media Center and Perseus Books.

The Hachette Speakers Bureau provides a wide range of authors for speaking events. To find out more, go to www.hachettespeakersbureau.com or call (866) 376-6591.

The publisher is not responsible for websites (or their content) that are not owned by the publisher.

Print book interior design by Trish Wilkinson.

Library of Congress Control Number: 2019057071

ISBNs: 978-1-5417-6279-4 (paperback); 978-1-5417-6280-0 (ebook)

LSC-C

10 9 8 7 6 5 4 3 2 1

For my mother

thank u, next

—ARIANA GRANDE

CONTENTS

The groom will keep his name.

BARONG TAGALOG

AT FILIPINO WEDDINGS, the grooms wear white. The classical attire for men is an undyed shirt, with sleeves up to the wrists and fine embroidery down the front. It's called a barong Tagalog, literally "Tagalog clothing." Most versions are cut from piña, a sheer fabric woven from pineapple leaves; silk but make it tropical. Of course, the barong is not a groom's only option. For five centuries, since our country was first colonized by empires, men in the Philippines have also worn the suit and tie—or, in the current Philippine parlance, the Americana.

Over the years, I've amassed a collection of suits in different colors, fabrics, and patterns. A suit can work anywhere, anyhow: with a turtleneck at the office, with sneakers at a bar, with a bow tie at a wedding. It's also something of a sartorial feint. A crisp blazer signals to colleagues that, yes, I can absolutely lead this meeting, even hungover. A fresh suit gives my dates the impression I do have my life together, even though I could only afford an appetizer at dinner. Suits exude power. I wear Americana as armor.

So to take off a suit feels especially intimate. Whether in my bedroom or the bedrooms of other men, disrobing leaves me vulnerable, my body exposed without the eye-guiding seams of a well-tailored garment. But, just like armor, a suit's component parts remain useful as separates. I once made good use of a tie and Theo's bedposts, while Gareth knew exactly what to do with a leather belt. Equally romantic are the rituals of the thing. Stephen liked to fix my pocket squares, and Adam would take my jacket, drape it over my shoulders like a cape. He admired it, he once told me, my confidence when I wore a suit, how it made me untouchable.

Barong Tagalogs, in contrast, are translucent. Piña fabric is chiffony, like organza; all the better to catch a cool breeze in the Philippines' humid climate in Southeast Asia. The garment evolved from precolonial clothing, as illustrated in the Manila Manuscript, a codex that dates to about 1590. It describes how local ethnic groups appeared to their Spanish colonizers. The manuscript says social status among natives was color-coded. For example, blue was the color of the nobility, while red was reserved for royalty.

I first saw these illustrations in a Wikipedia spiral about Filipino history. I'd just finished college and moved to New York, feeling untethered, particularly from my homeland. So I was ecstatic to learn about the manuscript, to see how vivid the ink and paint were still, even half a millennium later, digitized in a library archive. Here were my ancestors, catalogued like animals, but gallant nonetheless, draped in their silks and wielding their swords. How proud they looked, armed with jewelry and dripping in gold, opulent.

That was stolen from us. The Spaniards turned our various tribes, rajahnates, and kingdoms into a single colony, an appendix to their far-reaching empire. They brought their weapons, their own customs and class systems, and enforced them for over three hundred years. Unverified legends say that, under Spanish rule, men below the ruling class were forbidden from tucking their shirts into their trousers or wearing anything with pockets. This edict prevented Filipinos from stealing goods or cloaking weapons. Their Filipino clothing affirmed their status as subjects without agency.

There's no proof of such an imperial decree. Historians have not found any law in colonial Philippines that forbade men from tucking, as it were. And contemporary photographs exist of tucked Filipino men. José Rizal, a writer and our national hero, is often pictured with his shirt in his trousers, wearing European clothing—including suit and tie. This Western dress came to be known as Americana when, after war with Spain, the United States took possession of the Philippines, where white men in power wore their suits and coats, roasting themselves in the equatorial sun.

But then again, lived experiences of discrimination don't always find proof in official documents or laws, often scrubbed or never recorded. Whatever the truth, I like the reports of how Filipinos responded, allegedly decorating their barongs with bright colors—noble blue and royal red—an homage to precolonial ancestors to protest the Spanish social order. I've come to love this idea, redeeming Filipino clothing, the barong Tagalog as resistance.

The barong gained its status as the national costume after Philippine independence from the Americans at the end of World War II. In the 1950s, President Ramon Magsaysay wore a barong at all official and personal events, reframing the garment as a badge of honor. It has evolved with the times and the people: long-sleeved silhouettes as formal dress, short-sleeved versions as office wear. After centuries of dressing for others, my country reclaimed the barong Tagalog as a symbol of our developing identity outside the long shadows of empire.

I never wear it though. Occasions for Filipino formal wear are rare in my life in New York. Even in the Philippines, I'm more inclined to don a suit in a heat-friendly linen. I prefer the sharp creases of a tailored pant, the sleek shape of a suit jacket. The lines of a suit are in complete opposition to the classic barong Tagalog: where a blazer is tapered, the barong is loose; where a waistcoat is trim, the barong is long; where a suit is impenetrable, the barong is permeable. Since it's see-through, you must wear an undershirt, which, to me, defeats the one exciting thing about the whole outfit. It's just as well though, as piña fabric can be rough and scratchy.

The first time I wore a barong Tagalog, I was age three going on four, attending my uncle's wedding. My barong was itchy, so I ran and cried to my mother. She put me in a chair next to her, at a faraway table, reserved for those who were considered exiles at this court. She wore a tan silk dress and pearls that day. I remember because there's a picture of us, one of my favorites, one of the few I have left from the Philippines, before we immigrated to the United States. In it, she's leaning down to press her cheek against mine, so I can throw a tiny arm around her neck. Years later, we'd re-create that photo in Las Vegas, where we'd moved to by then. In both versions, I'm biting my lip, slightly cross-eyed, and my mother is flashing her unshakeable picket fence of teeth.

My stepfather took the re-creation; his shutterbug habits came in handy when we applied for US citizenship. I'm not sure who took the original. It was likely one of my aunts, that cohort of women who knowingly took the Ortile name, who pledged allegiance to sisters first.

After the photo was taken at the wedding, I whined to my mother. I was itchy, sweaty, and upset; why was she sitting so far away from me and my father?

Her smile did not waver as she told me it was all right. My mother took off my barong, wedged a clean dinner napkin into the back of my undershirt, and sent me off to play. I returned to my cousins and we tossed pisos into the koi ponds, making wishes, as the adults danced their usual dances, pivoting around and away from each other. I never told anyone, but when I tossed my coins, I wished for my mother to be happy, to no longer move in these balletic adagios—graceful, though exhausted, feigning composure. I was eleven when she told me we were going to live in the United States, putting an ocean between her and my father. Wishes come true, I believed then, when you want them badly enough.

I keep that original photo of us—my mother in her pearls and me in my barong Tagalog—as a reminder of how far we've come from where we began, for better or for worse. It's always with me, displayed in every bedroom I've ever had. In my early days with Stephen, when I'd just graduated college and moved to Manhattan, he picked up the photograph from my dresser. He noted how beautiful my mother was, that I'd inherited good genes.

He asked where she was. In the Philippines, I told him; she'd moved back to our birth country. As he undid my cufflinks for me, Stephen said, surprised, "Oh, I thought you were born here." This, to me, was a compliment. I said "thank you" with a kiss.

The other reason I never wear a barong Tagalog is that I've been habituated to suppress all signs of where I come from: accent, language, cultural habits. If I appear seamlessly acculturated, it's because I was diligent. I practiced my American accent in the bathroom mirror, rarely spoke Tagalog in public, and insisted on wearing my "outside clothes" at home. I grew up a run-of-the-mill immigrant, believing it gets better in America.

I fit in here, Christian once observed. We were at a table outside, summer in Harlem, before we went back to his place, before he peeled off my linen trousers and kindly placed them on a hanger. At brunch, I sipped rosé with bravado and an unchecked ID in my wallet. Christian brushed his leg against mine and told me, "You make this city seem easy."

I was twenty years old, just shy of a decade into my American life and gratified by his words. That year, I was interning at a magazine with virtually no pay but halfway through my education at an elite college, which wrote me a blank check. I was digging tunnels up to a glossy life, working as hard as I did when I first arrived to make it seem impossible that I was once designated by the US government as a "permanent alien" in this land.

"You need to relax," Adam said to me one night. I was tense, overworked. He was massaging my shoulders in the privacy of his dormitory before leaving me for his boyfriend, yet again. Adam removed my blazer and teased me, "We get it. You're brilliant."

At college, I had two majors, wrote two theses, earned double the honors at graduation. I was part of several student and faculty organizations, writing and dancing and extremely proficient in Google Docs. I applied for and won grants and prizes, decorated myself to the point of absurdity. In all aspects of my life, I did what I could to prove my merit. Take off the tailored suit purchased on credit, and you get an insecure kid who grew up in two countries, was bullied for being different in both, felt less-than for simply being himself.

Immigrating to the US at any age is difficult enough. Immigrating as a twelve-year-old, as I did, meant that middle schoolers, those so eagerly learning to brandish slurs with ease, were the peers I had to face. In Las Vegas, where we landed as new Filipino immigrants, I was target practice for everyone at school. To the white kids, I was a "wetback," and to my fellow students of color, I was a "faggot." Sometimes they called me both; there was one insult that involved me sucking dick, but the dick was a burrito. Though their hate lacked finesse, it was a powerful weapon, and they placed me in the crosshairs.

They were unable to name my Filipinoness. I was often mistaken for Mexican and once as "Arabian." They landed on the more general but accurate Asian only rarely. Since they were correct about my undeniable flamboyance, I had to come out at thirteen. That didn't stymie the bullying, but coming out early meant one less identity crisis for me to handle. I'd figured out I was gay in Manila; classmates at my Catholic all-boys school had figured it out as well, made it clear they knew my secret when they told me I was going to hell for being a sissy. In the Philippines, I'd already known what it meant to be a persecuted queer. In America, it took me a while to learn what it meant to be a Filipino—even longer to be both.

To dodge my middle school tormentors, I ate my lunch—usually rice and a slice of Spam—in classrooms, thanks to teachers who were kind, if confused by me. A guidance counselor placed me in ESL classes, assuming I needed them because of my accent. I transferred to honors English within a few days; at semester's end, I was awarded top marks. Once, in another class, the teacher called on me to recite a passage from a book aloud. So I did, in my fresh-off-the-plane accent, which was only starting to unspool. When I finished, I looked up to see her smiling face, beatific and wrinkled. She asked me when I had moved to the US. A few months ago, I said.

"But your English is so wonderful!" she replied.

In the moment, all I could manage was, "Well, our primary language of instruction in the Philippines is English." I felt my face grow hot. In the tense silence that followed, I excused myself to the bathroom. I stayed through recess, eating my lunch of Spam and rice in a toilet stall, determined to lose my Filipino accent as soon as I possibly could.

Add her to the list of many white adults who glowed at me with similar remarks. The silent implication was, I already knew, "for an immigrant." Because I was raised as a brown kid in America, taught to not cause trouble, I tried to bite my tongue when they patronized me. I didn't tell them that English language education in the Philippines was a vestige of their colonization of my country, after they won our archipelago of over seven thousand islands from Spain at the end of the Spanish-American War, which saw the rise of America's empire, a colonial history that cast the United States as defender of a world order that, in truth, was exploited to further US imperialism.

Here was an early lesson in my education as a young queer and brown immigrant: our talents and abilities are diminished when seen in the context of one or many marginalized identities. When you're in the minority, praise from the majority is too often laden with not-so-complimentary assumptions. It's because of attitudes like this that we have to work twice as hard to get half as far—a feature, not a bug, of centuries-old systems of power.

And I did work hard, certainly. Hard enough to gain admittance into a performing arts high school. As a theater major, being out was in. My graduating class was a veritable Benetton ad, varied in race, class, and sexualities, united in gleeful aspirations to dramatic stardom. Difference and diversity were celebrated here, but still I remained, to them, nominally perplexing. In what would become a recurring theme in my life, everyone had trouble with the name Ortile.

Thanks for asking: it's pronounced Or-TEE-lay. Sounds like how it looks—just like me. But intentionally or not, most people have corrupted my name ever since I could introduce myself. I have my favorite mispronunciations. In the Philippines, there was the accidental Or-tuli, which translates from Tagalog to "or-circumcised," and the nickname my bullies gave me, Or-titi, which translates to "or-penis." I was harassed, pranked and pantsed, passed over for teams in PE class. Only when the day's sport was volleyball was I chosen, and my skills envied; something to do, I think, with the limp wrists.

In the US, white people would chop my name into a shortened Or-til, or go for the obvious phonetics: Or-tile, as if choosing between granite, marble, or tile. A colleague once overcompensated, pronounced it Or-till-yay, and stuck with it. I liked the way it sounded—French, but not really—so I didn't say anything. I usually let these honest mistakes slide, rather than bear the exhaustion that came with correcting them. Though I was freed from the dick-related sobriquets to which my name lent itself in Tagalog, the harmless mispronunciations in the States could be equally embarrassing.

People sometimes made a show of my name's difficulty: "You know what, I'm not even gonna try." Even with those who meant well, their difficulty with my name made me feel guilty. I didn't want to be a burden. Over time, with enough tears and dick jokes and stifled exasperation, my name grew to carry the weight of all that marked me as different: my queerness, my foreignness, the color of my voice and my skin. I wanted liberation from being Other, from being Ortile.

Some years into our life in Las Vegas, my mother divorced my father. She dropped Ortile and reclaimed her maiden name. Then she married my stepfather, who made his usual Pacific crossing for the big day. He was still living in Manila, where he met and fell in love with my mother, where he was caring for what's now my extended family, where he is still a practicing surgeon in pediatrics. He's good with kids and me. For the occasion, he offered to gift me a barong Tagalog. But their American wedding, I insisted, required American style. So, while my mother shopped for a gown and made an appointment at the MAC makeup counter, my stepfather and I browsed the rental tuxedos.

My mother and I hate the pictures from that day. The white makeup artist ineptly painted my Filipino mother a burnt shade of orange. And while my stepfather was the perfect gentleman in his tux, I looked like I'd just come from a regional choir competition in mine. At fourteen years old, I made for a precocious picture: a little boy in a man's suit, giving a too-long toast in a hybridized trans-pacific accent. My parents humored me when I asked if we could have a do-over. They would get married two more times, in Filipino and Catholic ceremonies.

After the first wedding, I asked my mother if I could change my name, like she did. She laughed, and then again when I said I wanted to take my stepfather's name. She leveled with me: with all the paperwork and the fact that even she didn't take it—she kept her maiden name—it wouldn't be worth it. Besides, she said, when I grew up, I would thank her for saying no.

As a kid, I swore fealty to my mother (and still do, for the most part). I never did anything without her permission—except once. At the mall one day, my mother gave me an hour and thirty dollars to buy clothes for my last year of middle school. Normally, I'd have gone straight to American Eagle or Abercrombie & Fitch, those Mom-approved purveyors of suburban prep. But I was crushing on a boy who wore eyeliner and listened to My Chemical Romance. I wanted him to like me; I wanted to be like him. So I went to Hot Topic. I got a studded belt with a bracelet to match.

My mother lost it when she saw what I'd bought—accessories that were "punkista," as she called them—the most livid I'd ever seen her. It was a waste of money, she seethed, on our tight budget. Even though we were in public and, as was the credo in our family, forbidden from making a scene, she was so visibly furious, so terrifying, that I made one anyway. The choice was fight or flight, and I chose to flee my body. I fainted.

When I came to, I saw bystanders, a pair of mall cops, and my very embarrassed mother. The cops sat me down, told me to put my head between my legs, and asked my mother what happened. It was summer in Las Vegas, so she said I was dehydrated. We didn't speak on the drive home, but she let me keep the punkista leather. I never wore it.

We laugh when we tell this story now. My mother attributes her reaction to menopause and her taste. She hated the counterculture aesthetic I attempted to try on. It was incongruent with her style—classic and elegant, all crisp linen and sleeveless turtlenecks—and mine too. My fashion choices at the time were best described as "Nantucket on a budget." I'd dive into clearance bins at Polo Ralph Lauren and Tommy Hilfiger, at the Las Vegas Premium Outlets, in an attempt to keep up with my richer, whiter classmates with their double-popped collars.

Looking back on the Hot Topic incident now, I understand my mother's reaction. Those purchases were my little transgressions, a glitch in our coherent image as good immigrant mother-and-son, dressed like a diversity initiative at J.Crew, acculturating to our new country as best we could. The irony was that I had just bought what the other, cooler white kids were wearing.

Though I only attempted the studs and chains to impress a boy, I also admired that aesthetic—punk, emo, skater, whatever you want to call it. To me, it signified a resistance to authority I could never manage as a teenager. I was much more comfortable seeking the approval of the powers that be, wearing the prep-ista fashions my mother preferred. Though both styles were access points into pockets of American culture, being a prep was less objectionable, more compatible with the A-plus Asian fantasy that came naturally to me. I could assimilate by being the best, being undeniably worthy of my place in America.

My mother encouraged the method. Do your best so you won't be teased, I was instructed. Get good grades, get into good schools. Be a model student. Of all the high roads, it was the one where I'd meet the least resistance. Merit, it stood to reason, would prove my worthiness. Excellence, like armor, would make me bulletproof.

I think that's the confidence Adam saw in me, the sense of invincibility I tried to radiate while wearing a suit. Even when relaxed dress codes in Brooklyn, where I now live, deemed slacks and a pressed shirt sufficient for a

Williamsburg wedding, I persisted with velvet blazers and trousers in Glen plaid. I graduated from rentals and bought a tuxedo; I wore it to an office holiday party because I try too hard.

My colleagues and friends were, always have been, generous. You look amazing, they say, always so polished. What I neglect to mention is that it's all costuming. I work diligently to play the part. The goal was, always has been, to appear qualified, to present my excellence.

According to my mother, I got my personal style from her. True, in the way a young gay boy divafies women who've faced adversity and whose femininity was also a source of strength—like Judy Garland or Princess Diana—I modeled myself after my mother, a paradigm of grace under pressure. But it's hard to say if my predilection for oxfords at dinner or linen in the summer was entirely my mother's influence.

It was certainly something I doubled down on as an immigrant attempting to assimilate. I emulated my peers in Las Vegas, the ones who offered me a seat at the table and in their cars, in the sporty Audis and Mercedes SUVs their parents bequeathed them. Benevolent though they were, paying for my french fries at the Burger King drive-through before rehearsals, I was always conscious of how I occupied a caste below. At the outlet mall, I once bought a white cashmere sweater—something that, to me, screamed affluence—even though it was a size too big and we lived in the desert. I never wore it, only hoped for a day when I could at last fill it out.

If I had nice things, I thought, I would eventually grow into them. To Filipino immigrants who've gone stateside, nice things meant American things. When my mother and stepfather had their second wedding, this time in Manila, I skipped the rental tux and had a suit made. They took me to my stepfather's usual place, a haberdasher he had on retainer.

The shop owner asked if I wanted a barong Tagalog. I shook my head and said no. Instead, I requested, "Pwede po magpagawa ng Americana?"

––––––––––

THE BOSTON GLOBE published an interesting comic in 1899. It ran on March 5, barely ninety days after the Treaty of Paris was signed the year before, the provisions of which included Spain's relinquishment of Cuba and its cession of Puerto Rico and Guam to the United States. Additionally, as part of the treaty, the US purchased the entire archipelago known as Las Islas Filipinas from the Spanish crown for a cool $20 million (roughly $600 million in 2018 money, after inflation). History books, when they care to remember it, see the ratification of this treaty and the US victory in the Spanish-American War as the point where the nation began its ascent as a world power.

The comic from the *Boston Globe* is called *Expansion, before and after*. The central figure is a grotesque brownface caricature of a Filipino. He's smiling toothily in a suit, a stars-and-bars Americana, and labeled "The Filipino After Expansion." The crude "before" image has him in a grass skirt, bare-chested and barefoot, wielding a spear and bow. The surrounding panels portray him in similar befores-and-afters, that is to say, pre- and postcolonial makeover. In one, the description goes, "He could exchange his war club for the baseball bat readily." Another: "From the war dance to the cake walk is but a step." It's a slur in visual language, calling the Filipino population "savage" and "barbaric" without ever saying the words.

It's racist, obviously. That's not the interesting part. What's noteworthy is the comic's portrayal of Filipinos as uncivilized, which completely disregards Spain's role in Filipino history—that they had occupied the archipelago for over three hundred years, had already colonized, "civilized," and injected their DNA into the people who called that archipelago home, and organized them into a territory named after a boy who would become their king. By the time the *Mayflower* set sail, Las Islas Filipinas had been part of Europe's most powerful monarchy for a century.

But white America has long wanted to believe in its own manifest supremacy. The *Globe* cartoon pushed the notion that the United States had happened upon an exotic and previously unknown land, had baptized it with the name the Philippine Islands, and was divinely equipped to do the generous work of taming its unwashed ruffians ("His old habit of running amuck will aid greatly on the football field," jeered the cartoon) and bringing them into the fold of the Western world. In short, it was propaganda. It made a punch line of Filipinos and provided a model for how we must comport ourselves to belong in American society.

We're offered a path to acceptance and "civilization" by assimilating, shedding our Filipinoness, apparently so boorish and uncouth, and bolstering the greater American project. It remains the advertised path to this day, which can be seen in the promotion of English at the expense of Filipino languages. Common are the Filipino Americans who do not speak their family's mother tongue because their parents did not teach them. Such is an immigrant's gambit: speak only English at home to hone your speech and better fit into American contexts, to prevent the inheritance of impediments—hurdles we have jumped and don't wish upon our children.

Even teachers in the Philippines have greatly reduced the number of classes taught in Filipino languages. In 2003, the year I immigrated, the president issued an executive order that required no less than 70 percent of school hours be conducted in English. Given the over one hundred distinct languages spoken in the country—like Tagalog, Ilocano, and Hiligaynon—wider English education helps to develop a lingua franca among all Filipinos. It's also a tool of colonialization. The American colonial government used English education in the territory to homogenize its subjects under one flag. The United States promised the Philippine Islands a delayed independence, then made over this colony into a commonwealth in its own image, promoting myths of Western superiority that influence the Filipino diaspora to this day.

With my double-popped collars and penchant for the Americana, I used this colonial grooming to my advantage. But I made my choice under threat of violence. In the States, I was already targeted for being a "faggot"—peers threatened to beat me up if I so much as made eye contact with another boy. Even before a teacher grimly suggested that I research the killing of Matthew Shepard, I had known that to be gay was to be in constant danger. On top of that, my skin color—not white, but not black—made me a confusing Other in America and exposed me to racist stereotypes beyond the tropes commonly linked to Filipinos, or Asians broadly. A man once spat at my mother and grandfather in a parking lot, accused them of stealing jobs, and told them to "leave my country."

My mother had told me, when we were moving to the US, "You'll have a better life there." I had been indoctrinated to think that this American life was the favorable one. It was the refrain I'd heard growing up, from immigrants like me and those unlike me, too: from the undocumented and their families, from refugees and the stateless. We all came here for "a better life."

But to witness such prejudice, in my own time and in my history books, has taught me that racism, homophobia, and xenophobia are fixtures of life in the United States. The list of evidence is exhausting: The Asian Exclusion Act of 1924. The bombing of the Filipino Federation of

America. The internment of Japanese Americans in World War II. Antimiscegenation laws. Jim Crow laws. Slavery. The AIDS crisis. The shooting at Pulse in 2016. The Muslim travel ban. The teargassing of Central American migrant caravans at the southern US border. The existence of US Immigration and Customs Enforcement. That fucking *Boston Globe* comic. That this country exists at all on land stolen from indigenous peoples and nations.

Every day—even on the best of them, *especially* on the best of them—we despair at the possibilities of what might be stolen from us next: our homes, our loved ones, our lives, our dignity. They threaten to nullify the citizenship we have—as in, the quality of being seen as a citizen, a being with rights and ensured humanity. It is that citizenship of ours on which white supremacy has waged war.

And in war, I decided to do what I thought was best. When the enemy firepower was too great, I avoided being attacked entirely. I opted for camouflage. I chose safety by blending in. I chose to be invisible.

THE MODEL MINORITY theory is a myth. It suggests that Asian Americans are the ideal foreigners: they are productive and respectable, proving that, in America, anyone can succeed, regardless of ethnicity or race, as long as you pull yourself up by your bootstraps. It is a popular fallacy that hangs its believability on the fact that Asian Americans have achieved significant levels of socioeconomic mobility in the United States: above-average household incomes, high rates of educational attainment, overrepresentation at the top forty universities and among US honorees of Nobel Prizes.

This is related to contemporary stereotypes of Asians: the studious, diligent Asian; the upwardly mobile, law-abiding Asian; the inoffensive and unremarkable Asian. It positions Asian Americans as minorities of merit. I played into this model stereotype while growing up in Las Vegas, at Vassar, in New York. It was a safe role to play, one that flew under the radar.

In the framework of the *Boston Globe* comic, it's the "after" in the assimilationist makeover for Filipino, Korean, Japanese, and Chinese Americans. From being seen as lower-class and uneducated blue-collar workers, in the age of exclusionary acts and the so-called Yellow Peril, we became, by the latter half of the twentieth century, paradigms of middle-class mobility, well educated with white-collar jobs. Quite the progress we've made, said white sociologists in the 1960s. One of the earliest mentions of the model minority theory was in an article in the *New York Times* titled "Success Story, Japanese-American Style." A positive stereotype if there ever was one!

But the idea of a model minority pits minority groups against one another. If one group can do it, the thesis asks, why can't another? It's a construction that views Asian Americans as a success story and regards, for example, Black Americans—among other demographics—as lazy or irresponsible. It's an apples-and-oranges comparison that flattens the distinctions among the experiences of nonwhite people, erases the specific challenges of different groups in the US.

Though we are all subjected to white supremacy in America, the ways we face it are informed by divergent histories. How the institutions of slavery and racial segregation have impacted Black Americans—and continue to do so, as proven by the prison-industrial complex and pervasive police brutality—can't be easily equated with how the September 11 attacks on the World Trade Center and the mythic War on Terror have fed Islamophobia and violence against Muslims, just as the lasting effects of centuries-old genocide campaigns against the native peoples of North America are different from the consequences of American imperialism and the country's Orientalist meddling in "The East."

Even within the umbrella term "Asian," we are ethnically diverse and thus experience America differently, have built our lives here with varying rates of what's considered "success." US census data from 2017 slices the Asian American pie chart by ethnicity and markers of social mobility: about 74 percent of Taiwanese adults and 72 percent of Korean adults have a bachelor's degree or higher, compared to 26 percent of Vietnamese adults and 13 percent of Laotian adults who do; average annual incomes range from $100,000 in an Indian household to $83,000 in a Filipino family and $53,000 in a Laotian home.

Pointing to the educational or financial achievements of Korean or Indian Americans, for example, and decreeing all Asians a model minority masks the socioeconomic struggles of groups like Vietnamese and Laotian Americans—many of whom first came to the US in the 1970s as refugees during the crises set in motion in part by American military involvement in the Indochinese Peninsula. To homogenize us and put us in a neat "Asian" box is to discount the varied privileges and difficulties we have in this country, what America's past has charted for our present. Not all Asians are Taiwanese. Not all Asians are Filipino.

However, because I was unreadable to the white majority, I jumped at the chance to be a model minority. Any legible, more "positive" stereotype would be an improvement, a safer kind of othering, so I elected to be a success story, a poster boy for the American Dream. I consented to have others write my narrative for me, but I didn't fully understand the terms. I believed that if I did well in school and looked the part and kept my head down, I would be protected and elevated by a meritocracy, that I would belong—in and to America. An easy lie to believe when your ancestral inheritance is an inferiority complex.

From 1521 to 1946, Filipinos were the property of empires, subject to colonial conditioning, the systems and codes that drilled into us our subalternity. As Las Islas Filipinas, Spain placed us into castes based on how Spanish one's blood was, colorism by DNA. It's why Filipino pop culture today still puts light-skinned celebrities on a pedestal (just look at our Miss Universe winners). To help the census and tax collection, a Spanish colonial decree in 1849 required all Filipinos to take on Spanish surnames, chosen from the *Catálogo alfabético de apellidos*, a book of 61,000 options provided by the empire. Our clothing, our bodies, and even our names were reframed as inferior to those of our colonizers.

This "mis-education," as the late Filipino historian Renato Constantino called it, retrains colonized peoples into thinking that survival under imperial rule is achieved by behaving as a model subject. "The ideal colonial was the carbon copy of his conqueror," Constantino writes. "He had to forget his past and unlearn the nationalist virtues in order to live peacefully, if not comfortably, under the colonial order." After the US purchase of the Philippines, Constantino describes how the colonial conditioning was remixed: "The new Filipino generation learned of the lives of American heroes, sang American songs, and dreamt of snow and Santa Claus."

"Benevolent assimilation," as President William McKinley put it, was the premise of American colonization. He was convinced by God, so he said, that the Philippine Islands would descend into anarchy without Western guidance. By annexing the archipelago, he took on what the imperialist poet Rudyard Kipling called "the white man's burden." Across the newly claimed territory, the American government rolled out judicial structures, legal codes, and public schools modeled after those in the United States.

In and out of classrooms, Filipinos were "mis-educated," to use Constantino's term, to believe "Spain was the villain, America was the savior," to see their history through the eyes of their new teachers. As governor-general in Manila, William Howard Taft presumed that Filipinos needed fifty to a hundred years of American oversight "to develop anything resembling Anglo-Saxon political principles and skills." He saw Filipinos as America's "little brown brothers."

As I later found in the US, as a well-behaved little brown brother, I was permitted a path to get ahead, but only up to a point. Worse, I was used as a tool to bolster an agenda that kept my fellow people of color oppressed, an agenda that says those unlike us—and unlike the white authorities and culture from which we seek validation—are our competitors. The model minority myth tells us as people of color that we must fight among ourselves for seats at the table in America and cages us in roles as unthreatening yellow, brown, and black folks in predominantly white spaces. It gilds and promotes a tokenized position that keeps us minor, subservient to the majority. To keep white people at the top, we were divided and conquered.

I wore the model minority costume too proudly. As I walked through the lasting effects of US imperialism, I traded my Filipino clothing for Americana, armor I smithed under fire in the country of my colonizers. This was how I survived in my youth, by leveraging the allowances permitted me as an Asian in America. I relied on my honors, looked toward better futures, better lives, and neglected to honor my past, what continues to shape me today. It's no wonder I felt disconnected from my homeland when I arrived in New York. Decorated and overworked, I'd come perhaps too far. I planted my flag in fifty square feet of my own with no regard for the name under which I claimed it.

By then, I'd given up my Filipino citizenship to be naturalized in the United States, to acquire a status with which I wasn't born. To this day, though my mother filed all the paperwork and paid all the right people to make our place in this land inalienable, her rights and mine to simply be in the US remain under assault. For a great many of us, our citizenship in America is seen as contingent on the acceptability of our customs and faiths, our humanity on the legibility of our skins and our names.

———————

THERE'S A LITTLE Manila in New York. In the Woodside neighborhood of Queens, along a roughly ten-block stretch of Roosevelt Avenue, stands a collection of restaurants, grocery stores, salons, driving schools, and shipping centers that cater to the city's Filipino community. There's also a Pinoy neighborhood in Jersey City, but it's too far from my apartment in Brooklyn; getting there, crossing rivers and a state line, is not an easy ride on the train.

In fairness, neither is Woodside. Though Queens and Brooklyn are literally next to each other, they're notoriously difficult to traverse using public transport. Two to three transfers are mandatory to get to the land of Jollibee, Ihawan, and the Phil-Am grocery. Whenever I go to Little Manila, whether for a Chickenjoy meal or on an errand to get banana ketchup, I go with Mia—and often her partner, Sarah—to make a day of it. On one such occasion, we went there to work together on a photography project.

The plan: we approached Filipinos in the neighborhood and asked them what they missed most about the Philippines. Then I charmed them into being photographed by Mia, as they held up a large notebook on which they wrote their answers. We got twenty-seven responses, not counting Mia's and mine, numbers twenty-eight and twenty-nine. Naturally, most of the responses were about food and family.

A young woman, standing in front of Jollibee, said that she missed her favorite dessert, snack, and meal: "Halo-halo, kwek-kwek, bangus." Down the street, a lady getting a pedicure replied, "I miss everything about my life in the Philippines." A dude was heckled by his friends as he wrote, "I miss my girlfriend." We met a woman on the sidewalk carrying a bouquet of flowers. When Mia asked her who she'd like to see when she returns to the Philippines—if she could—she wrote down six names, with the simple note: "I love my kids. From Mama with love."

Mia and I published the photographs online in May, to celebrate Asian American Pacific Islander Heritage Month. Commenters replied with what they missed most about their own lives in the Philippines: "Chika-chika with my neighbors." "Watching kids play patintero." "The taho man shouting at the crack of dawn on the street—and then the balut man shouting in the middle of the night!" "The sweetest mangoes you could possibly imagine." "My uncle's dog and the sound of tsinelas."

Beyond their beloveds and beloved food, they celebrated the ambient rhythms of a Filipino life. These were things I missed too—the smell of freshly cooked rice and fried fish, the singsongy cadence of the Hiligaynon language, the familiar flatness of a Tagalog accent, the feeling of my tsinelas on a wooden floor polished with a coconut husk—things I had eagerly left behind when I came to the United States. I'd traded them for what I believed were nicer things, American things—accents, tastes, clothing—that signaled my right to belong stateside.

I tried to drain myself of my Filipinoness to fit the role of a model American minority so much that I ran on a cultural deficit. Though habits and traditions and cuisines and languages alone do not comprise an identity, they make up a big part of it. Severed as I was from my family and homeland, to deprive myself of what made me Filipino only exacerbated my feelings of separation and lack, how I felt unrooted in America and uprooted from the Philippines.

It was up to me to reframe the facets of my Filipinoness as nourishing things, to reclaim them from my internalized colonialism, this parasite that made a host of me. I fed it by eating up myths that upheld the status quo, myths I accepted as truths universally acknowledged about structural inequalities that seemed natural because I was mis-educated to think so. Colonialism is a structure built on lies, tricks its subjects into being the architects of their own oppression.

Deconstructing a colonial mentality is an active and everlasting process. For me, part of decolonizing has been to hold myself accountable, to think more critically about my actions and experiences as a gay Filipino immigrant; my writing is part of that project. Crucial too is the banal and invaluable goal of learning to love myself, especially the parts of me I've been taught to hate—among them my skin color, my queerness, where I come from. In my life, as well as in my peoples' histories—that of immigrants and queer people and people of color—we've been punished enough by powers that have benefited from our traumas. To love ourselves—and one another—is an act of resistance.

After our day of photo taking in Little Manila, Sarah, Mia, and I grabbed a drink at Jeepney, a Filipino restaurant on the Lower East Side of Manhattan. Over San Miguel beers and a bowl of talangka fried rice, Sarah asked me and Mia what we missed most about the Philippines. Mia missed her lola's kisses, she offered first, the love of her mother's mother.

When it was my turn, I hesitated. There was so much I'd lost, I realized, so much with which I was eager to reconnect. I didn't know where to start.

"Kuya," Mia said to me. "Just write what you know."

I took the notebook and wrote in huge letters, falling back on what was true, "I miss my mom."

Days like those with Mia and Sarah—who has learned from Mia to douse everything in Datu Puti vinegar and how to eat with her hands, kamayan style—are fortifying. Here was someone on a journey like mine, and another willing and excited to walk alongside us. Such friendships have been vital in my adult life, in how I unlearn the teachings of our oppressors, both historical and contemporary. We support one another in a system that often does not support us.

"Wear more color," Krutika loves to tell me. It's the same advice she's given throughout our friendship, ever since we met each other in the newsroom at work and decided, "Yes, that one."

I do wear color, I once defended, reminding her of my camel coats, cognac pants, and chocolate suits. When she laughs, it's contagious. She said, "No need to wear brown when you already *are* brown."

For a friend's wedding we were both attending, Krutika went into my closet and picked out a green suit for me. We could match, I said to her, thinking of her new sari in bright celadon. No, she replied, she'd only wear that at an Indian wedding; besides, she didn't want to steal the bride's spotlight. We laughed. She then paired my suit with a blue shirt.

"Everything else you own is blue," she said, going through my clothes. "I guess that tracks." It was no secret

I was a Harry Potter nerd and habitually dressed myself in the house colors of smarty-pants Ravenclaw students—my A-plus Asian tendencies manifesting at a slant.

Then Krutika spotted a tuxedo jacket. It was still blue but decorated in a floral pattern of scarlet and blood orange. I put it on and we looked into a mirror. Satisfied, she said, "You should wear more red."

Blue for nobility, noted the Manila Manuscript, but red for royalty. I'm reminded of those early colonial Filipinos who allegedly embellished their barong Tagalogs with ornate designs that harkened back to our ancestors. Though their methods and causes are unsubstantiated, these fables motivate me to reclaim my Filipino clothing too, to wear it proudly. With that in mind, I bought a pair of sneakers in red, blue, and sunshine yellow—the colors of the modern Philippine flag, fitting for a new myth I'm fashioning for myself. The toes are even spiked—a little punkista, for good measure.

When the time comes, I'd like to wear a barong Tagalog for my wedding day. I'll still wear a suit or tux for the reception. After all, I'm Filipino American and a two-outfits kind of groom. But now, in the way that little kids dream of their wedding dresses, I've got lots of ideas about how my barong could be designed. I would definitely put a tailored spin on it since I'll always love a streamlined shape. Maybe my trousers will be linen. Maybe I'll wear a piña cape.

And I dig the idea of wearing the barong Tagalog without an undershirt. Not only would it be fucking sexy, I see it as a subversion of the idea that the barong's translucence was a way to oppress Filipinos during the Spanish colonial period, intended to prevent my ancestors from concealing weapons, from planning resistance. It'd be an itchy outfit, without the protection between the scratchy fabric and my skin. So call it a symbol, then, of what I know I can handle, for the sake of my style, to wear my Filipinoness my own way.

To go seminaked with the barong Tagalog, to me, feels right. It conveys a sense of vulnerability, openness, even bravery: *This is who I am—and I have nothing to hide.*

QUEEN BEDS

I PRESSED THE heels of my palms into the headboard. I was trying to not get lube on its tufted fabric, since silicone is so difficult to get out of velvet. It was an elegant thing; I had seen a knock-off like it recently, but it was still well beyond my price range, even on sale.

My fingers, claw-like and slick with Wet Platinum, were cramping. I began to shake. To stabilize myself, I grabbed onto Gareth behind me. Stop for a second, I told him, and he obliged. He held me tightly, his chest hot against my shoulder blades, both of us tangled in his plush duvet. I'd once asked where it was from, but he couldn't recall. I wanted to order something like it online, but packages tended to disappear at my sublet, left alone in the lobby of someone else's building.

"Ready to go again?" Gareth asked.

He was a gorgeous doctor from England. He'd been in New York for ten years, as long as I'd lived in the United States. Whereas I'd purposefully lost my Filipino accent years before, in an assimilationist panic, Gareth seemed to have cultivated his Yorkshire accent to an almost comedic thickness. As a charm, it worked. I'd kiss him when I didn't understand him.

We always understood each other in bed. I pushed Gareth back onto the pillows and straddled him. Reentry was more difficult this time. I grabbed his cock to guide him. Once he was in me, I tried to resume our previous frantic pace. Gareth put his Platinum-covered hands on my hips and found a new rhythm, something smoother, easier. My sigh slid into a moan. He smiled and kissed me.

After, once Gareth began to snore, I slipped out of his arms and into the shower. As the water warmed up, I inspected the aftermath on my body. We'd been rough before, when I asked for it. My first time here, there were scratches striping down my back, a hand-shaped mark on my ass. But tonight, there was not a trace of him on me. In the mirror, there was only my body, covered in brown skin and fucksweat. After washing myself, I wore Gareth's white terrycloth robe, one size too big for me.

I put the kettle on, as Gareth would say, and made a cup of the tea he always drank for breakfast. I didn't want to wake him up, so I turned off the heat just short of the kettle whistling. As the tea steeped in a mug, I opened the glass door to the balcony. The air felt different up here, dozens of stories above Manhattan. It had been a hot day, the kind of hot that left even the kids in my neighborhood listless, too parched and leaden to crack open the fire hydrants. The evening was hot too. Despite my best efforts to dress for the weather in a white button-down shirt and linen pants, the summer had smothered me on the sidewalk on the way to Gareth's. But up here, the warmth was friendly. The hot stones tickled the bottoms of my feet.

Past midnight, Gareth's Movado chronograph said, dangling like a tennis bracelet on my wrist. It had been on the bathroom counter, as usual. I'd borrow the watch, just to try it, always careful to return it to the same spot, next to his wallet. I pressed the watch into my skin, relishing how cold and rich it felt. To think, only hours ago I'd been worlds away—a hundred blocks uptown.

I'd spent the evening at my sublet, glued to my phone, while Gareth was doing his rounds at the hospital. Once I'm done, he'd said, I'll let you know. Just as well, I'd told him, pretending "I have to write anyway." I could've whiled away the night with my friends, my fellow seasonal transients, but they were sunning themselves in the Hamptons or on Fire Island, stealing champagne and time, or else shuttered in their own borrowed homes, keeping cool as our weather apps advised.

Tonight, it was my roommates' turn to keep the sublet's one portable air conditioner in their bedroom. They'd worried about me going without it on such a hot night. Don't worry, I'd told them, I probably won't be sleeping here anyway.

Around ten, Gareth finally messaged me via Grindr: *you can come over now, if you like ;)*

I brought my overnight duffel. It was my second summer in New York, and I'd long since learned the advantages of having such a bag at the ready. That first year, I interned at a glossy magazine that gave me a measly stipend that barely covered rent. My internship grants from school barely covered drinks. This summer, I had a bit more money; now I could afford to order cocktails even after happy hour. Though I could pay my rent, I came to count more often on those drinks and my eyebrows to put high ceilings and expensive rooftop terraces over my head. And tonight, here I was—at the end of a hundred-block journey to a queen bed and a park view.

From the balcony, I could see Central Park, a few blocks north. To the west, cars orbited Columbus Circle. It was there I first spoke to Gareth. I was parked at a café with a latté, laptop and Grindr open, when he invited me over for a writing break. I couldn't quite call it a writing break— that would imply I'd actually been producing paragraphs, rather than trawling apps for men and willing 1,500 to 2,000 insightful words to magically appear on my screen, to be exchanged for a byline in an online magazine for no pay.

I'd let this happen because I didn't know better. None of us did. Like my fellow transients, I thought exposure—the idea that I need only present myself, and someone would see me, see my worth, and say yes—was all I needed to find roots and be fixed.

Out on the balcony, I sipped the tea. Tepid, bitter. I returned to the kitchen. Maybe Gareth had some honey or milk or something. But I couldn't find anything in the dark, not in this place where I didn't quite live.

———————

I DIDN'T SPEND a lot of time at the sublet on 151st Street. The apartment was perfectly nice though. Two friends and I were subletting it from a Columbia professor on holiday in France. On the bookshelves, I found a first edition of Roland Barthes's *Mythologies*. I worked through the original French that summer, doing my best to interpret old myths.

Most of my time was spent at a website known for its lists and quizzes. Their fellowship program paid ten bucks an hour. It wasn't much, but it was a step up from my unpaid gigs at print magazines. The assistants who managed me and the other interns at the glossies had us calling in thousand-dollar wine decanters to be photographed, or researching their pitches, which their bosses always shot down.

At the website, we posted memes, drank cocktails on summer Fridays, and raked in the clicks. My college classmates asked if there were always dogs in the office. (Unfortunately, no.) But those halcyon days weren't without stressors. As fellows, we were in a three-month job interview, our editor explained. We were expected to thrive in a "high-pressure environment." Not all of us would get to stay.

Everyone in my fellowship cried at least twice. I cried publicly at my desk when I got brutal rounds of edits from conflicting editors, then privately at a bar called Harlem Public to my roommates. I was afraid I wouldn't get a spot at the website after the fellowship. The mere prospect of getting so close and ultimately failing, of having to return to the drawing board, gutted me. I wasn't even up for the job; I still had a year to go at school. Still, I childishly wanted to be wanted.

Outside the office, I spent most of my time at coffee shops in neighborhoods that weren't my own. I'd ride the downtown 1 train at least eleven stops from my sublet and station myself at a place with croissants and outlets. There was no lack of such spots at Columbus Circle and in Chelsea and the West Village. I told myself there weren't places uptown in Harlem or Morningside where I could sit and write. This was a lie. In reality, I camped out in expensive zip codes to see the apartments and the men that lived there. On Sundays, some people would read the real estate section in the *Times*; I would browse Grindr.

Casual sex was like an open house. My fantasies were built on beefy forearms and exposed brick, so I'd made a habit of running sex apps when in proximity of doorman buildings and million-dollar co-ops. After every 150 words, I'd check my phone for messages, then inspect their selfies for hints of marble bathrooms or windows with cityscape views.

Like most Filipino immigrants I knew, I traded my accent for class anxiety. I would respond to any pricey-looking man with biceps, then we'd exchange the requisite facts: HIV status, sexual positions, safe words, etc. Once the rules of our engagement were determined, I'd uproot myself from that day's café and pay him a visit for, as it were, a "viewing."

As their pants and shirts came off, I'd ask them how long they'd been in their apartments, how much they were paying—customary first-date chatter in New York. There was the trust-fund bro in Chelsea who mumbled five-figure rents against my lips; the gallerist who'd seen his place through a decade and three renovations; and the hotelier with a bed from which we watched the sun set over the Hudson.

I was lucky, with most men and their apartments, but, of course, there were dud days. Sometimes they were bad kissers, sometimes they "didn't hear the safe word." Sometimes they couldn't host me because of roommates. Sometimes messages led nowhere, sometimes no one messaged at all. But I stuck with it. I'd carried over this routine from the previous summer, my first one, in the city. I was subletting then too, spending most hours at the old Condé Nast building in Times Square, at a Starbucks near Lincoln Center, or in someone's Restoration Hardware'd bedroom. Over two seasons, I managed to fuck grooves into various blocks. I plumbed certain neighborhoods so deeply that I knew some buildings more intimately than I did the men they sheltered.

Not that I conducted my visits impersonally. If anything, I prided myself on my knack for small talk and in-bed banter. There was once a French chef who, perhaps meaning to say I was "vocal," called me "expressif." I practiced my prepositions with him: Je te veux *sous* moi, je te veux *sur* moi. I was "*sous* chef," I joked. I was insufferable. He laughed anyway.

I lost track of him, never saved his number. At Harlem Public with friends, I'd cried because I'd gotten my hopes up for a job. It seemed safer then, in all things, to be distant.

By force of habit, I rarely worked outside this mode. Even on proper dates with proper men, I kept them at arm's length. I rarely followed up, left messages unanswered. I ghosted often and well, long before those who despised boys like me coined the term.

I blamed my involuntary transience. I was between years at school, between countries, between homes. I was in New York for just a short while. I didn't know if I could ever come back. I was borrowing the city, seasons at a time, and borrowing as much as I could. A private joke, a sunset, a queen bed with a park view.

But these were places where I didn't quite live. I was subletting the lives of men on a per-hour basis. When you sublet, you put yourself in someone else's shoes. You occupy someone else's home, read someone else's books. I could drink Gareth's tea, wear his watch or his bathrobe, but they were not mine. Nor did I need them to be. All I wanted was to try on lives that I could return after an evening, the price tags still attached. So whether by sunrise or dinnertime, I was free to pursue the thrill of waking up in other queen beds, with other possibilities.

It was a modus operandi befitting New York, I thought, the city of options. If I couldn't have it, not yet or ever, I could glimpse it. I wanted to glimpse real homes with real adults—ones who'd taken root on this island, woven themselves into its fabric. I wanted to glimpse what my promised future in America could be. I wanted this city, so I made it want me in return.

———

THE FIRST TIME I moved to New York was the summer after my sophomore year. I bought my ticket at Poughkeepsie Station, a one-way to Manhattan. On the train, I sandwiched myself between two overpacked suitcases in a forward-facing seat, chosen specifically to savor that literal sense of approach. Despite the well-publicized heat wave, I insisted on dressing for the occasion—expectantly coiffed and blazered—like an actor auditioning in costume.

I also brought props. I'd purchased a copy of E. B. White's *Here Is New York* from the college bookstore and read it on the way to the city.

"It is a miracle that New York works at all," White writes. Toward its implausibility, he counts its overpopulation, its vulnerability to plague and famine, its severe lack of land and excess of sea. But the city, this city in particular, provides its citizens with a balm White calls "the sense of belonging to something unique, cosmopolitan, mighty and unparalleled."

He squints at the city, is stunned by it, and does not mean to defend it, and so sees its absolute truth. In spite—and because—of New York's physical constraints, here, it seems, there's nowhere to go but up. White compares the city to a willow tree in Turtle Bay, a neighborhood I had to google at the time and, frankly, still do. They've been through hell and high water, this tree and New York, both standing for "life under difficulties, growth against odds, sap-rise in the midst of concrete, and the steady reaching for the sun."

I'd long wanted to bear witness to that, to New York. I first saw it through the lens of pop culture as a kid in Manila. My mother watched *Sex and the City*, *The Nanny*, and *Will & Grace*, so I did too. When I discovered musical theater, I inhaled the New Yorkiest of them, particularly *Company* and *Rent* (let the early aughts gay kids who didn't stan the movie cast the first stone), with their anthems to life and love in this city that challenged them to have both. That I became a theater major in high school, aspiring to perform lives unlike my own, was a little on the nose. (My bio, instead, picked up credits like *Miss Saigon* and *West Side Story*.) Then there were the books. *The Devil Wears Prada*—the novel, then the film—introduced me to a particular class of gilded New Yorkers: the so-called media elites who are lampooned and exalted so fiercely that I actually grew to crave a taste of the gold leaf they wore.

If my adult life at times resembles a romantic comedy, it's by deliberate design. I read those scripts as maps to and through American adulthood. Whether by nature or nurture, I came to want very much to banter with friends in great clothes, in greater apartments, in the greatest city in the world, much like the characters I loved. Carrie Bradshaw was an especially strong early influence. The math of her life and style were unsustainable; a weekly newspaper column alone cannot pay for an apartment near Barney's, an appetite for Manolos, and lunch with friends at Pastis—in any decade! But all I knew, watching the PG-ified cuts of *Sex and the City* at an impressionable age, was that, however improbable, this art must be imitating life.

Even at a distance, I wanted to join the ranks of a storied people, those who, as White describes, see New York as "the city of final destination, the city that is a goal." They're the immigrants, born elsewhere and pulled to New York in quest of something, who carry with them electric passion to power the city they so desire. Carrie was one of them—as were Andrea in *The Devil Wears Prada* and White himself. They came to this city as writers, living as and among the "young worshipful beginners," as White called them, those called to New York for that balm of belonging, yearning to begin. It's tempting to say that the life I enjoy today as a writer and editor was preordained. But really, I was just stubborn.

This early exposure to an ideal of American culture informed my answer for the question I was never asked. When the time came for my mother to leave the Philippines—and my father—she was determined to take me with her to the United States. In my memory, that fallible thing, I believed I was asked, at eleven-going-on-twenty-one, to decide where I'd rather live and grow up, where I wanted my future to unfold, and, by extension, which parent I'd prefer in it. As I recall it, they gave me months to think it over. I knew instantly I wanted to go. But it would've been impolite, I remember thinking, to choose so readily between countries, between parents. In reality, my mother reminded me recently, I didn't have to worry about the optics of the decision. She made it for me.

Around that time, my father took me on a trip to Singapore. Perhaps he was attempting a farewell tour or trying for pleasant father-and-son memories. If it were the latter, the plan backfired. All I remember are how much my feet hurt walking down Orchard Road and how often he told me to "stand up straight like a man." He said the same at home in Manila too, a regular sermon on posture delivered in public and in private. I refused to obey. A hand to my waist and a pop to my hip became an act of civil disobedience.

My mother appreciated it, I think. She never seemed to mind how I stood, spoke, cried. I'd tell her about how the other kids at my school would tease me for being effeminate, how they reminded me of my father. Whenever my parents fought—"heated discussions," they'd call them—I'd hide in my mother's car. Hers was always closer to the gates, and I'd wonder how far away I could get if I just grabbed her keys from her vanity. Had it been my choice, to go to the US with my mother or to stay in the Philippines with my father, it wouldn't have been a difficult one to make. It would've been, was, a choice between everything I had and everything I might want.

When we left, I was under the impression we were to live in San Francisco, where my mother's parents had lived, by then, for close to thirty years. I'd visited before and grown familiar with the fog and the Muni and the whispers about the Castro I didn't yet fully understand. But I understood enough to believe that Frisco, as my grandfather called it, had kinship enough with New York and so was a place where I could see myself living—cosmopolitan and sophisticated, in contrast to what I saw as the parochial theocracy of Filipino culture and its regressive views on sexuality. West Coast or East Coast, I didn't care. I looked forward to coming of age in America, a place that would accept me as I was.

I was mistaken. My mother said San Francisco was a stopover on our way to Las Vegas. There, jobs and houses and fellow Filipinos were plentiful. Convenience, apparently, was in the middle of a desert.

What New York lacked in lateral space, Las Vegas had tenfold. Nothing stood in the way of real estate developers but sand and dry heat. There were no natural disasters to speak of, save the odd inch of rain that could scare non-essential government offices into closing. Local drivers rarely saw water on the roads. The slightest precipitation sent BMWs spinning off the freeway. My mother, though, could handle it. In Manila, she drove through four-foot-high floods just to take me to school.

When she got a job in pharmaceuticals, she found us a new house to go with it. It was there in the suburbs I spent my adolescence, either in rehearsals or in front of my computer, attempting to conjure worlds onstage and online. But whenever I say I grew up in Las Vegas, I'm inevitably asked if I lived in a hotel. I may as well have. I spent so much time at the hotel where my mother had worked retail to get us on our feet when we first arrived that I memorized its map, learned intimately the alleys and aqueducts of a faux Venice.

Las Vegas and its themed resorts made a business of pretending you were elsewhere: in Venice, in Paris, in Caesar's Rome. Not that their architects paid much respect to verisimilitude. The Las Vegas Strip was such an exaggerated collage of signs and symbols that homage became parody. The Eiffel Tower was erected to straddle the Paris Opera House. A tram was built to shuttle tourists between a medieval castle and an Egyptian pyramid. A water-logged palazzo was engineered in a town so afflicted by drought its citizens were on a lawn-watering schedule. Though that was the whole point, I guess, of Las Vegas. It was a fantasy.

Of course, there was an imitation of my own fantasy towering over the Strip. In my seven years as a Las Vegas resident, I never set foot in the hotel based off Manhattan, for no reason other than I didn't have one. I once mentioned this fact to my high school boyfriend. He'd been my best friend until I decided he would be my boyfriend, for no reason other than I didn't have one. We were having a heated discussion as we drove by the hotel itself, that counterfeit of the New York skyline. As a Checker Cab roller coaster whizzed around a replica of the Statue of Liberty, he said it was because I was saving myself for "the real thing."

Whenever I told my family I was bound for New York, they'd raise their eyebrows. In Las Vegas and in Manila, people would click their tongues and sip San Miguel beer, dismissive. Don't bother, an uncle said, don't waste your time, don't dream too big. You'll learn, they said, you'll see. That was part of New York's allure to me, that I'd be the only one in my family to try it. This city scared them, and I thought, "Good."

My mother encouraged my cross-country ambitions, threw me a surprise party when I got my acceptance letter from Vassar, a small college in New York's Hudson Valley. She and my stepfather dropped me off on move-in day— the first of only two times they could afford to visit Vassar, the second being graduation. After we unpacked the last box, she teared up. I offered my mother some tissues from my pocket; I'd been sobbing in the bathroom while they picked up extra hangers at the nearby Target.

She was proud I was "moving on," even if it meant being apart. She'd long braced herself for this because, as she said, "this is the whole point." We immigrated to the US so I could have what I couldn't in the Philippines: a choice to stand however I wanted, wherever I wanted. In that immigrant shorthand: a better life.

"Promise me," she said, "you'll make good choices, OK?" We cried, we hugged. Perhaps that's why I recall my mother's choice to come to America as my own. It's thanks to her I have so many.

By the time sophomore spring rolled around, a pneumatic tube opened up between college and the city: an internship. Knowing that Vassar nepotism was alive and well, I had found an alum in Manhattan who needed interns, and he offered me a spot for the summer.

I didn't dare tell anyone—apart from my mother—that my ambition wavered in the face of terrifying potential, of unscripted events. I didn't want to get there and fail—or worse, hate it. I'd fantasized for too long what living in New York would be like. What if it was a film its trailer greatly oversold? What if everything I'd been told about America, the promised land, was false?

This was my shot, what I'd worked for, my mother reminded me, what we'd worked for. There was no use in giving up before I even started, no way to learn unless I tried it for myself. Here were my next steps forward, ones I had to take alone.

My mother encouraged me: "Kaya mo yan. Mana ka sa'kin."

True, I'd inherited from her many things. An immigrant life, a series of stopovers. A talent for moving and moving on, visits within visits, one after the next. If San Francisco was her stop, Las Vegas was mine. She'd immigrated to Las Vegas. I was immigrating to New York.

Reading the first page of *Here Is New York* on that train from Poughkeepsie, I wept without irony. "It can destroy an individual," White writes of the eponymous city, "or it can fulfill him, depending a good deal on luck. No one should come to New York to live unless he is willing to be lucky."

I believed I was the luckiest twenty-year-old entering the city that afternoon, with work and a place to sleep already waiting for me. My first job: an internship at a men's magazine. My first apartment: a sublet in Harlem that belonged to my mother's gay best friend's husband's sister—a veritable aunt, my Tita in Filipino terms. I paid $700 a month for a sofa and a folding screen in her living room. I couldn't wait.

The rolling banks of the Hudson turned into the dirt and steel of Yonkers turned into the elevated platform at Harlem-125th. I'm here, I pinched myself, I get off here. My sense of an approach became a sense of beginning. I could see the unfinished Freedom Tower gleaming to the south, steadily reaching for the sun. Here was the city that was a goal. Now I, young and worshipful, got to stay.

Just for a few months, I told Tita's doorman, just visiting, really, and he was always kind enough to let me in after four in the morning. Since I was rarely at home in the evenings, Tita didn't bother with the folding screen but left me dinners kept warm in the oven. Whenever I went out, I brought my passport, as Tita advised, blue and American and incontestable, just to be safe.

I brought it to dinners in Nolita and to parties in Amagansett, to dates in Alphabet City and to happy hours at bars that never cared to ask for it. It was my only valid identification at the time, stuck between an expiring learner's permit and a student ID.

I spent that summer learning to gild myself. I borrowed Ferragamo loafers that chafed my Achilles' heel from the fashion closet at my internship. I tailored H&M blazers to forge Prada, fooling only fellow pretenders. I feigned champagne out of water by finessing the right Instagram filters, embellishing plastic flutes with golden light. I learned to perform lives I wanted as my own. I allied myself with club promoters to land on the right lists. I used a twenty-one-year-old friend-of-a-friend's Venezuelan ID to gain entry. To convince the bouncers, I affected a Spanish accent that was almost certainly inappropriate and incorrect. And I learned to sketch with my body the storyboards I'd drawn long ago. I took up the role of a Filipino Carrie Bradshaw who read Barthes and trolled Grindr. I bantered with friends in stolen clothes, in borrowed apartments, in the hottest city in the world.

That summer felt episodic. As if inhabiting the sitcoms I devoured as a kid, I acted without consequences. The men I met were just characters, their homes my sets. Any mess I'd made, I thought, would be resolved by moving on to the next scene. I penciled the episodes and acts I wished to perform, then restarted each day on a blank page. This performance continued into my second season, at the website, at Gareth's. I reprised my role as the funny, promiscuous gay filler you could write off after sweeps. It was easier that way. If you wrote me off the show, I wouldn't leave lube on the headboard.

Transience was what I knew best in those days. Subletting, borrowing, moving. I had a talent for living out of a duffel. This was part of my immigrant conditioning—the dual fear of stagnation and desire for stability. Stability required roots. But to stay put would be to rot on the vine; movement was synonymous with merit. My immigrant mind-set begat these mental gymnastics and the exhaustion that came with it. My impermanent summers, then, were my adequate in-betweens.

Let me enjoy the foreplay, I thought, and let me live in the trailer, with no conflict and no resolution. Each season, I chose New York for the fantasy.

———————

IN GARETH'S KITCHEN, I gave up on the milk and honey, then poured the tea into the sink. I put everything back where I found it, left no sign anything had been moved. I returned his watch to the bathroom counter, his robe to the hook, my body to his bed. He stirred, shifting toward me. I turned away to face the windows. I watched the restless city outside, beyond the glass, until I fell asleep, not quite visiting, not quite living.

When I woke up, Gareth wasn't there. Normally, we'd be woken up by the sun pouring into his bedroom. I'd offer to get going, to "get out of your hair," and he'd tighten his arms around my waist, hold me hostage in his sheets. Today, his queen bed seemed so much roomier without him. Sunlight sliced through the curtains and across my legs. He'd drawn the shades. He hadn't wanted to rouse me from my sleep.

My phone rang. It was my mother. I automatically did the calculation: 9 a.m. in New York meant 6 a.m. in Las Vegas. She was awake at this hour because she liked to rise with the sun—who, for her, was my stepfather, conditioned to be up at daybreak for morning rounds at the hospital. Gareth didn't have his rounds until later, so I was welcome to stay the night.

I picked up my mother's call. "Hi, Ma." She said she was at church and asked where I was. I could hear Gareth puttering about in the kitchen. "I'm at Starbucks."

My mother was calling to ask for an address. She had some things to send me, vitamins among them. When my grandmother's cancer killed her, my mother's interest in holistic health kicked into overdrive. She'd already been mindful of her personal fitness, but now her efforts extended to me and my stepfather. Last time I was on the phone with him, he'd whispered that dinner had been fibrous but bland.

This time, in addition to capsules of ginger root, my mother was mailing over a cocktail shaker she hadn't been using. "You're sending mixed messages," I told her.

"We have to empty the wet bar at the house kasi," she said. They were preparing to move back to the Philippines. "Lahat na lang sana para sa'yo, pero I can't send Cointreau through the mail."

I said, "You could try." She laughed.

When my parents decided to return to Manila, they sold the house in Las Vegas for half the price they'd paid for it five years before. To break even, they began to sell the house's interior. First to go was the rarely used formal living room furniture, which only functioned as a backdrop for three years' worth of Christmas cards. My stepfather insisted that the recliner in the den go last; he used it for naps in between packing sprints. They sold the custom dining table and chairs to a friend, who said she'd hold on to the set for them, in case they came back. As my parents stood to eat dinner, take-out pasta in tin containers, in the upgraded granite kitchen that cost extra, my mother reported an ache of regret.

She FaceTimed me when it was time to tackle my bedroom. They had never turned it into an office like I suggested—"Why would we need two?"—so the place was untouched whenever I wasn't there. Since I had no plans to go back home before their transpacific move, I'd effectively moved out of the house when I left it the Christmas before. This left me with the task of tying up loose ends remotely. My mother pointed her phone's camera at every article of my youth and asked, "Keep, toss, or donate?"

I told my mother to get rid of everything. Clothes, video games, my tear-stained Harry Potter books. I didn't think anyone would want to buy my junk, its worth only sentimental. Everything went to the nearest donation center. The contents of my life, I realized then, comprised a storage unit upstate and the two suitcases I brought with me to 151st. The only permanent address I had left was Vassar, which I could call home for one final year—nine months, maybe less.

Still, it was the only one I had. So when my mother called asking for an address while I was at Gareth's, I told her to send the package to my box at Vassar. I could've had it sent to 151st, but there was too big a chance I'd miss the courier and lose the package to the labyrinthine postal service. There was the website's office address, but it would've been presumptuous. I was just a fellow and leaving soon. I never stayed in one place for too long.

"Ay, pero may kasamang cookies."

I laughed. "Vitamins, a cocktail shaker, and cookies?"

She had a smile that could be heard through the phone. "All good things in moderation."

Gareth's kettle began to whistle. Before hanging up, I told my mother, "I'll figure it out. Love you."

In the kitchen, Gareth was cooking eggs in his underwear. Light flooded the place through floor-to-ceiling glass, the smell of fresh toast in the air. Gareth asked if I wanted tea. I understood him. I kissed him.

"Who was on the phone?" he asked.

"Me mam," I said, in a poor imitation of him. He snorted. "She's sending me a package. I'm just not sure where I could have it sent."

"Here, if you like," he said, putting fried eggs and toast on our plates. "You're here all the time. The doorman must know you by now."

He offered me a fork. I responded, "That wouldn't be weird?"

Gareth shook his head and smiled at me, his dimples like canyons. He poured tea for us both in his-and-his cups. It was strong, warmer than what I'd had before. No need for milk and honey.

The apartment at 151st was empty when I returned that evening after work. My roommates had moved out. One had gone back to Vassar early for preseason field hockey training; the other was finishing the summer at her boyfriend's. I took the portable AC and rolled it into my bedroom. I hooked it up to the open window, turned it to the highest setting, and squatted in front of it to blast the sweat off my skin.

My room was a mess. Knowing I wasn't staying for much longer, I'd become less diligent about cleaning up. Clothes were spilling out of my suitcases, open on the floor. I'd already begun the packing process, which was easy enough as I hadn't fully unpacked to begin with. On one of the suitcases, my roommates left a note with move-out instructions, how to clean up and return the keys. I'd told them I wanted to be the last one to leave. Now, alone, it was time to go again.

School was starting soon. I still had a handful of dates lined up. "We should hang out before you leave," they said. The quality of their company was not exceptional, but they offered in spades the attention I craved—tickets to worldly domestic elsewheres.

My duffel, however, had become a burden. I'd stopped packing light. Last night, I brought my blow dryer. Gareth didn't have one and laughed at me that morning as I coaxed an "effortless" swoop into my hair. He suggested I leave the blow dryer in his bathroom, that I come back for it another time. I brought it with me to the office. It used to be simple, dropping into someone else's permanent address, sliding in and out of another life. Now it was labor to bring with me bits of mine.

I was tiring of places where I didn't quite live. Open houses had been easy when my life had a home base, had two. But I would soon lose the keys to both: within a year, my parents would leave the States and I would leave school.

I wouldn't have a place for all the stuff in my temporary storage locker, a home where I could unpack my two suitcases.

I was welcome, it seemed, to leave a few things at Gareth's permanent address. A blow dryer, a package, myself. I could leave some things now, perhaps pick them up during a visit, or I could visit and never leave. If his clothes weren't a fit, then perhaps his life. When I left his apartment that morning, I entertained the idea that what was his, what was not mine, could become ours. His front door could become our front door, our building, our doorman, who tipped his hat as he showed me the exit. He did recognize me, for a moment, but only in the cursory way of doormen, nodding at a guest who's on their way out.

The summer, this season, was over. Back up the Hudson I'd go, on that train, sandwiched between two overpacked suitcases. I'd face those final nine months, maybe less. There would be my next steps forward, ones I'd have to take alone, toward the city that was my goal, toward terrifying potential.

I was afraid of my future because I'd charged it with such fantasy. My aspirations for life in the US had found a proxy in New York, an antithesis to repressive Manila, to garish and empty Las Vegas. To find a place for myself in the city, I imitated performances I'd seen on stages and screens. Pop culture, inevitably, teaches a big lesson to immigrant students in what an American life might look like. Ever the teacher's pet, I wanted to stick to the script.

Now the trailer was ending, the feature about to start. Without the safety of my parents in the country with me, we'd gone off script. I had to write a new one, my own narrative. At a prospect so intimidating, to do it all from scratch, I thought it easier to slide into scripts and queen beds already made for someone else.

I looked to others to give my life shape, others I saw as more adult, more rooted in this land than me. I saw myself as a recurring guest star, since I could never shake the feeling I was a guest in America. What began as casual visits became petitions for refuge. Look here, I offered, see my work, see my body, see me. Take me from transitory to permanent. Give me your roots. Let me be fixed.

I unlocked my phone and opened Grindr, canceled my remaining dates. Maybe next time, I said, when I'm properly in town. None of them seemed too disappointed, as far as I could tell. Not that you could gauge sincerity all that well on the app, an opaqueness on which I'd relied.

Then I looked at my Grindr messages with Gareth. When he invited me to come over, I'd gone straightaway; I already knew where he lived. I'd been welcome more than once. Now, all I needed was his zip code.

When I picked up the package from my mother, I asked Gareth, "Why have you been so good to me?"

I'd never given him my number, never promised him anything beyond great sex and infringement of his personal space. Gareth swiped two more cookies from the tin. They were "scrummy," he said.

He'd suggested we spend the afternoon in bed. He didn't have his rounds until later, and I was all packed at home. So Gareth threw open the shades in his bedroom. We were naked, save for our socks, for all of Columbus Circle to see.

"Because I'm a good person," said Gareth. "And you're a good person." I kissed him.

When I left for Vassar, with my back to the city, I messaged Gareth with my number, saying, *if you like :)*

He never texted me. I like to think he eventually found someone who was fine leaving lube on the headboard.

———————

A LEASE IS, by definition, temporary. You agree to borrow a home for a fixed amount of time. In New York, I've met people who've changed apartments yearly, others who've spent decades in one place. Though circumstances vary, uniform among them is the commitment to making it work, the privilege in getting to stay. Money is a requisite in this city, almost as vital as our foolish brand of bravery. When we sign a lease, we make a promise we'll give it a shot. Such is that terrifying potential: we might fail, or we might not.

After graduation, I found a place to sleep for two months, a too-expensive sublet in Harlem. Then I signed for an apartment nearby on Central Park North. I shared it with a couple I knew from college. I took the smaller of the two bedrooms and most of the closets. We didn't have a doorman, so rather than receiving packages at home, I used my office address back at the website, where I started a full-time job two days after a very sweaty graduation.

I did put it on my first New York ID, though it would need to be replaced whenever I moved, new impermanent addresses, four in my first three years. I kept up my habit of carrying my incontestable passport instead. I liked that it only assigned you a home country. Though, of course, "home country" came with its own nomenclatural idiosyncrasies. It would take me half a decade in New York and a visit to the Philippine consulate before I could officially lay claim to two.

When I visited my parents in the Philippines, my mother gave me her cookie recipe. I had to learn how to make them from scratch, now that she and my stepfather lived abroad. Though, I guess, with respect to my family, I'm now the one overseas. But my mother made it clear I have a home there, that I was welcome to move in with them. They'd renovated their Manila townhouse, with his-and-hers offices and more than enough guest rooms to spare. To turn one into my bedroom needed only my say-so. She offered in person and over the phone, whenever I called from New York, whenever the city proved challenging. I had a safety net, after all, however far away.

In those early years, I spent most of my time at work, laughing at memes and writing well into the night. We all did. No longer those seasonal summer transients, my peers and I were the young and worshipful turned perennial, in New York for our first falls. This difficult city was, all ironies considered, a perfect place for starters. We came here to begin. Though it destroyed us repeatedly, granted us many little deaths, we came alive, again and again, by the grace of our friendships and a good deal of luck. Though some come and go, we carry with us still the pride of having tried as immigrants to this island—passionate, electric, ever-reaching for the sun. Whenever this city scared us, we would say, "Good."

Occasionally, I paid visits to open houses. I tried to not lie to myself when I did, remembering that these were indeed visits, that I had my own high ceilings to come home to. Over time, I had less use for my overnight duffel, so I left it unpacked. The blow dryer stayed at home, to be deployed whenever I landed dates with potential leading men. One of those occasions was with a man I met on Twitter. We cooked dinner, and he suggested that we break in the new dining table that I'd built myself with wood and steel. We fell apart soon after that, the ghost now the ghosted. The table outlasted us, has outlasted all of my relationships. A friend tried to buy it off me, which was a pleasant surprise. In an inversion of roles, someone wanted a piece of my life.

The table has stayed with me, came with me when I left that apartment along Central Park North. I used to thrill at the possibility of seeing that apartment from Gareth's balcony, though I never got to check. I miss that balcony, that bathroom, and the idea of him, of sharing a life already rooted. Since I can no longer borrow his, I've begun to build my own, according to my designs.

Sure, I've taken some cues from Gareth. I splurged on the same plush duvet that I so loved in his bed, the one in which I remained a permanent visitor. I now have a bathrobe and a Movado watch, both exactly my size. I even attempted a morning tea habit, but I'm staunchly a coffee drinker. And I've moved into a parkside apartment, this time in Brooklyn. It's a studio where I live by myself and sleep in a queen bed. It's a lot of space in which to wake up alone, but now, at least, I wake up in a place in which I've come to live.

READING THE STARS

It started, as it often does, in my DMs. A direct message appeared in my inbox on Twitter when I tweeted about a novel, posted a photo of a page that referenced John Keats's "Ode on a Grecian Urn." The DM was from a man whom, for now, I'll call Nate. He said something about how he too loved truth and beauty. He asked if I was a Romantic. I said I was more of a Greek. We flirted like insufferable honor students, and once we exchanged enough texts to establish mutual attraction, I invited my Twitter crush on a date.

There are unwritten rules to digital etiquette. They vary among platforms, as each has a purpose unique to its users. Even on one app, different users will have different aims. Just as I repurposed Grindr to scope out real estate beyond my price range, Twitter's functions are variable. For some, it's a place to promote themselves or their small business, be it a bakeshop or laxative teas. For others, it's a venue to espouse white nationalist beliefs, with knowledge they won't be banned by the website, claiming "free speech."

For my colleagues in journalism and digital media, they're chained to the nightmare platform du jour to catch breaking news and find sources for their reporting. And some of us are here for the memes and the thirst.

Of course, as it's social media, there's a social aspect too. As depressing and anxiety-inducing as Twitter can be, it's also a way of connecting with like-minded people in real time, meeting and engaging with those who speak the same language, whose lives rotate around the same axis. There are politics around who follows whom and whether it's mutual or not; the meaning of a "favorite" or "fave," signified by marking a tweet with a star; and whether that meaning shifted when Twitter changed them to "likes," indicated by hearts. These codes are often dimly understood but strongly felt, especially on a platform where the personal bleeds into the professional and vice versa.

Look at the profile of anyone in, say, Media Twitter. You'll find their tweets about the latest industry bloodbath and links to articles they're promoting or skewering, mixed with photos on holiday with their mutuals—often also in Media Twitter, or adjacent neighborhoods like Book Twitter or Gay Twitter—and jokes they've workshopped with their therapists. Many of them are "Twitter famous," small-scale celebrities in their own realms, and their followers read them precisely for this chaotic mélange of content, everyone faving and retweeting and discoursing in public. It's today's virtual café society, sustained by iced coffee and Xanax.

Nate started following me on Twitter after reading something I wrote online. At the time, I was publishing essays on breakups, mental health, and mortality; this was circa the tail end of the it-happened-to-me personal essay–industrial complex. For every three commenters who enjoyed my work, there were two who labeled me "another navel-gazing millennial." (And, thankfully, only ever one death threat containing racist and homophobic expletives. It was then I knew I'd made it.) I didn't mind any of it. But I did worry that my extreme candor on the internet, public and on the record, would deter future gentleman callers and their courtship. So it was a pleasant surprise when Nate was intrigued by my honesty. Here was a man who didn't mind all the baggage I'd unpacked.

I read Nate's tweets as his own microconfessionals. Of all the major social media platforms, Twitter's the one where users most easily undress—emotionally, at least. (Though there is, absolutely, Porn Twitter.) Compared to all the curating and "plandid" posturing more common on Instagram (of which yours truly is unashamedly guilty), Twitter is where you can exhibit the multitudes you contain, talking openly about your antidepressant regimen, which celebrity you'd like to spit in your mouth, and how black lives matter, all on the same account.

From Nate's Twitter, I surmised that he was a smart, liberal, handsome twentysomething. A man who, like me, worked in media and, unlike me, had his shit together. When he messaged me, we were already following each other—mutuals, in the local parlance—and familiar, the way you're acutely aware of your schoolyard crush. I caught sight of Nate when my mutuals retweeted his jokes, admired his left-leaning politics during election season, deemed him dateable whenever I faved his tweets about his favorite animal. I suppose he thought the same of me when he slid into my DMs.

But at that point, well before our first date, Nate had access to far more of my truths than I to his. Mine were displayed freely online, not all of them beautiful. He could read me like an open book, all my anxious neuroses and romantic failures. My cards weren't just on the table; my cards were in the cloud. I feared this put me at a disadvantage. Nate would face no surprises, but I might face many. He could take advantage of my transparency, as my well-meaning friends reminded me. I may've been too eager to claim "radical vulnerability" in public, to take control of my narrative by baring everything online before someone else could expose me.

Ironic, given how guarded I was on the internet of the 2000s as a teen. In the era of GeoCities and Angelfire, anonymity was the default. Terms and conditions were loose guidelines, the Wild West laws of a sheriff who couldn't be bothered. Users blew into those pioneer towns, message boards and chat rooms, running away from "real life." In those corners of the web, no one could see my face or hear my accent, Filipino and fading. I took advantage of the freedom to present however I could.

I bounced around those early sites—particularly Live-Journal, DeviantArt, and FanFiction.net—deploying various personas. At one point I pretended to be a white teen named Jonathan, using a stolen picture for my profile photo. When I came clean, my rightfully freaked-out internet friends stopped talking to me—or, I guess, to Jonathan, who never existed anyway. As an adult, I've flipped into an opposite mode. I treat my writing like interstellar radio messages, announcing myself to the void, seeking friends among the stars.

Nate picked up my signal, suggested a casual coffee on a fall afternoon, after rain-checking our first dinner. It was then that he called me "beautiful"—not in spite of but because of my messy truths. He knew me, I thought, and I knew him. And so, our thirst seemed pure.

HERE'S WHAT I knew about Nate.

Nate was tall. In his mirror selfies, his coiffed hair was always just out of frame. When we hugged for the first time at a café, I rose onto demi-pointe to throw my arms around his neck. Over iced coffees, we discussed past jobs, current books, and future homes, our elbows on the table as our knees grew familiar.

Nate was funny. I'd laugh to myself while reading his tweets at happy hours, drinking with other men. On a dinner date, our banter had me on my toes, and I smiled even as I chewed. I couldn't help but kiss him in that Thai restaurant, where his hands easily found my back pockets.

And Nate was sexy. He'd DM me and my pants would come off. To break in the new dining table I built, we cooked a meal together and had sex thereafter. He tiptoed naked through my kitchen, and I learned his silhouette by the light of the refrigerator.

But Nate was busy. He made a habit of rain-checking our dates. A new job gave him mountains of work, absurd hours, and a title he wanted to live up to. Still, he thought about me and about what I'd already been through with other men. I didn't have to wait for him, he said, I'd waited long enough for a man to be my lover. I can be patient, I told him. After all, as Barthes said, the lover is the one who waits.

Nate was perceptive. He picked up on my little tells and always knew what to say. When he noticed my aching tweets (an excess of T*ylor Sw*ft lyrics from her *1989* era), after months of drawing out our sporadic dates, he gave me a mutually convenient out. But that endeared him more to me, deluded and twenty-three. We were compatible, I thought, because he knew me—a gift when all I wanted was to be known.

Nate made me feel heard. And in this comfort, I came to see him exactly like the constellation I had drawn: that brunette twentysomething, who worked in media and read me like an open book. I thought that because he understood me, already knew me before he even met me, it meant we'd get to skip the hard parts, the growing pains, and slide into a relationship.

And Nate, it should be said, was a Gemini. He was good at saying what I needed to hear. In return, I tried to meet his need for constant mental stimulation. (I'm a Libra, obviously—an eternal people pleaser.) The friction between our schedules raised my hackles—my Mercury is in Virgo—but whenever our calendars aligned at last, Nate's heartening company—his Venus is in Cancer—very much made up for it.

Despite this analysis, I admit I don't take astrology too seriously. But it's humbling to think that the skies and the stars, things bigger than us, shape our constitutions from the moment of our birth—that we (and our parents) are not the only ones to blame for who and how we are.

My skeptical friends consider astrology a scapegoat, an excuse to leave personal traits unexamined: "Sorry I'm so blunt, my sun sign is Sagittarius." I see it as a challenge. To overcome allegedly predetermined faults, to reverse the shortcomings to which your birth chart condemns you— that's fucking impressive. It's satisfying to overturn a trait ascribed to you by a rubric that feels false; for example, to experience moments of perceptive empathy when a personality test says that you're rigidly judgmental. As the Twitter meme goes, "Myers-Briggs is just astrology for straight people."

Astrology is a tool I use to examine my reality. As with all myths, the truth of it takes a backseat to the beauty of its logic. Like Greek mythology, it lives on not because it's scientifically viable, but because it provides insight into how we view the world. With fewer empirical facts to get in the way, the realm of possibility becomes more expansive.

For the Greeks, more things were possible in a time before, say, telescopes: What was there to prove that the moon was not the goddess Selene, who rode her lunar chariot nightly across the sky, who fell in love with the astronomer Endymion, who asked Zeus to bestow upon the man eternal youth and eternal sleep that he might remain a thing of beauty and a joy forever?

Fair to say I'm a dreamer, as most Libras are. We air signs, Geminis included, are said to leave our heads in the clouds and live as social beings. This much was true: Nate flitted among many friends and interests—par for the course for the Twins, but anathema to me as the Scales, who sought harmony and balance with a complementary partner.

Nate constantly postponed our dates, while maintaining a schedule of hyperactivity. This was a red flag, said my friends, he should make time for you. But I told them about his frenetic attention span, his overscheduled calendar, his new important job at an up-and-coming media company, his friends who shared him and his time. I'm a master of Libran diplomacy, able to argue on behalf of another. It's not a willingness to play devil's advocate, but one to give chances, to move through the world in good faith.

Though we didn't get together as frequently as I'd have liked, Nate and I spoke often. I'd see texts from him in the morning, @mentions from him in the evening. When I tweeted that I'd be getting an Apple Watch, with its haptic perception and constant presence, Nate replied, for everyone to see, "Promise to send me your heartbeat."

This is another application of Twitter: a public forum for horniness, flaunting your interest in someone or their interest in you. It's evident in Gay Twitter, where the playful negging and flirting makes it all feel like high school, even when we're grown men. Since many queers in my generation didn't come out until their late teens or even adulthood, it's said we experience a second, sometimes perpetual, adolescence after coming out. And there's no better place to perform our boyish psyches unchecked than social media. In this virtual cafeteria, those I considered the cool kids offered me a seat with them. I seized my opportunity to join the followed and verified in this court of favorites, this theater of likes.

Sometimes, these invitations happened IRL. At happy hours, whether at XES, The Boiler Room, or Boxers, I rubbed shoulders with gay men in a way no different from how we moved online. They were friendly and entertaining, our interactions fast and casual. Not all of them were quite for me, and I suspect I wasn't everyone's favorite either. But there was a satisfaction in being with them, getting tagged in their photos and @mentioned in their tweets, acquiring mystique by osmosis.

Part of me enjoyed the homosociality. In Las Vegas, I didn't have gay male friends. I only had crushes and boyfriends (including the best friend I turned into a boyfriend).

Now, given the chance to be with other queer men, I didn't care so much that I was usually the only Filipino at these gatherings, maybe one of a minority of nonwhite gays. Occasionally there were other Asians, there with white boyfriends. While no one meant any harm, sometimes I felt like a token. Being new in New York and not knowing other gay men, I figured this was my lot. Whenever I got invited to happy hours, I thought, *Paupers can't be choosers*. I was content to be chosen at all.

At these gay bars, I could never shake the self-imposed expectation to hook up with someone. Whether friend, acquaintance, or stranger, anyone would do, anyone who saw me and said yes. I'd learned to center sex in gay male spaces—and most of them did too, the spaces and the men. (It's hard not to have sex in mind when gay porn is playing next to the bottles of house vodka and gin.)

Later, Twitter would provide me a way to meet people without the pressure to take anyone home. I guess gay dodgeball leagues and sales at Zara are good for that too, but Twitter demands little exertion, transcends physical limitations. We could chat from our beds or our offices, whether in Brooklyn or Manhattan, London or Los Angeles. It also makes the times you hang out in real life feel special. You make the choice to share space with each other, toast to being queer together. But at this point, I'd yet to critically examine the possibilities of queer sociality. I conflated the carnal with the communal because what else, I thought then, did we gay men have in common?

Given the temperaments of queens, I fell in and out of favor at court. It made sense; on any given day, there are more than enough gay men in New York named Matt. To differentiate, people usually referred to me by my last name. It was nice, actually. I had to correct the pronunciation only once; I suppose word of me eventually got around.

They knew about Nate too, followed us both, and it was clear from my heart-eyed tweets how hard I had fallen. I prioritized him in the way you can only in your early twenties: with an open heart and an open schedule. When we agreed to meet outside the theater where we were seeing *Into the Woods*, I was ten minutes early and Nate was twenty minutes late. But when he arrived, distracted and suave, I was just happy to be wrapped in his arms, to smell his cologne on his neck, to call him my "very nice prince."

Afterward, we went to a bar with a backyard. We sat on a bench to drink, my arm looped around his. Talk of witches and woods led us to ask each other, "What do you wish for?"

I wished to publish a book—wish to publish many books. Nate said he'd throw me a party when my first one came out. I was swift to fantasize my toast to him. He believed in my work, in me, and so I believed in us.

On the topic of books, I asked Nate, "What's your Patronus?" In the Harry Potter series, the Patronus Charm conjures a protective force that wards off evil creatures. Your Patronus takes the shape of an animal that is, per the affiliated site Pottermore, reflective of a crucial yet unseen aspect of your personality. It was another semiserious way of getting to know Nate—astrological sign, Hogwarts house, Patronus. I'd have asked him about his wand wood, but I didn't trust him to let slide the opportunity for a sarcastic remark. I was two chardonnays deep, feeling tender.

"I have to think about that," Nate said. He sipped his IPA. "What's yours?"

Nowadays, Pottermore offers a quiz that determines your Patronus. But we old fans had to conjure ours on our own, have held onto our personal myths for ages. Mine, I'd long felt, was a peacock. Since that's also my favorite animal, the lore of the spell suggests that I "may not be able to hide [my] essential self in common life" and "parade tendencies that others might prefer to conceal." How readable I am, it's true.

Since my most recent breakup—one I'd written about, one Nate had read about—I'd been feeling an existential shift toward something else. One's Patronus might change, it's said, when one undergoes trauma or falls in love. After all my peacocking, I fancied myself an owl, a bird who'd learned its lessons. But with Nate, I became a romantic once again.

"A peacock," I told him. "Flashy, showy, a master of courtship dances."

Nate laughed. He stopped to think of his.

I studied him in the faint light of the bar. The dark circles under his eyes were looking permanent. Nate had mentioned to me how stressful his new job had been. But all he tweeted about was his excitement for big projects and new directions. Perhaps he was not so readable as I'd thought. Here, tonight, I saw that this handsome twentysomething, who worked in media and had his shit together, was holding it together by a thread.

I closed the space between us, linked my fingers with his under the clear and starless sky.

"OK," Nate said. "I think I know."

Wagering I knew him too, I took a shot at naming his Patronus—and, by extension, him—this passionate, charming, considerate, clever creature whom I'd had the luck of meeting, of constellating.

I kissed his cheek. "A panda."

But I was wrong. Out of nowhere, it began to rain.

"A hummingbird," Nate said, as he got up to leave the backyard. "It loves one thing for a moment, before it moves on to another the next."

A week later, Nate called me ten minutes before our dinner reservation. He said he couldn't see me anymore. He blamed his job, cited anxiety, and claimed I deserved someone better, someone who wouldn't keep me waiting. I'd arrived fifteen minutes early at the restaurant, so I gave up our table for two and hailed a cab to his apartment. Nate answered the door with heavy shoulders and a sigh I echoed.

In his bedroom, I alternated between reasoning and crying. I had already written him into my life, placed his name on the dedication page of a manuscript I'd begun in a fugue state. So fervent was my desire to know and be known easily and immediately, to skip the hard parts of starting fresh, that I tried to slide into his life and slide him into mine.

Still, I kept trying. We don't have to escalate this, I offered, we can keep it casual, things don't have to change. If not a ready-made relationship, one that grows from knowing, then let us compromise, agree on eternal youth, forever midchase, like the etchings on that Grecian urn. But this was not the right offering—not for a Gemini, who's easily bored; not for Nate, whose decision was final.

When I ran out of tears and he stopped saying sorry, we lay in bed together. Nate wouldn't let me hold him or his hand, but he did let me gather my breath. He took pity on me, kissed me, and offered me my coat. "We can still be friends," he said, and I took that as his good-bye.

I really liked him when he really liked me. And then he didn't, when I still did. I told myself it was as simple as that. So I stepped out of his building and onto the Manhattan streets. I looked up at the sky—nary a star above, no constellations from which to divine meaning. It's easy to lose sight of them, those heavenly bodies, when the earth keeps turning and this city is too bright.

I'VE IMPROVED SINCE then, I hope, at interpreting signs. Two writers in particular are my role models. Both are very good at deciphering mixed messages—indeed, have made whole careers of it. The first is Carrie Bradshaw; the other is Roland Barthes.

In 1957, Barthes published his third book, *Mythologies*, a collection of articles that reflect on the cultural symbols of his time. He calls them the "myths" of everyday French life—wine and the latest Citroën, steak-frites and Greta Garbo's face—from which he extracts meaning. He interprets such images as markers of how the masses live their lives—or are told to live their lives. (The book is unfailingly assigned in media studies courses.) As a semiotician, one who studies how signs come to mean things, Barthes regards myths as popular concepts that have been drained of their initial meaning and repurposed to mean something else, as dictated by the ruling powers of France's bourgeois society.

In one section, Barthes examines a photograph in *Paris Match*, the French weekly, in July 1955. It depicts a young black soldier wearing the French military uniform, saluting with eyes ascendant. On one level, the picture of the boy in uniform saluting is just that—a picture of a boy in uniform saluting, a pure sign in the semiotic sense. In this case, the sign consists of the picture of a boy, the signifier, representing the concept of a boy, the signified. Other examples: the word "horseshoe" representing the concept of a horseshoe; an eggplant emoji representing, innocently, the concept of an eggplant.

But Barthes also sees the "second order signification," the image as a constructed myth. The photo as sign, published on the cover of the country's national magazine in the '50s, amid rebellion in its African colonies, now acts as a signifier for a new signified: "That France is a great Empire, that all her sons, without any color discrimination, faithfully serve under her flag, and that there is no better answer to the detractors of an alleged colonialism than the zeal shown by this Negro in serving his so-called oppressors." The myth constructs the soldier as compliant, a model minority in service to the majority. Barthes understands myths as a system that furthers agendas, be they capitalism or imperialism. Today, he'd do well as a writer for *The New Yorker*. Some contemporary myths he might dissect: the color "millennial pink," Calvin Klein ads, why people on Twitter want celebrities to hit them with a car.

Another entry in *Mythologies* that feels eternal is "Astrology." Barthes finds that the horoscopes in *Elle* merely describe its audience's quotidian routines, in banal sections like "At Home" and "Outside." Though astrologists appeared to work with magic, Barthes writes (he mentions how, in his day, the French spent 300 billion francs on "sorcery," a field that apparently included reading the stars), horoscopes merely reflect a reader's reality. They do not distract nor offer escape from daily life; they reiterate it instead. Barthes compares astrology to literature: both are exercises in dealing with the real, seeking to know it by naming it—just as the Greeks called the moon Selene, as Keats called beauty truth.

By naming Nate, whether by Patronus or birth chart or signs, I'd hoped to know him. If I could know him as well as he did me, I could be as prepared as he was. Then we could go toe-to-toe, be a match for each other, a twenty-first-century match made via social media. If astrology confronts reality by reflecting it, then technology goes even further. It aims to, in Tech Twitter speak, *optimize the experience*. This is apparent in dating apps, which aim to reduce the friction in romance.

Tinder plays messenger ("He likes you!"), while Hinge plays matchmaker ("We thought you should meet!"). OkCupid makes algorithmic matches ("You're mathematically compatible!"), while Grindr does the literal least ("He's online and nearby, so you might as well."). We use these apps because, as their ad campaigns tell us, we've got better things to do than sit through bad date after bad date, or prowl bars and clubs and gallery openings. Dating apps cut down on time and reduce the energy required. Searching for a mate takes our attention away from important things, like work—the petty tasks we accomplish at our standing desks and in Slack, as we inhale Sweetgreen salads that were preordered for pickup.

Millennials like me have been told constantly to organize our daily lives in pursuit of maximum productivity. Time is capital, so preaches the Church of Optimization, and every year is the Year of the Hustle. We devote ourselves, then, to work and what it offers us: a salary, health insurance, proof of our life's worth under late-stage capitalism. As investments, courtship and matters of the heart are too volatile. We turn to technology to reduce the risk and effort. In a way, this faith in tech requires grand optimism: Stop trying so hard, we tell ourselves, and be chill. Let love come to you. Leave it to old Cupid and his arrows.

Meeting Nate through Twitter appealed to me because it's not the app most geared toward romance or sex (Porn Twitter aside). To bend the platform for his own purposes, Nate had to take an active role in the pursuit. He admitted it too. He said it felt unfair of him to end things when he was the one to message me first. That's the thing about the Twitter meet-cute: the favorites, retweets, @mentions, replies—this nascent courting conveniently done from your commute, your bed, your bathroom—all transpire online. Your thirst is on record. Unless, of course, you delete that record.

Nate eventually unfollowed me. I returned the favor. We didn't block or mute each other, so I saw him around my digital neighborhood as I had before our first iced coffee date. I'd see him when my mutuals retweeted him, believe he was dating someone when he'd @mention another man. I childishly assumed I would know him better, interpret him online more easily, once we had known each other in the biblical sense. But even then, I only knew him as well as his ten thousand followers did.

Social media can create an inflated sense of familiarity. It tricks you into thinking that those you follow are knowable and accessible to you. That's the whole premise of the game, one celebrities and influencers have mastered. Since Twitter's design frames itself as a user's stream of consciousness, the id to Instagram's superego, Twitter can feel like the platform where you are at your most authentic, unguarded.

But technology is a malleable thing. It offers the power to control a narrative. I took advantage of this as a teenager when I presented a false identity online to protect myself and play a role I never could in life. Today, in an internet landscape where we can monetize the myths of who we are, an allegedly candid authenticity is our best armor. There will always be other essential parts of ourselves that we keep hidden—even for me. That we seem so open online is just part of the performance.

So it's logical, the need to vet someone online before meeting them. I do so before going on a proper date but rarely before a hookup. I should probably make a habit of it because, these days especially, physical safety is imperative. Consider all the acrobatics we perform when going on dates: first meeting in a public place, making contingency plans with friends, all just in case. A friend once gave us access to a GPS tracker on his phone before meeting a headless torso on Grindr who seemed too good to be true. We'd just heard about a series of gay hate crimes in Texas, where gay men invited Grindr users to their homes, only to find a group of men at their doorsteps. The gay men were attacked, restrained with tape, and called "faggots" as they stared down the barrel of a gun.

"Text us when you get there," we say in our group chats. "And text us when you get home."

When I meet someone new, I dive deep into their social media to probe for signs it won't work. I pass on dudes who want kids, since I don't; on guys who, judging by their pictures, only have white friends, since I'm not. I swipe left on men who say their political views are "conservative" or "moderate." To possess an ideology that's right of left evinces a heart that considers the lives of queer people, people of color, women, the poor, the disabled, immigrants and refugees, and combinations thereupon as lesser than one's own.

It's a snap judgment, yes. One that saves me the psychic burden of sitting through dinner with a boy who might insist, "But *all* lives matter." Isn't this the point of tech-assisted dating? It's to optimize the experience, to reduce the friction, to make the slide into a relationship as seamless as possible.

But even when a suitor is a match on paper, I've found that nothing replaces the fact-finding you do together. Zodiac signs, in theory, might tell you if your fighting styles are a match or if your silences are harmonious. But neither the stars nor Twitter can tell you what their lips feel like against yours, or if they fit snugly in your bed, or you in theirs, in the place where their neck and collarbone meet.

THE YEAR AFTER we met, I published an essay about Nate. One of his colleagues DMed me about it. Great piece, he said; no, I haven't talked to him about it, and yes, we saw your flowers. As I wrote in the essay, I had sent flowers to Nate's desk on Valentine's Day after we ended it. I'd wished him well in the card and sealed the envelope with a golden hummingbird. Only now do I realize that, by doing so, I'd brought the theater of Twitter to life; I'd sent him my heartbeat, as promised, for everyone to see.

At the time, I told myself I was just being a gracious ex. A power move, said my friends. But it's not a power move when you secretly hope the flowers send him running back to you. I never heard from Nate about the essay, but he eventually published one of his own, about burning out and building a home in the woods. He briefly mentioned what I'd written about him (he called it "self-aggrandizing"), but he didn't write about me specifically. While I didn't think he would, a naïve part of me hoped he would return the gesture. It's human nature—or at least my self-aggrandizing nature—to want to believe we can affect someone so greatly that we become a part of their story.

It was nice to read Nate, though, to finally learn about him as he had me. Other than his essay, he didn't flinch. Nate moved on easily, as if nothing had happened between us. It was a familiar tactic, one I've deployed too. It's the old principle: Never show your romantic failures. Only allow the spectacle of someone new appearing in your profile picture, in your timeline, in your stories.

However incompatible we were, I'm glad Nate and I met. I acknowledge he read the signs clearly, saw my own red flags, and put up with me longer than he should've; I was a recent college grad who dedicated a book to a guy I'd only been seeing for a few months—yikes. He was right to end things, even while I remained enamored and hopeless. This story, whether or not it's true, is one of many I believe in order to move on and let go. To do otherwise, to begrudge the many men I've met, would make my heart too heavy.

I still entertain DMs on Twitter, still check a new date's zodiac sign, but I take it all with a grain of salt. I don't avoid Scorpios, and I'll give a Pisces a chance. Astrology's less prescriptive, more descriptive—to me, at least—and I'd rather use it to read myself. It's self-interrogation, naming possible personal tendencies, whether good or bad, to know myself better. Libras, for example, are allegedly pragmatic in love. This is a trait to which I aspire.

Birth charts don't set the course for our lives. They just determine the cards we're dealt. Greater influences are the earthly circumstances of our births, which can hold immense sway over our characters, our lots in life. The families into which we're born. The borders that we cross. The genes and dominant alleles that determine the courts we may join, the tables at which we may sit.

So there's merit to studying the things bigger than us, the forces that shape how we rise and how we fall. All the better to live up to an expectation or overcome a shortcoming. A Libra, it's said, bends to the will of others to avoid conflict. This is a habit I'm currently fighting.

RICE QUEENS, DAIRY QUEENS

I WAS IRREVERSIBLY drunk, I'm told, by the time I screamed at Christian.

He'd arrived with someone else, as the guest of a reporter in our newsroom. I saw Christian, he waved hello, and I decided to obliterate myself. Given the open bar for our annual holiday party, this was dangerously doable. I doubled my self-imposed maximum of six drinks to twelve, slamming flutes of prosecco, one right after another. Stressed as I was by the various crises of that year—romantic and domestic, familial and professional—I figured, what the hell, I deserved it.

The photos from that night resemble my memories of it: blurry, messy, awkwardly cropped. The pictures have a neon pallor to them, washed out by nightclub lighting at the venue we rented out. My colleagues and I wore our holiday best, all velvet and sequins and MAC Ruby Woo. My suit was brown with cobalt accents. In hindsight, the accessories were overkill. I wore a tie, lapel pin, pocket square, and tie bar. I looked like an inexperienced soldier, laden with excess equipment I didn't yet know how to use.

By the time we got to the photo booth, Krutika and I were terribly sloshed. Our eyes were half-lidded, my tie and her blouse askew, stumbling to compose ourselves for the camera. We'd grown close and quickly that summer, as each other's anchors amid a period of stormy weather in our lives. Our bond was bolstered by how much we had in common—queerness, Disney villain cackles, and gleaming open-mouthed smiles (the rewards of orthodontia paid for by parents who wanted only the best for their only children in this strange new country). For the photo booth picture, Krutika kissed me on the cheek and smeared lipstick across my face.

She lost track of me, she says, when I left for the bar. That was probably when I saw Christian and drowned myself in bubbly. It's impressive, to think now, how the booze kept flowing for a crowd that size. Though we were a huge company by then, plus-ones were still allowed, as evidenced by the presence of my friendly ghosts, Christian being just one of them. All night I'd been running into men I'd kissed before, now on the arms of my better-looking colleagues.

According to my pickled memory, Christian found me at the bar. In reality, I likely stumbled over to him. I can't remember our small talk, but Christian had always been a gentleman. He probably saw me, off-balance and transparent, and offered a sage yet teasing aphorism: "Never drink to feel better." I would have agreed: "Only drink to feel worse."

We met on a Grindr date, remained occasional lovers during my formative New York summers. Our kisses were incandescent and then we peaceably lost touch. Seeing Christian at any other time would've been refreshing, would not have upset me the way it did that night, on the heels of too many breakups and rejections in this school of queer desire where he was once my tutor and I still had much to learn. His arrival hammered home the facts of our small world, an incestuous one where, it seemed to me, men loved only men who looked like them. In that moment, it was clear to me how few options I had, how I would always be the one passed over.

Why not take me home, I asked Christian, for old times' sake? His no was firm and clear, but I was deep in my prosecco fugue and persistent. I wasn't hearing him. The neon lights flashed and strobed, and I was seeing red. I'd been given too many flimsy excuses lately, variations on the themes: it's not you, it's me; you're cute, but; sorry, just a preference.

So, with pent-up rage in my heart and frizzante in my veins, I yelled at Christian, "Is it because I'm not *white*?"

I couldn't believe I said that. At least not out loud. But it was coming back to me. The shape of the words became familiar in my cottonmouth, even through the fog of my hangover, as Krutika recounted the evening on a morning-after phone call. It was the first of many to come. Phone calls, yes, but also times we'd tell this story, so representative of who we were at the time: her, equal parts supportive and assertive (a Sagittarius), and me, clumsily parsing sex and racism.

This is how the story goes: I was at the bar with Christian, making a scene (I am a huge gesticulator), and Krutika came over to investigate. She tried to pull me away from him, but I insisted on confronting my old flame, on finally screaming at him in a room full of reporters and middle managers. At my outburst, Krutika immediately dragged me away to get water and my coat. I was tripping over my feet, so she and our friends had to hail me a cab, reassure me I was in the right as I shifted from angry to ashamed, and give the driver my address.

"And then you got home," Krutika said. "I mean, I hope you did."

I did, but first I threw up in the cab. I found my trousers on my bedroom floor, which had a suspicious stain at the hem. Further confirmation: the "bodily fluids" fee charged to my credit card by the cab company. At that point, I remember, I was already in front of my house. Had I just stuck my head out the window, I could've saved myself a hundred dollars and a dry-cleaning bill.

"I think I need to call Christian and apologize," I said. Krutika didn't think I owed him anything, but I cared about him and our history. It bothered me that, in a drunken rant, I implied he was a racist.

"Oh, you didn't imply," Krutika said. "You fully yelled it at the bar." I pulled up my bedcovers around me, to hide from the sunlight and the embarrassment. She asked, "How do you know that guy, anyway?"

Christian was an editor at a wonkish magazine, which was probably how that reporter knew him. We all ran in the same circles, but Christian and I had known each other for years. We met when I was twenty and a rising junior at Vassar, spending my first summer as an intern in New York. In addition to our mutual attraction, we were an intellectual match. In our early conversations, we went toe-to-toe on Wilde, Bataille, and Barthes's *Camera Lucida*. (I'd just declared my double major in English and media studies.)

I once found another Barthes on Christian's nightstand after we had brunch and sex. It was one of the writer's later volumes, called *A Lover's Discourse*. As I thumbed through the yellowing pages, Christian suggested I read it.

"It's very much like you," he said, then planted kisses down my spine with each word. "Sexy. Romantic. Overly analytical." After another orgasm, I got a copy that afternoon.

We weren't, nor would we ever be, boyfriends. He was in a long-term relationship, now marriage. But they were open, of course, as most learned gays I've met seem to be. Given the arrangement, I didn't expect much from Christian beyond vigorous academic debate and sportive sex, the kind that makes you smile when you come. We didn't know what to call ourselves, other than "just friends." But we joked how we loved in the manner of Greeks, adopting a pedagogic model, conscious of consent and age.

Christian made for a good set of training wheels. He showed me, by example, what my life in New York could look like after school: literary, joyful, filled with camaraderie. At one point, he even invited me to go out dancing with him, his partner, and his friends. We wound up at his favorite gay bar, dancing with drag queens and tossing back vodka sodas until three in the morning. This queer world felt so much bigger then; it and Gay Twitter hadn't yet shrunk around me. I think I owe these good times to how safe I felt with Christian. He always asked for permission, whether to treat me to dinner or take me to a club or kiss me, in public and in private. He never patronized, always treated me as an equal.

I was subletting a living room when we met, so Christian and I would hook up in his immaculate uptown apartment, where he and his partner kept two cats. Once, when we were disrobing, he asked me if I was all right. Look, he said, your eye. He brought me to the mirror. My left eye was swelling in its socket, an allergic reaction to the cats who said hello with their tongues.

I removed the contact lens, but it left an imprint around the iris as the sclera became inflamed and angry pink. It didn't hurt and I could see clearly, but I was visibly shaken by the incident. Christian was gracious: "We can stop if you want!" It was fine, I assured him, nothing Benadryl couldn't cure. I kept my left eye shut, giving the impression of a twinky Cyclops, and carried on.

We were about to have sex for the first time, and I couldn't pass up the chance, not with him. Christian was classically handsome, as if sculpted, wore a crown of curls that'd make the Apollo Lyceus jealous. He was in possession of an eternal grace, as close as art historians could get to a bona fide Praxiteles. That he was considerate and good in bed made it almost unfair. But it was hard to begrudge him such gifts when they benefited me. When I came, I smiled. When he did, we kissed.

Historically, Christian had been available to me. So when he refused my invitation at the holiday party to go home with him, I was taken aback. Sure, we hadn't hung out in a while, but we had grown apart naturally with no ill will—so what was the problem?

"You kept yelling something about Dairy Queen," Krutika said on the phone. "I was like, bitch, there's no DQ here!"

I probably meant dairy queens, I explained, the slang term for gay men who only date milky white men. In my alcohol-fueled frenzy, I had thought I was seeing Christian clearly for the first time, that he had a preference for white men—like his partner, like all his friends, like that brawny reporter he came with. He was white too, after all, and so many of the white men I'd tried to date after him ended up with men who looked like themselves. Christian was a dairy queen, I concluded, just like the rest of them, because he didn't go home with me after the party.

Krutika scoffed, called me out on my bullshit. Christian and I used to go out years ago, she reminded me. It wasn't as if I was white then.

"All right, you know I love you," Krutika said, "and I don't mean any harm by what I'm about to say."

She has always been very good at taking apart my delusions and self-deceptions. We built this disclaimer into our friendship early on, so as not to overstate the given: *I love you and I want you to be better.* But on that phone call, I hadn't steeled myself enough to hear what I immediately knew was the truth.

"If anyone's a dairy queen," she said, "it's you."

FOR ME, IT began in the men's underwear section. It was there that I first saw them, that carved alabaster lot, a pantheon of idolized physiques. David Beckham, Freddie Ljungberg, Jamie Dornan, and—of course, the archetype—the classical Marky Mark. Long before the Greek antiquities room at the Met in New York, I had Macy's at the Fashion Show shopping mall in Las Vegas. That gallery of bodies informed my sexual ideal, those aisles of men seemingly hewn from marble. Many pubescent gay boys go through this rite of passage, stealing glances at the packages on such packages, imprinting on men who've come from Olympus itself.

I would abscond to that PG-13 corner of Macy's whenever my mother gave me money and time at the mall. After taking in a visual feast of chiseled bodies, I'd rearrange my erection and pick a package I could take home. Just as I once bought a studded belt and bracelet at Hot Topic to better resemble the classmate I was crushing on, I took those opportunities to buy what I hoped would make me desirable, would link me to other men.

The blinding whiteness of those underwear aisles was not lost on me. From the first Calvin Klein ad in 1982, featuring the Olympian Tom Hintnaus viewed from the bottom, to Mark Wahlberg in his Calvins in 1992, to David Beckham smoldering in repose for Emporio Armani in 2008—those campaigns and images were persuasive, even when they were diluted into less intentionally provocative images on packaging for Fruit of the Loom. They gave the impression that to be white and muscular were prerequisites to being sellable, worthy of being wanted. Here were two lessons bundled into one for queer little boys: what to desire and what to desire to become. As a young Filipino immigrant beginning to engage with American culture as practice, I didn't question the messaging and bought into it instead. These ads didn't just sell garments. They sold the very myth of American masculinity.

Underwear ads have been a site of this mythmaking for ages. Well before Calvin Klein, there were the decadent ads drawn by J. C. Leyendecker in the early twentieth century for men's outfitters like Kuppenheimer, Cooper Underwear (now named Jockey). He drew his men not only as jocks (rugby boys and crew captains) or as dandies (dashing bachelors in white tie), but as both (squash players), always in contexts of WASPy affluence. What Leyendecker and Calvin Klein created was an image of the archetypal American man—one whose attractiveness was charged with classical ideas of masculinity and whiteness.

Recently, men's underwear ads have featured more people of color. In the late 2000s, Calvin Klein enlisted Djimon Hounsou, a black model and actor from Benin, and Hidetoshi Nakata, a Japanese footballer, into their campaigns. These castings expanded the masculine ideal, but they still had their limits. Like their white counterparts, these idols still had carved abs and bulging biceps, as if sculpted by Michelangelo himself from bronze and brass, rather than the marble he saved for David. The lesson, then: desirability could be accessed through whiteness or sheer brawn, most easily through both.

Underwear ads alone don't dictate the gay male obsession with whiteness and masculinity; various cultural phenomena also teach racism and internalized femmephobia. Still, the people behind such ads and images—very often queer men themselves (who do you think drew the swollen muscles on Hercules and Zeus in the Disney film?)—set the standards of male beauty. They then use those standards to sell their products to anyone who will listen, queer or otherwise, implying that their products provide an avenue to that beauty. That's how advertising works. And I bought it. Calvin Klein capitalized on my need for validation, for mythic signs of virility. Whenever I met up with Christian, or Gareth, or Adam, or any of my nameless men, I always made sure to wear my Calvins, even though they couldn't make me look like Marky Mark or David.

I didn't see myself as anything but a twink, at the ages of twenty and twenty-one, with only the nubile charms of a Filipino boy to leverage in uber-competitive New York. While some men took this bait, more common were those who disclaimed in their profiles, "no fats, no femmes, no Asians." (Or "no spice, no rice.") Sometimes, men who wrote such slurs fucked me anyway, reminding me how racists might make exceptions in the name of conquest. Even in my Calvins, it was clear I wasn't one of them, the men who held me at arm's length even when they were inside me. But I took such evenings as concessions and kept on with the chase. Like them, I was a product of conditioning, taught to think only these white muscular men were desirable.

Christian appealed because he knew all this, understood the theory that animated my anxieties. Over dinner, we'd skewer the masc4masc habits of our fellow queens who idolized stereotypes of hypermasculinity, who couldn't intuit, as we did, the oppressive systems at work—the code in the matrix, as it were. We thought highly of ourselves, we admitted, and yet maintained our ambitious gym routines, stuck on that hamster wheel.

When he conceded that he loved French cooking and butter too much to possess the coveted six-pack abs, I felt camaraderie in that admission, though he was still white—like them, unlike me. But I focused on how we reflected each other instead. We fancied ourselves aesthetes, learned in the ways of epistemology and camp, heirs to a more cerebral and sibilant tradition, one that celebrated reading queerly.

Christian taught me about the homoeroticism in Leyendecker's art—the men's macho suiting, homosocial schemas, and dextrous glances as if cruising. Leyendecker mapped the men's gazes to circumvent their women companions, to point instead to men they resembled. When I noted how all the men looked alike, Christian explained they were facsimiles of the artist's young lover, Charles Beach, who became the template for the Arrow Collar Man.

This man was in most of Leyendecker's ads: for Arrow and Cluett, as men with golf clubs exchanging flirtatious glances; for Kuppenheimer, as two men eyeing a third, ignorant of a woman drawn as a literal siren; and for the Marines, as a pair of them on a cliff, eyeing a ship on the horizon, one on his stomach, ass up, with the other standing behind him, waving a flag positioned as if he himself were at full mast.

I loved Leyendecker's style. His distinctive brushstrokes in oil and turpentine complemented the strong lines in his art, from the pleats and creases in clothing, to the jaws and cheeks of men who mirrored Christian, debonair. I identi-fied with them as much as a passion for suits and Ivy League drag would let me. But I didn't see myself in this art, in these homosocial worlds. In fact, growing up, I didn't see anyone like me in American popular culture at all.

Though I could project myself onto Carrie in *Sex and the City* or Will from *Will & Grace*, the fact remained: They were white. I was not. With Will, at least, there was a smidge of identification in that we were both gay men. When it came to Asian representation on screen, I saw characters and bodies with which I shared only a par-tial resemblance. There was Lucy Liu in *Charlie's Angels*, Jackie Chan in *Rush Hour*, Thuy Trang as Trini the Yel-low Ranger in *Power Rangers*. They were all Asian, yes, and powerful ones at that. But none of them were Filipino. Or gay. Or gay and Filipino.

Even in private, my imagination was limited by what I saw in pop culture. When I wrote a very bad novelization of my first year at Vassar, I cast Darren Criss, a mixed-race American actor, as myself. Though Darren is Filipino (his mother is from Cebu), he's white-passing; his break-through out-and-proud gay character on *Glee* was portrayed as white. As much as I admired what Darren represented, I didn't feel like he represented me. By that same token, I envied his ability to pass in America. In casting him as me in my book, I wished for the same privilege of passing, even if only in art.

I'd done the same when I first started exploring who I could be on the internet. I concocted a whole other persona, a white boy I named Jonathan. My profile picture was a portrait I'd stolen from someone's blog. My internet friends were under the impression I was an out teen from Baltimore, with a doting boyfriend and accepting parents. In those days, we were told to be anonymous online. Protect your identity, never put your name in your email. So why not be someone else? There were so many more white images in America to choose from anyway, to pass off as my own. So the decision to pose as white was a matter of convenience. That was the lie I told myself.

In his essay "The Decay of Lying," Oscar Wilde argues that life imitates art, not the other way around. "Literature always anticipates life," he writes. "It does not copy it, but moulds it to its purpose." Barthes might contest this thesis. He says in *Mythologies* that literature's task is a delayed, rather than anticipatory, confirmation of the real. Either way, these white gays might agree that meanings are consciously grafted onto what we see in nature.

Wilde makes an example of London's fog. People see it as a phenomenon with "mysterious loveliness," he says, because that's how poets and painters have rendered it in art. Of this mystique and romance ascribed to fog in a collective imagination, Wilde writes, "They did not exist till art had invented them." That makes art, Barthes might say, the grand exercise in mythmaking. In this case, it's fog as signifier, with a hazy and dreamy London as signified, to create a sign, a language, deployed by artists that their audiences, in turn, template onto life.

Whether by art or advertising, I was taught what to see and how to see it. Michelangelo's David. Leyendecker's Arrow Collar Man. Calvin Klein's Marky Mark. I saw them as prescriptive, rather than descriptive, signs of beauty, of masculinity in the absolute. But I didn't see myself in these images, nor in so many televised and canonized imaginations. As a gay Filipino immigrant kid, Western culture gave me no reflections, no confirmations of my lived reality, only aspirations to whiteness. My life then, I had decided, must imitate this art, however inaccessible. I learned to want what I could never be.

———————

FILIPINO SOCIETY AND its internalized colonialism have similar ideas about desirability. In popular culture, the highest tiers of beauty are populated by mestizo celebrities. The term "mestizo," in the Philippines today, refers to mixed-race Filipinos, often those who have a white parent. The term, and the beauty standards that follow, were passed down to us over three centuries of Spanish colonization.

Mestizos dominate the media landscape. They appear in ads, act in films, and win international beauty pageants. Two of our Miss Universe titleholders are mestizo: Filipino Australian Catriona Gray and Filipino German Pia Wurtzbach. As one of the nation's most beloved love teams, mestizo actors Sam Milby and Anne Curtis were a celebrity power couple who starred in (and marketed) everything together. These superstars share airtime and commercial space—via endorsement deals across all sectors (I once bought a Pia-sponsored medical throat spray)—with their nonmestizo yet light-skinned counterparts too. In short: Filipinos, myself included, look to lightness to know what to desire.

I moved to the US as a tween and visited the Philippines almost every summer, splitting my time and my puberty between the two countries. Each had a say in my sexual education, and I realize now, they were consistent. Both emphasized a heteronormative masculinity and Westernized standards of beauty in the bodies they honored.

In Manila, my Marky Mark was Sam Milby, a Filipino American celebrity with a white father. He was a stateside import—from Ohio, of all places—who first gained prominence on the local *Big Brother* franchise. When he first got his start as the handsome Am-Boy (meaning "American Boy," naturally), he exuded boy-next-door charisma. I had a similar charm as a stateside import too. Then the studios engineered Sam into a star. Whenever I visited for my teenage summers, I saw how he and I were growing up into two very different Filipino men. I remained scrawny and twinky as Sam became ripped and hunky. Where his body was chiseled, mine was just fleshy. He was carved rock and I soft clay. I'd see Sam shirtless on roadside billboards for the underwear brand Bench and go home to touch myself, thinking both of him and of me *as* him, unsure if I wanted to fuck him or be him or maybe even both.

Celebrities are sculpted like this in the Philippines, positioned as aspirational—as literal models!—in the culture at large. It follows that the images Filipinos see most frequently are ones that do not reflect the majority of us. Every time I land at the Manila airport, I compare the stars featured in ads plastered on the jet bridge, in duty-free shops, and all over the terminal to the people waiting at the gates, at baggage claim, at the arrivals area. The difference is day and night. The Filipino majority is not mestizo but moreno.

It's another term inherited from Spain. "Moreno" comes from "moro," the Spanish exonym for North African Muslims. In Filipino contexts, it describes someone with dark hair and dark skin. That's most of the Filipino people, who were sculpted, as a precolonial creation myth goes, by a divine being who took for their materials the islands' fertile soil, clay, and ash.

That said, there are pedants who insist "all Filipinos are technically mestizo." Scientifically, it tracks: We're descendants of indigenous peoples, such as the Aeta and the Ifugao, and ethnic groups who came from parts of Oceania, East Africa, and Southeast Asia, who speak languages from the Austronesian language family. Add to that millennia of migration from places near (China, Japan) and far (Spain, duh), and you get the Philippine population. So, yes. In a way, we're all mixed.

And sure, in the Spanish colonial period, the term "mestizo" applied to anyone of mixed race: mestizo de Sangley for those who are part-Chinese, mestizo de Español for part-Spanish people. These were classifications that existed within a caste structure determined by the Philippines' Spanish colonizers, one similar to the casta system enforced in Spanish colonies in Latin America.

In Las Islas Filipinas, mestizos and their variations stood in the middle of this caste pyramid. At the bottom were the Indios, the Austronesian locals, and below them, the Negritos, like the indigenous Aeta. Near the top were the Insulares, those of wholly Spanish descent but born on these islands. This was a key marker that indicated their difference from the Peninsulares, who surpassed them on the social ladder, who ruled at the very top, who were born on the Iberian Peninsula and granted ancestry deemed "pure."

The construction of the contemporary Filipino mestizo is an artifact of this system of social stratification, one organized by proximity to whiteness. In this schema, as in today's, your lot in life is determined by the circumstances of your birth, by the color of your skin. So, the current use of "mestizo" isn't so far off from the original. It has simply been reconfigured into a new myth of mestizoness: that a mixed-race person possesses and represents the class mobility offered to people who are light skinned, a privilege often denied those who are dark skinned, which describes most of the Philippine population. To dismiss the word's current popular usage is to deny the racism, classism, and colorism in this country's past, as well as their continued prevalence today.

While a sliver of the population can look to mestizo celebrities for representation, the moreno majority can find reflections in the presidential palace. I've seen Gloria Macapagal Arroyo's short stature on my titas; Rodrigo Duterte's dark brown skin on my titos; Noynoy Aquino's lighter brown complexion on myself. In contrast, Noynoy's sister Kris Aquino is known for her porcelain skin and Americanized English. She's also dubbed "The Queen of Philippine Media" for her ubiquity in all forms of Filipino entertainment—historically as actress, more recently as meme, always as product endorser. Idols like Kris and Sam, light-skinned and conventionally attractive, are purposefully installed in the upper echelons of our society by studios and star makers. Though Filipino presidents make (and break) the laws of the land, it's the celebrities who reign over our culture, our desires, and our imaginations.

As such, the old casta structure lives on today. Skin-lightening products are a huge industry in the Philippines. Our parents pinched our noses as kids, "para tumangos," to better resemble narrower, more "Spanish" noses. Most of my Filipino American friends don't speak a Filipino language because their parents feared its attendant accent would invite ridicule or marginalization in the United States. They wanted their kids to blend in, to survive unscathed. Wherever we go, we still carry with us a colonial mentality, the one beaten into us over centuries by colonizers, whether by the Spanish who called us Indios or the Americans who considered us their "little brown brothers." Western and white ideologies have drilled into us the view of our inferiority, those standards and those caste-ings.

This gave me an advantage once I moved to Las Vegas and became Filipino American. I flexed my Am-Boy charm through my accent, by sharpening the dull edges of my Filipino English—with its mixed-up f's and p's, v's and b's—and honing it to an American crispness in its sound and vocabulary. It was a survival tactic in the States. In the Philippines, my Americanness could be a tool to move up in the world. On my visits to Manila, my relatives encouraged me to move back and enter showbiz. "You're from America now, and you have the accent, so people will love you," they said. "You're Filipino, but you don't look like it. You look like you're mixed. They love that!"

It's true I have some physical features that deviate from the Filipino norm. I'm considered tall in Manila but decidedly average in New York. I have comedically thick eyebrows, which my father once described as "Basque." My nose isn't particularly flat, which makes me think all that childhood pinching might have worked. My skin is lighter than most; both my birth parents are relatively light skinned and I spend most days indoors and out of the sun. As such, my melanin isn't as prominent as Duterte's or my Tito Ronnie's, but my color doesn't come close to Kris Aquino's porcelain-doll complexion.

Variations in skin color among Filipinos the world over are explained by our ancient creation myths. According to one myth of many, the divine being who shaped us out of mud used a kiln to bring us to life. One batch of Filipinos came out dark, another light, and the third at a midpoint between the two shades. This divinity was like Goldilocks, the story goes, who preferred a happy medium, who thought the middle was just right—but came to love all three batches equally, remembering they were shaped from the same materials, brothers by the same clay.

In reality, it's all just genes and Punnett squares. Alleles will simply deal you genetic cards from the decks stacked by history. From there, culture does the rest. My mother and father didn't choose which physical traits I inherited, but they made sure to pass down what societal privileges they had, like a middle-class education and upbringing. My passably mestizo looks were merely an unexpected yield.

Strangers have asked me, "Where are you really from?" even in the place where I am really from. They don't believe I'm "full," as in full-blooded Filipino. On Grindr in Manila, a guy said I was handsome because I was biracial. (I'm not.) "Gwapo mo," were the words he used, "halo ka, no?" Halo, as an adjective, translates to "mixed." He couldn't disentangle the myth of mestizoness from who he found attractive.

It reminded me of the Filipino clothier Bayo and a notorious ad campaign they ran in 2012 with the slogan

"What's Your Mix?" It featured mixed-race models with captions like "40% British and 60% Filipino" and "60% African and 40% Filipino." I kid you not, the ad copy said, "Call it biased, but the mixing and matching of different nationalities with Filipino blood is almost a sure formula for someone beautiful and world class."

Bayo spokespeople and their defenders insisted the ad didn't imply that "pure Filipinos" couldn't be "beautiful." But the subtext played into that colonial framework of how class mobility might be achieved: "The mixing and matching of different nationalities," the augmentation of one's DNA into something Filipino-*plus*, as the "sure formula" that produces someone of "world class" status. This is colonialism in action. It's in action when Filipino elders tell kids to "stay out of the sun because you're gonna get dark," when skin-whitening cosmetics promise "more radiant skin," and when I slept with white men as the dairy queen I was.

I had believed I was above the colonial brainwashing so apparent in the Philippines. I refused the whims of my relatives, said I'd never do show business in Manila, even when I was literally an acting major at my Las Vegas arts high school. Admittedly, I would have enjoyed being bootcamped into a young hunk, like Sam Milby, into a golden and imported American boy. However, I was a young gay man, too out and proud to go back into the closet for a Filipino studio system in a de facto theocracy. Instead, I let my queerness and my internalized colonialism run free in the hemisphere of my colonizers. I planned to marry a white boy, looking at white men with a queer desire complicated by a colonial mentality: Do I want to fuck that white guy or do I want to be him? Groomed by colonialism and racism on both sides of the Pacific, I was shaped to become a dairy queen.

That said, colonialism is a two-way street. Dairy queens are just one side of the equation—one inversion being rice queens. In contrast to men who insist on "no spice, no rice," rice queens specifically seek out Asian men. Such gay men, both white and others of color, saw me as an exotic conquest, something to pillage, literally booty to be taken. One said, with his cock in my mouth, "I've never fucked a Filipino before. This'll be fun." Another wanted my skin color, saying, "I want skin like this. You never have to go tanning!" And there have been plenty of slurs about what my brown body must taste like. One said, "I bet you taste like soy sauce." I left him at the bar right then and there.

What's worse, many of these men thought their fetishization of me was a compliment. The white man who said he'd never had sex with anyone Filipino before had mentioned, earlier that night, he'd always wanted to visit Manila or Bangkok, "anywhere in Southeast Asia, really." In hindsight, that should have been a red flag. I was fodder for his colonial fantasies, an object imported for his sexual tourism. It was demoralizing, being reduced to a stereotype, an extra in *Miss Saigon*. At first, I allowed it, figured it was just another tool in my arsenal to bag a man. But it came to a head when I was with a fellow Filipino, whose internalized colonialism jumped out.

I'd been cruising him (and his non-Filipino friend) in a steam room for a while. He seemed sweet and polite, someone I might actually bring home to meet my mother, who might fit into my family, given the culture we both shared. One night, we finally had the place to ourselves, to do as we pleased. We shared orgasms, and I learned his name was Paolo. I also learned, when he asked for mine, that he and his friend had been calling me "Island Boy."

That name traded on colonial ideas of Filipinoness, of exotic and servile bodies. I felt like I was the butt of his joke, as if he were one of the upper-class Peninsulares, relegating me to the lower rungs of this tiered room, where even steam couldn't obscure the sexual caste system. Look who's talking, I wanted to reply. But that would've been my own colonial mentality rearing its poisonous head.

Besides, to contest him wouldn't have made a difference. Incidents like these remind me that, in racist and colonial imaginations, I inhabit a fetishized body, one marked as Other, even by the men who desire it. With this comes the difficulty of parsing a man's attraction, whether he wants me for me—my charm, my intellect, my smile—or as some island fantasy, a box to tick, a flavor of the month.

At the holiday party, when I offered myself to Christian and he said no for the first time, I misnamed him. I drunkenly called him a dairy queen, lumped him with the white men who'd refused me and made me feel undesirable because of the mere facts of my body. In my inebriated rage, I thought I saw it clearly: he said no to me because I wasn't white.

In the light of the morning after, I realized I had named the wrong fear. I was actually afraid that Christian was a rice queen, who fucked me only as a fetish and cast me aside once he was done with his sexual tourism. In the past, he'd made me feel safe, like an equal. I got riled up at the prospect that he might be just another white man taking advantage of me. That he might have lorded power over me, duped me into thinking I had any at all, felt like a betrayal of my trust, of our lovers' discourse.

Under colonialism, rice queens and dairy queens reign— as do bean queens, curry queens, and variations thereupon. As a dairy queen, I wished to join the ranks of men made of marble. In the eyes of rice queens who were white, I was desired precisely and only because I didn't look like them. As a model minority aspiring to whiteness, I would relinquish my power to these men, however they may have seen me, othering my own body in the process. All that mattered, in those deep wells of doubt, was that they witnessed me, picked me, and ultimately said yes.

———

"I SAID NO, Matt, because you were drunk."

I asked Christian why he didn't just tell me that at the party. "I did!" he said. "But you were drunk!"

I had reached out to Christian against Krutika's advice. I wanted to have a conversation that cleared the air. I also needed to collect scraps of dignity, rather than ignore the drunk elephant that stormed the room the night before. I would've had to own up to it sooner or later; we ran in the same circles in our small world.

As always, Christian understood my anxieties, what had instigated my outburst. He offered generous words as I described to him how my year had been drawing to a dismal close: the disintegration of my friendships with my roommates, my mother's and my stepfather's cancer diagnoses, the instability at work, and, of course, how I'd been picking the wrong men who only picked me for a night.

Christian was as kind as ever. I believed him and appreciated his continued respect of me and my body. To have taken me home in that obliterated state, I understood, would have been an actual betrayal of my trust, an abuse of power.

But when he offered to get together again soon, just as friends, I was too embarrassed to take him up on it. Moreover, my paranoia insisted, what if chivalry was merely a convenient excuse? What if he had simply tired of me or no longer saw me as attractive, despite his being a rice queen?

"Matt, my husband is white," said the imaginary Christian in my head.

What if it was true then, that his tastes had changed, that he had become a dairy queen, grown to prefer the company of men who resembled him, copies of other young lovers, and would prefer that I be made of porcelain rather than clay?

Imaginary-Christian echoed real-Christian: "You're sexy. Romantic. Overly analytical."

So what if none of this answers or negates or assuages my doubts?

"What difference would it make," Krutika had asked, "to have that conversation?"

This was why Krutika had advised against speaking to Christian. It wouldn't have solved anything. I was good at advocating on behalf of others and contradicting myself, see-sawing on a fulcrum like a set of unstable scales. Krutika knew I'd just enter another downward spiral. Such was my orbital path, repeatedly falling to the earth and crashing because I centered the lives of other men, allowed mine to revolve around theirs.

I spiraled like this often when I was seeing Nate. My college friend Vincent, bless him, was patient with me. He offered a warning, packaged in restaurant metaphor. With these white boys, he said, they'll happily try Ethiopian food one evening, or Malaysian another; their Wednesday night go-to may be Thai. But what do you think they long for, he asked, when these boys go home for Thanksgiving, for Christmas, for Purim?

The analogy is brilliant; it sparkles to me now, having had years to process it. But back then, when I was fresh out of school, green and hopeless, I had furrowed my brow at what I considered an unproductive tribalism. Aren't we all in this together, I thought, as gay men? Wouldn't such a worldview only further balkanize our broader community? I was an idiot, safe to say, who couldn't see the forest for the trees. Vincent had once said that I wasn't cooked yet, that I would get there eventually.

I was smart enough, at least, to shut up and listen to him. Vincent said he wouldn't give the same advice to our white friends; they don't face the same problem. "But we're boys of color," he said. "We have to have each other's backs."

Vincent was advising that I need not wait on Nate, not prioritize his interior life and perspectives over mine. And Krutika was doing the same thing now, telling me to de-center Christian, white men, and whiteness, to put myself in the center of my own universe for a change.

The misgivings I harbor in my relationships with other men are not about them. Not always, at least. My anxieties about desire and masculinity, race and colonialism, how they intersect and challenge each other, are mine, finding their center of gravity in me. The relationship I must develop is the one with the body I inhabit, which I had been reading from a position of aspirational whiteness. My desires to transcend the contemporary casta system were rooted in my own imagination, one I'd allowed to remain—to be—colonized. I had given consent. I'm working to revoke it.

I recall that episode at the party with Christian, however embarrassing and public, as an edifying one. While the execution was off, it was an overdue attempt at kicking down the doors that kept slamming in my face. With enough distance from the incident, I'm now proud of who I was at the time: someone beginning to unlearn.

Unlearning the colonialism I was taught, the stories I've been told and I've told myself, is a constant process. It's self-instruction by daily practice, like learning a language. You learn it by watching films, listening to the radio, reading books. Your ear gets attuned to it. You pick up the vocabulary, learn the system's grammar and mechanics. From there, you can understand and deconstruct it. Sure, learning a language is a solo task, but it helps to have conversation partners.

Friends like Krutika and Vincent have helped me along. They hold me up emotionally—and sometimes physically—when I spiral, help me unpack my ideas, whether wild or reasonable. I'm lucky to have a Greek chorus to check my hubris—and to do the same for them. In group chats and on phone calls, we have our everyday acts of solidarity, hearing one another across the gaps in our experiences. They encourage me to reflect on my theories, to engage in the praxis of decolonizing myself. After all, heavy is the head that wears the crown of dairy queendom. Freed of that burden, I've gotten better at discerning the difference: whether a man might fit nicely into my life, or he's just a white guy with a beard.

When I look at Calvin Klein ads now, I don't search for myself in them. And I don't try to sleep exclusively with those sculpted bodies either, whether carved from marble or bronze. (Of course, if Trevante Rhodes is up for it, I am wholly available.) Such images helped me understand my sexuality as a boy, but I can finally see through their mythologies, disentangle the myths of what makes a man beautiful. They're beautiful bodies, yes, but they're not the only ones worth desiring.

As it turns out, the whiteness of classical sculpture is itself a myth. In 2018, *The New Yorker* ran a piece about art historians studying the whitewashing of ancient art. For years, the powers that be in the worlds of archaeology and museums have led the public to believe that Greek and Roman statues have always been purely white when, in reality, the ancients were fans of polychromy. They painted their gods and heroes in robes of pinks and patterns, their hair in black or auburn or blond, and their skin in various shades, from olive to dark brown. The evidence has always been there on the marble bodies, millennia-old pigments that prove the ancients lived in color.

This becomes visible to the naked eye, an art historian told *The New Yorker*, when you begin to see objectively, to set aside institutionalized myths that have long linked whiteness with idealized beauty, banished color to the realm of the vulgar and exotic. "Ancient sculpture was not pure white—and neither were the people of the ancient world," argued a classics professor. She wrote essays against the whitewashing of classical sculpture to counter the disturbing trend of white marble statues being co-opted as symbols of white supremacy by racists, who hoped to "affirm what they imagine to be an unblemished lineage of

white Western culture extending back to ancient Greece."
In a way, Wilde was right: People will aspire to art's ideals,
however falsely constructed. Barthes too might find satisfaction in ancient polychromy—a confirmation of the real,
delayed for centuries, that art reflected life.

There was a sculpture show at the Met that I was supposed to see but didn't. Christian had suggested, one au-
tumn, that I have a look. The exhibit was *Bernini: Sculpting
in Clay*. I'd known Bernini was another one of those men
who worked in marble, as the creator of Saint Teresa's divine ecstasy. At the time, I didn't think I was missing out;
looking back, I know I did. The exhibition had on view
Bernini's sketches in clay, fired as terracotta, which were
the bases for his grand Baroque works that decorate the
eternal city of Rome at every turn.

To have walked through that gallery would have been
to witness angels and gods and whole royal courts in the
colors of sand and ash and soil, everyday humans molded in
rich browns and gleaming blacks. It would have been to see
stories of creation, to behold how art could begin as—and
ultimately be—beautiful figures made of mud.

VASSAR GIRL

Every year, we prayed for Meryl Streep. The class before mine claims they actually got her. And they did, kind of. She was sitting onstage, with her fellow alums and trustees, and she ran up to hug her daughter, midwalk to get her diploma. But it was Kirsten Gillibrand, the junior senator from New York, who stood at the podium at Graduation Hill and gave a speech to the youngest Streep and her Vassar classmates. So, no. Technically, they didn't get Meryl.

Neither did the class before theirs, which was addressed by Leymah Gbowee, the Nobel Peace Prize winner for her work in ending civil war in Liberia. Quite the upgrade, joked the class prior, who had been addressed by Chip Reid, the chief White House correspondent for CBS News. He did, at least, have the distinct honor of being the first male alum of our former women's college to give a commencement speech on home turf.

I sat in the crowd that year, as I did every year I was at Vassar—in the rain, in the sun, in the wind, in the sun again.

I was a freshman at the time, watching the male journalist address the seniors, dreaming of the day it would be my turn. Not to speak; my dreams were not yet that big. But I looked forward to the day it would be my turn to sit there in the black robes while overlooking Sunset Lake, my turn to cry and eat up clichés about oh the places we'll go. I couldn't wait. And I was hoping, as we all did, that we'd get Meryl.

Instead, in 2014, Vassar College's sesquicentennial graduating class was addressed by the woman who discovered God.

At least that's how *The Miscellany News* put it. Our class woke up one morning in the spring thaw, emerged from our townhouses and terrace apartments, bleary-eyed and bogged down by senior theses, to grab coffee and huevos rancheros, and read in the *Misc* that our commencement speaker would be a physicist named Sau Lan Wu.

The article listed her qualifications. Wu had been part of three major discoveries in particle physics: in 2012, of the Higgs boson, known as "the God particle," the subatomic particle that gives mass to all matter; in 1979, of the gluon, which glues together the nuclei of atoms; and in 1974, of the J/psi particle, for which her research team's leader won the Nobel Prize in Physics. She was also a distinguished professor at the University of Wisconsin–Madison and herself a Vassar graduate, class of '63.

At commencement, we learned that she was more than just her credentials. Wu was an immigrant to the United States, like I was. She was born in Hong Kong under

Japanese occupation. As a teenager, she applied to fifty schools in the US, asking for a full scholarship; she came from a poor family and couldn't afford to attend otherwise. Only Vassar picked her, told her, "You're in."

The school's generosity, she said, was invaluable to a young immigrant like her. Wu was met by Vassar alumnae when her ship from Victoria Harbour docked in San Francisco and again when her train pulled into Grand Central. In addition to the full scholarship, her books were on the house and her classmates gave her clothes to wear. For some spending money, a professor gave her a job.

"I ironed her suits and burned a big hole in one," Wu said. The audience laughed. "My new job was to move piles of mud from one side of her garden to the other." The audience laughed some more.

Since she wasn't financially preoccupied, she explained, she had the freedom to focus entirely on her studies, hiding in the library basement while her classmates cavorted with the "weekend busloads of Yale men." Wu emphasized her gratitude to Vassar: "All of the support—emotional and financial—provided me with great inspiration to be a successful scholar."

Wu went on to recap her career and the three scientific discoveries, all adding up to immigrant excellence personified. She owed her successes, she said, to Vassar. So then, what did she owe back? As an alumna coming home to campus with those three breakthroughs under her belt, I couldn't help but feel that her speech was something of a song and dance, payment for her scholarship. I thought of how a college footnotes itself in the careers of its alums, claims their wins as its own.

Isn't that why we extolled those names—Streep, Kudrow, Fonda, Hathaway, Bourdain, Bouvier? Wu was now among them, cast in a narrative that framed her potential for excellence as something only fulfilled because Vassar picked her. And now it had picked her again, to inspire us, to offer a model of life after Vassar. Here was a Vassar Girl, an excellent immigrant, a model minority.

But as Wu wrapped up and dedicated her address to her mother, I was all tears, no shade. She spoke of how her mother had wanted for her daughter the choices in life that she herself had been denied. I looked at my own mother, rows behind me, with my stepfather, both in their Sunday best: she in a blue jumpsuit, he in a linen Americana. They had flown in from Manila, crossed seas and states once again, to escort me out of Vassar, just as they'd dropped me off here, with the freedom to make choices they hadn't been afforded.

Professor Wu's story reflected mine and my gratitude mirrored hers. My tears mixed with my sweat as she reminded us of what we had sharpened in the confines of this campus: friendships, creativity, tenacity. She tasked us to face the world beyond our campus and live up to our terrifying potential. After a standing ovation, we fell into a procession as her words continued to ring in my ears, her message clear as a bell.

"That accent was a shame, though. I could barely understand her!"

The mother in Ralph Lauren went on, waving around a skewered shrimp, counting the years Professor Wu had been in the US and wondering to me, a friend of her daughter, who was fetching a drink at this graduation reception, why that thick Chinese accent hadn't been stamped out or, at the very least, neutered into legibility. I was too stunned to laugh when the shrimp on her cocktail stick went flying.

"How about you, Matt?" She wasn't slurring; her diction was perfect. "How long have you been American?"

Instinct kicked in—*play along*. "I immigrated ten years ago."

She threw up her hands in a there-you-have-it gesture. "And your English is so clear!"

When my teacher gave me the same pseudo-compliment in middle school, months after I landed in the US, I'd responded instinctively: "Well, our primary language of instruction in the Philippines is English." Though I flushed at my boldness then, I refused to be embarrassed by her ignorance. I could have answered my friend's mother similarly now—even more elegantly, after four years of studying the theory, sparring in seminars, critiquing such aggressions whether micro or macro.

In praxis, however, we show our true colors. Since my instincts had been neutered over those ten years, as I learned to take the path of least resistance, I tried to change the subject. I offered to get her another shrimp. I asked where her daughter went. I said I should go look for my parents; they're probably lost. I did what I could to avoid a scene and flee unscathed. Professor Wu wouldn't have kicked up a fuss, I thought, her message now unclear to me too.

Immigrants and people of color are forged in such fires, shaped by heat and pressure. But in my four years at Vassar, I was chosen to be privileged. As a model student and Asian American, I never risked getting burned.

WHILE SAU LAN Wu applied to fifty schools, I chose just the one. I applied Early Decision and heard back before Christmas. I was at rehearsals for *West Side Story* when my parents rolled up to my school in my mother's company car. They handed me an envelope, their faces expectant; they'd held it up to the light. I ripped it open to confirm: I got the letter that begins "You're in," got the only acceptance I wanted.

Vassar had been my first choice ever since I read the name in *The Devil Wears Prada*. In the book, Andy (played by Vassar alumna Anne Hathaway in the film) works at a fashion magazine as an assistant to the editor in chief Miranda Priestly (played by Vassar alumna Meryl Streep). At work, Andy befriends a gay male beauty editor and Vassar alumnus named James (he didn't make it into the film). The book makes a point of noting that, despite the career and college choices, James's parents didn't know he was gay.

I took it as a sign. *Prada* was a notorious roman à clef of the author's time at *Vogue* under Anna Wintour. There must've been some gay guy at Condé Nast that James was based on—perhaps all of them. Since James's path was possible, I chose the same one, hoping Vassar could play its part. The subsequent casting of alums Hathaway and Streep were affirmations of the theory I conjured. I said as much in my Vassar admissions essay, predictably titled "The One," and peppered it with generous helpings of the word "destiny." When I finally moved into my dorm room, my paperback *Prada* had a place of pride on my bookshelf.

On campus, I grasped that, though the joke about James was cheap and hackneyed, it held truth. On college tours, we always said Vassar wasn't any gayer than other liberal arts colleges, in terms of pure numbers. But it was true that queer kids here were more visible, felt more open to play with sexuality and gender. We seem gayer than most because there's only twenty-four hundred of us; there's little room to hide. This is a good thing, tour guides would tell prospective parents. On any given day, your daughter, son, and/or genderqueer progeny will encounter all walks of campus life, behold Vassar's quotidian diversity.

We were diverse in interests and race too, categorized by student organizations: Dance troupes. Drama clubs. Sports teams. Cultural and racial identity alliances. A cappella groups. Newspapers and journals and magazines. Bands and orchestras and choirs. New organizations popped up every year. Some were founded by my friends who had the foresight to leave legacies, alliances for those who'd come after us.

Among founders, I was an explorer, especially in my first year. I was eager to shed my high school self, who I considered plain and green. I'd been limited by the constraints of a single-minded focus to get here, to college, which promised to blow doors open to what would come after. That was how my mother and I saw it, one of many immigrant goal posts: get into college and you can get in anywhere.

Now that I was here, I took as many well-trodden paths as I could. I joined and auditioned for everything. By integrating myself into campus life, I managed to shed my past so well that my peers were often shocked to learn that I hailed from Las Vegas. I took this as flattery. We joked that I came from Vassar itself, sprang forth from the Shakespeare Garden's flowering columbines as did Athena from her father's skull, fully grown and armed.

Instead of Greek life, student organizations were our sororities and fraternities. Such affiliations were our identifiers: "You know, Matt Ortile? Dances with FlyPeople and Vassar Repertory Dance Theatre; does musicals with the Future Waitstaff of America; does social media for the *Miscellany News*; student-teaches that class on women and gay men in pop culture? The syllabus is pretty white? Yeah, him. He tried to make out with me last night." Like me, much of the school was overcommitted. There were lacrosse boys who made time for choir as well as Quidditch. There were theater girls directing one show while performing in three others. And there were student presidents on premed tracks singing solos in touring a cappella groups.

We were exhausted but, for the most part, happy. This was how we found our people, how we met new ones too. I remember fondly one of my birthday dinners. We went to the sushi place off campus, a ragtag group of friends I met through dorms, classes, and extracurriculars. Over sake bombs and Maki Combo Bs at Tokyo Express, my people became each other's people—dancers, musicians, writers, and, yes, athletes and scientists, too—becoming a small but chosen family.

This was also how we discovered people with whom we might jump into bed. Sex at school was often preceded by parties. And parties were accessed by affiliation. On a typical weekend, we'd hop from bacchanal to bacchanal as a squad, a veritable roll of tickets into parties otherwise off-limits. It's how ballet boys met Frisbee girls, rugby ladies met actresses, and a cappella dudes met yours truly.

I kissed set designers, swimmers, and tall men who ran track. I hooked up with class presidents, would-be doctors, and rowers in conference rooms and parlors. When a boy and I had roommates and neither of us could host, we spent the night in the languages hall; I could swipe into the French lounge. I then lost my VCard, which, surprise, is what we called our Vassar ID cards. And yes, we joked often how easily we lost ours.

I did have my first time at college. I'd tried with a Las Vegas boyfriend, but we weren't the right fit. Compared to high school's tiny wading pool of eligible gay men, Vassar was a buffet. I needed to get it over with—and did my first year, with a nice senior who held my hand during and let me spend the night—so that I could freely explore as I'd promised I would.

And explore I did. Despite our myriad student denominations, queerness cut across them. The women welcomed their sapphic inheritance at one of the famed Seven Sisters. And the men were curious, flexible; notorious were the tales of princes seeking the favors of we queens, the answers to questions they felt free to ask us. The "gay by May" bets might have been callous, but our queer peerage was rarely wrong. We were bitchy little things, in the way people can be when the tables have turned finally in their favor.

After all was said and done, my experience of being gay at Vassar was one of solidarity. Whether against homophobic graffiti that appeared on campus overnight, or the Westboro Baptist Church who picketed us, an alleged "Ivy League Whorehouse," I felt solidarity with friends I made, both queer and not. My time at Vassar was idyllic, befitting a college catalogue, a commencement speech. From the first bonfire at orientation to the graduation pyre into which we tossed what we wished to let go, I was privileged to be among people I loved, people like me. Vassar was a place where we could be fully ourselves, maybe for the first time. I understood little of Sau Lan Wu's physics, but her gratitude I knew well.

Vassar gave me such a hysterical sense of belonging, of being so rooted in its earth, that whatever the campus's terroir, I'm sure my blood would taste of it.

———————

As I EXPLORED new interests at school (semiology, ballet, Adderall), I dropped old habits. No longer did I pack a lunch of Spam with rice to eat in the bathroom while hiding from bullies; I bought pasta salads to eat with friends instead. I never asked them to go shoeless in my room, even when they sat on my bed. In public, I'd pick up calls from my mother and answer in a wide and nasal English I'd never use at home.

My Filipinoness was secondary to me at Vassar. Though I belonged to the well-publicized 35 percent of the student body that was nonwhite, my being Filipino—or brown or Asian—rarely came up, if at all. No professors cared to comment on my perfect English; no directors hesitated to cast me as a romantic lead. I wasn't denied parts in dances or talked out of writing articles for the paper. My merits got to function simply as merits, didn't have to protect me as they did in middle school and high school. At college, I seldom experienced racism personally. In fact, I seldom experienced race at all.

This was a relief to me. My Filipinoness had been a burden in Las Vegas. As I adjusted to life in the US, I faced peers who bullied me for being a gay brown immigrant and teachers who patronized me. As a teenager, I was othered, lacking. Now, I was welcome. More than that, I was chosen. I was selected for my talents, beloved for my charms. I wasn't limited by the circumstances of my birth—how could I be, when I said I was birthed by Vassar itself?

And, in a way, I was. It was then I began to fill out the mold I'd made for myself as a kid, what I'd hoped I would one day become. I grew into a thinker, a writer, a scene stealer, and a performer. On and off campus, I took these versions of me on test drives: in seminars, at internships, onstage, and in bed, respectively. Vassar gave me tools to define myself anew. It made my path possible, as *The Devil Wears Prada* had promised. Like Sau Lan Wu, I was chosen by Vassar, permitted to hone my potential within its walls. I became a proof of concept too, a model Vassar Girl.

While allusions to the Vassar man are rare, the Vassar Girl is a long-standing trope. Films and TV shows as varied as *Some Like It Hot*, *Designing Women*, and *Living Single* have used her as shorthand for an educated, often well-to-do woman. She's also, at various turns, the nonconformist (*The Simpsons*), the lady-loving lady (*Orange Is the New Black*), and the coddled artist (*Veep*). The Vassar Girl has also become symbolic of ambition and class mobility. Gina Torres's character on *Suits*, the no-nonsense Jessica Pearson, earned the title of managing partner at her law firm (and the view from her corner office) by working her ass off: "Full scholarship to Vassar," she says, looking down on New York from her glass tower, then "three years at Harvard law, and one year as the first black woman to clerk in the third circuit." I'm sure the Vassar PR machine loved that plug.

Pearson is a modern take on the Vassar Girl of yore, who's been sidestepping the shadows of her Yale father or Princeton brother since the school's founding in 1861. She's the one in a 1936 *New Yorker* cartoon whose mother warns, "I hope, dear, that you won't come back from Vassar with a lot of *ideas*." She's the one in a 1942 book of comics sighing, at the dinner table, "Mother, how can I explain the position of organized labor to Father when you keep passing me the chocolate sauce?" and on the phone with her beau, "But darling I *can't* marry you on Thursday—I have an Art 105 slide quiz." She's the one who chooses her own path.

In her 1951 essay "The Vassar Girl," the writer Mary McCarthy (class of '33) describes the school's transformative qualities. Most first-years, she writes, "come through Taylor Gate, as I did, with the hope of being made over, redirected, vivified." They're emancipated from pasts that didn't suit them, she says, via intellectual liberation. The Vassar Girl is tasked to offer her opinions and to spar in classrooms. She must "think for herself."

McCarthy notes that most Vassar grads leave inclined toward the liberal and heterodox, with a yearning to make something of themselves. "Vassar has a peculiar power," she writes, "of conveying a sense of excellence." Decades later, it's a sentiment, however pompous, that echoes in alums fictional and not. Jessica Pearson gave the school a proud place on her impressive CV. Her origin story was one of undeniable excellence, which used Vassar as a keystone—as it was in Sau Lan Wu's, as it was in mine.

Like McCarthy, Pearson, and Wu, I attended Vassar on a scholarship. I took out loans for my first year, as my mother's career in pharmaceuticals meant we didn't qualify as financially needy. Then she lost her job in the recession. For my next three years, as the child of a single unemployed parent (my stepfather and I had no legal relationship), I was paid by the college to come to school. Tuition, books, room, and board all on the house. I spent my work-study money on Chinese delivery to the library, bedsheets from Crate & Barrel, and bottles of chardonnay, purchased through friends with fake IDs. After four years, I left with only $15,000 in loans—not an insignificant amount but a small percentage of the $200,000 ticket price.

Fair payment, my mother reminds me, whenever I get my monthly student loan bill. Vassar opened doors for me: internships through alumni, grant funds from endowments, and proximity to New York City. I'd parrot these sound bites at scholarship receptions, where kids on financial aid were made to schmooze with the school's donors. These benefactors, usually white and wealthy, endowed scholarships for us, we who were at once privileged and poor by virtue of our attendance.

Over shrimp and cubes of cheese, we'd sing for our supper, wax grateful for opportunities the school bestowed on us. I was very good at this. I'd tell donors how I immigrated from the Philippines, didn't feel like I belonged in the US—not until I came to Vassar, where I was free to be myself, revel in my friendships and my studies, against the bucolic backdrop of its stately campus. I could pursue my career and life ambitions without financial worry, I'd tell them, thanks to generous donors like yourselves.

And, oh, how they'd glow, taking pride in my pride, so believable because I believed it too. I never had to fake my love for Vassar, which made me a favorite of the institution. The offices of financial aid, career development, campus life, admissions—I was their poster boy. The Vassar homepage featured me four times. The school photographer knew my name. I was exhausted but, for the most part, happy.

I looked the part too. At college, I dressed like Leyendecker's Arrow Collar men, ever blazered and pressed, a picture of affluence however feigned. It was part of my not-entirely-ironic Vassar Girl drag. I took my cues from McCarthy's description of the school's "dazzling girls . . . in pale sweaters and skirts, impeccable, with pearls at the throat and stately walks like goddesses." I buttoned up in oxfords, wrapped myself in clearance cashmere. Had I the mandatory gloves to wear for afternoon tea, I would've worn those too. (It was only when busloads of Yale men visited on weekends that I wore a pearl necklace.)

My middle school impulse to double-pop my collars in budget-Nantucket costuming had taken a new shape. The irony was that my Ivy League disguise often stood out at Vassar, where many of my white peers were making problematic attempts at what they considered counterculture, from putting their blond hair in dreads to declaring they were Hindu. They did all they could to shed their Connecticut skins because they wanted to be different. I wanted to be the same.

To style myself as a Vassar Girl, I thought, was to simply uphold the storied spirit of the Seven Sisters. On graduation day, as I listened to Sau Lan Wu and then the mother in Ralph Lauren, I realized my self-expression on this overmanicured arboretum, this daycare center for trust funders, was, in fact, assimilation. College wasn't so different from my days role-playing online, pretending I was someone else. Though I was my own avatar now, I'd learned to perform another character, however naturally she came to me.

———

VASSARIAN AMBITION PAIRED nicely with my class anxiety, so common among Filipino immigrants. Growing up, I was well exposed to this strain of colonial mentality.

In Las Vegas, my mother worked as a pharmaceutical rep who convinced doctors to prescribe her company's drugs. This meant she got to know the staff at local hospitals well. In the parking lot during a visit to my pediatrician, my mother told me, "Look at the cars." Though some of the BMWs and Mercedes-Benzes belonged to the well-to-do doctors, she said, a fair number belonged to the Filipino nurses too, so eager to display their stateside wealth, their achievement of the American Dream.

During college application season, my parents' friends asked me where I planned to go. Most had never heard of Vassar, pronounced it in that Filipino way—"vuh-*sahr*," emphasis on the second syllable. Then they'd offer where their kids or grandkids went with great fervor, as if the "Har-bard" or "Yell" diplomas were their own. But there was one father who knew of Vassar. He was a friend of a friend of my parents, a man we hardly knew. I was pleasantly surprised that he'd heard of my future alma mater, but the conversation went south when he told me, "Hindi madali makapasok diyan, ha." Apparently, his daughter hadn't gotten in, so he didn't like my chances. He acted as if it were a competition.

It does sometimes feel that way when you're Filipino, whether in the Philippines or abroad. We talk a lot about crab mentality, named after the behavior observed in crabs caught in a bucket or barrel. When one crab scales the sides to escape, the others grab onto it, dragging it down and sealing their collective fate as dinner. It can be read as an analogy for the way a group will undermine a member who ascends beyond the rest.

The myth that one person's gain is another's loss is not exclusive to any one cultural group, of course. But it's a common topic in Filipino articles, morning shows, and forums. When FilipiKnow.net published "12 Annoying Attitudes of Filipinos We Need to Get Rid Of," "crab mentality" was number one. Fair enough: I've heard as much from my relatives, who say, "Crab mentality lang yan," when dismissing other people's attempts to thwart their excellence by way of sabotage or gossip. Since crab mentality centers the individual, the indignation at such behavior might be attributed, more optimistically, to the Filipino cultural concept of kapwa. Translations vary, but in essence, it is an ethical concept that values a collective "we" or "togetherness with others." Crab mentality is anathema to this virtue and so exasperates those who witness it.

The laws of kapwa, however, might also animate the crabs themselves. As I once heard a Filipino anthropologist on the talk show *Good Morning Kuya* point out, crabs in a bucket aren't pulling each other down; they're all trying to get up and out. If they could work together efficiently, they might escape the bucket or topple it entirely. That would be the Filipino spirit of kapwa at its best, the classical kind that fueled resistance against dictators and Spanish colonizers. At its worst, kapwa can be an impulse to maintain a group's status quo. In a bucket, all the crabs are trapped. When one crab ascends, it disrupts a shared destiny to be killed and eaten.

When the skeptical father told me "hindi madali makapasok diyan," my instinct was to think, "crab mentality lang yan." How petty he was, I told my mother when I accepted the spot I was offered at Vassar. It wasn't as if his daughter and I were fighting for the same seat. To think so was to throw kapwa at its best out the window. Shouldn't he encourage a fellow Filipino, simply wish me good luck, and leave it at that?

My resentment wasn't exactly noble either. I took his skepticism as an insult, wanted to prove him wrong. Filipino families are competitive, whether first generation or fourth. For years, Filipinos have told their children that the most selective schools, the ones with the fewest seats, would open doors for them. Our parents want us to have those seats, the choices they never had, especially in the United States. As brown immigrants from a brown country once owned by our new home, it's instinct to center our self-interest, especially when we all land in the same bucket. Maybe it's the crab mentality we learn in the Philippines. Or maybe it's what we've been taught in America: belief in the bootstraps and the meritocracy and the unwinnable competition of being the model minority.

My mother voted for McCain in the 2008 election. As an employee of Big Pharma, she believed Obamacare would shoot her industry in the foot. It was the first year she could vote, as a newly naturalized citizen. I was seventeen at the time, too young to cast a ballot in the interest of my future. Her vote protected her interests, her means of supporting our lives in America, of scaling that bucket. The lives of those in the US who needed affordable health care were of little significance to her and to those who voted likewise—not in the grand scheme of things but certainly in the scheme of our American Dream.

On election night, when Fox News called the election for the first black president of the United States, my mother said, "I knew Obama would win anyway."

She wasted her vote twice over: first, by casting a ballot without actual faith in her candidate; second, by refusing participation in an epic historical event (which she apparently believed was inevitable) in favor of upholding the status quo. That year, my US history teachers had taught me how elections were supposed to be free and fair, to allow the American people a choice. (I'd yet to study the finer evils of voter suppression, gerrymandering, and the electoral college.) In the Philippines, I'd learned from my family how elections were likely rigged at all levels of our government, how our presidential candidates manipulated their way to Malacañan Palace.

On one of my visits to Manila, in June 2005, all anyone could talk about was the Hello Garci presidential scandal. Wiretapped phone calls allegedly proved that, in 2004, Gloria Macapagal Arroyo had colluded with the election commissioner Virgilio Garcillano to secure her presidency. A snippet from the recordings, Arroyo saying "Hello Garci," became everyone's ringtone that summer and remained so for the rest of the year, even after Arroyo's allies blocked an attempt to impeach her that September.

It's par for the course to see presidents behave badly in the Philippines. Apart from Arroyo, there's Rodrigo Duterte, who sanctioned extrajudicial executions of alleged criminals in his "war on drugs," and Joseph "Erap" Estrada, who plundered an estimated $80 million, according to Transparency International's Global Corruption Report. Given the malfeasance, political nepotism and dynasties (Arroyo is the daughter of a president; various families control entire cities), and overreaches of power so deeply woven into the fabric of Filipino government, it's easy to feel helpless.

Filipinos who speak up against such unethical administrations have, historically, been arrested or killed. Those who resisted Ferdinand Marcos during his presidency of twenty-one years—and his nine-year rule of the country under martial law—were "salvaged." That was the term my mother used, describing how Marcos's cronies would torture and mutilate activists and political enemies, then dump their corpses to be found by the public. It was meant to be a scaremongering tactic of the police state. It worked.

My mother grew up near Malacañan Palace. She recalls the evening curfews, how the police would visit her neighborhood in the middle of the night. They'd take all the men, young and old, and line them up on the main road. By then, one of my uncles was already living in San Francisco, but another uncle and my grandfather would be among those rounded up. They'd be inspected and intimidated, while my mother and grandmother were left to wonder if their loved ones would return.

The streets near the palace would be barricaded at night, my mother says, and under constant surveillance. To get past those standing guard, my grandfather needed a permit whenever he came home after a late shift. "And it was—well, not exactly *funny*," my mother said of how her dates would escort her home after curfew and then willingly walk alone in the dangerous night. "They must have really liked me."

No one in our family was ever harmed under Marcos's martial law. Everyone stayed in line, took paths of little resistance. They'd heard about peers and friends and friends of friends being salvaged, turned into examples, statistics. They didn't dare protest publicly for fear of being killed, leaving their families to fend for themselves.

In 1986, on February 22—my mother's birthday—the People Power Revolution began. In total, an estimated two million Filipinos participated, with many demonstrating for days and taking to the streets, particularly Epifanio de los Santos Avenue—EDSA, colloquially. My mother remembers how, on the following day, she and her colleagues at the pharma giant Glaxo were given the afternoon off. "If you want to go to EDSA and march," said their managers, "then go."

The crowds, paradoxically, were festive. My mother witnessed the civility of demonstrators in their civil disobedience. People traded stories in solidarity, shared food (my father and his buddies packed sandwiches for the soldiers aligned with the resistance, then joined a human chain to protect protestors from loyalist tanks), and, of course, prayed. Ultimately, Marcos caved to public pressure and resistance. He fled the country with his family to Guam and then Hawaii, where he died three years later.

In Manila, my classmates and I were taught how the EDSA Revolution was a testament to the strength of prayer. People Power, the story goes, was rooted in the people's faith—faith in a higher power and a better future, faith that they'd be protected from the police, be spared from the state's violence. In my mind, the stories from the revolution of civil disobedience, of actual "People Power" from family members and friends who were there to see it, were more significant. Such was the good, I believed as a kid, that came from being together with others.

These days, the people's power, kapwa at its best, has felt like a thing of the past, something to be nostalgic for rather than to practice. Duterte won the popular vote by a landslide, on a platform of violence that promised a war on drugs but which revealed itself to be a war on the poor. In the 2016 US election, I knew Filipino Americans who voted to deny undocumented immigrants the freedom of physical movement that they, the ones with papers and passports, could afford.

Why should others get a pass, they ask, when we had to work so hard? They see themselves as the deserving ones, who performed the immigrant gymnastics and "earned" documentation, their right to take root in the US. The boot-straps mentality aligns all too well with traditional Asian American conservatism: to go through all our hardships, they think, only to see rules relaxed, exemptions made, costs mitigated for others. They're crabs who have scaled the bucket, who want those still trapped to have to work at least as hard as they did to earn their freedom.

At seventeen, I would've voted for Obama (and did so at twenty-one). I would've been happy to negate my mother's choice to vote for McCain. I didn't tell her this, didn't want to start a fight or make a scene. This was the tack I took at the graduation reception too. Up against the mother wielding a cocktail stick and Ralph Lauren, I picked flight over fight, trained as I was to feign politesse. The rare times I faced racism at Vassar, I did so with what I thought was grace.

Much of the racism I faced at school could be viewed as misunderstandings, if I tried, as harmless apolitical gaffes. One in particular comes to mind: when I was a faculty intern, a student found me in the office I shared with my boss and asked, "Are you Professor Chang?"

It was easy to overlook the less overt instances, blissed out as I was on college life. If every rose has its thorns, I thought, Vassar's weren't so bad. At least the school lavishly indulged me, a gay brown immigrant with little to no money, and spent hundreds of thousands of dollars to give me a home. How wonderful it was on campus, I'd report whenever I visited Mother and Stepfather, refusing the steamed rice at the dinner table, that we were all treated the same.

I neglected to tell them the ways we were treated differently: how my merits were never disqualified, unlike the black professor who was told that she had nothing to offer the predominantly white faculty; how security was never called on me, unlike the students—a group of black and Asian women in my year—who had to explain they were just washing their clothes in the laundry room; how the police were never sicced on me for being loud in the library, unlike the black teenagers from town who were detained and questioned, while we students—we who had laughed and wailed among the stacks just as loudly at the height of our academic deliriums—stood by and watched.

I didn't tell my parents how we responded differently either: how some of my classmates took the school to task for these acts of racism; how they defiantly and valiantly addressed the president and her deans at town halls where the topic was "the campus climate"; how both students and professors wrote articles critical of this old white institution that enacted violence on brown and black bodies; how a handful of students created and distributed posters that spoke truth to power in our cloistered park.

"Racism happens here," they said. Racism happens here.

I didn't tell my family that racism happened here—happened to me, subtly, and to my friends, who faced aggressions that went well beyond micro. On phone calls and visits home, I only ever told them that all was good—as expected. "Classes are good," I'd say, on autopilot. "Grades are good. Rehearsals are good." I wanted to affirm that college, this American institution to which I had the honor and privilege to belong, was everything I was promised it would be.

That was the story I told myself. I upheld the myth of the idyllic ivy-covered campus, gorged on the utopist ideals of academia. In believing the myth of meritocracy, I leaned into the power structures designed by white architects and performed as best I could, in order to protect my seat here. I was happy to be decoration in the admissions videos, to be part of a well-publicized statistic, to be a model and a minority.

When people I loved asked Vassar to do better, I couldn't bite the hand that fed me. At scholarship receptions, I had the ear of donors, those apparently so invested in "diversity and inclusion." Here was an avenue to those who might listen to civil resistance. But I was afraid of rocking the boat, making them uncomfortable, having them discover that I wasn't a Vassar Girl but a difficult and different brown boy all along. Though I had the platform, I chose to maintain decorum and the status quo. I benefited from Vassar's legacy of whiteness, was subsumed by it, rooted in its earth. This institution loved me. I loved my position at this court. So I kept quiet.

Deluded and comfortable, I insisted that my peers' experiences were not mine, so how could I speak someone else's truth to power? The school gave me everything I needed, and I should leave it at that. I kept my head down and protected my interests. I'd been told stories of how resistance could burn you—even get you killed. Though I knew what resistance could look like—civil and disobedi-ent, motivated by solidarity and kapwa and the drive to do good—I feared retaliation.

When my mother dropped me off at Vassar, she told me to "make good choices." Too afraid to make the wrong one, to endanger my seat not at the table but merely in the room, I didn't make any choices at all—which was a (bad) choice in and of itself. Rather than think for myself, I thought only of myself. I failed to come home with ideas, to choose my own path.

IN MY FIRST job out of college, I worked in a newsroom. As part of our standards and ethics guide, leadership enacted a policy that forbade employees from donating money to political causes or participating in demonstrations or pro-tests. They insisted we not do anything that "would make our fellow journalists' jobs more difficult."

My colleagues were frustrated by this. They resisted the policy to, well, resist. Despite explicit orders, some attended the Women's March. Two friends made do-nations to presidential campaigns via siblings or parents (one friend, for Hillary; the other, for Bernie). And there was nothing in the ethics guide about calling our elected officials.

I wasn't as willing to potentially draw negative attention. To rock the boat with a salary on the line was a risk I wasn't yet ready to take. I did what I could. I was the editor for our site edition catering to Filipinos in the Philippines and abroad, so I curated those feeds to share and retweet the good work of my colleagues, the ones from whom I learned the most. From 2014 to 2018, I tried to amplify their reporting—on immigration, on American police brutality, on the Philippine drug war. My hope was to combat the misinformation proliferating on Facebook, especially the fake news articles being shared by my titas and titos (many of them not actually my parents' siblings), who'd insist on friending me, then guilt me when I hadn't yet accepted their friend requests.

From comments on my edition's articles to the status updates of my Filipino network, I watched the collective "we" of kapwa become an "us versus them." The shape of their "us" shifted depending on context, but it often looked like "we who are privileged with power." I witnessed demands for a border wall, for the banishment of undocumented immigrants from Central and South America, from those who called themselves "legal." A woman I knew on Facebook whose brother was a police officer insisted, "Blue lives matter too." And "good riddance," said an auntie, as the drug war death toll rose; she wanted "safe streets" the next time she went home to Manila for Christmas. Kapwa at its worst.

Not everyone was so terrible. There were friends deter-mined to duke it out, criticizing the hypocrisy on display, the American police state, the pervasive sense of Filipino classism. But Facebook is rarely the best place for produc-tive discourse. It proved the rule of thumb we had at work: "Never read the comments." If you do, we were warned, you'll only want to give up.

Our jobs were taxing that way, I explained to my fam-ily when they asked me, "How's work?" I couldn't pretend anymore. In the lead-up to the 2016 US elections, I was clearly tired and anxious. So much so that they invited me to join them in Rome that fall. My stepfather's brother was an archbishop and summoned to the Vatican; might as well make a trip of it, they said.

Over dinner near the Piazza Navona, they asked who I was voting for. My incredulity at the question, I have to say, was justified. Who do you think I'm voting for, I de-manded, when one of the two candidates disparages whole immigrant populations as "criminals" and "rapists," believes he can just grab women by the pussy and was caught on tape saying as much, regularly retweets white nationalists, and was endorsed by a former leader of the Ku Klux Klan?

I was so upset that I refused the plate of cacio e pepe offered me. A vote for him, I explained, not quite slurring, would be to embolden white supremacists in America, an already deadly force responsible for the loss of so many black lives. Black lives matter, I said, period. To counter that "all lives matter" is to dismiss the specificity of anti-black racism, how the gradations of violence inflicted on nonwhite bodies is dependent on the darkness or lightness of our skin.

Take Peter Liang, for example, the Asian police officer who shot Akai Gurley, a black man in Brooklyn. When Liang was indicted, Chinese Americans marched across the Brooklyn Bridge, demanding that the charges against him be dropped. They believed Liang was being used as a scapegoat; after all, the white officers who had fatally shot unarmed black men and boys that year—Darren Wilson, who killed Michael Brown; Timothy Loehmann, who killed Tamir Rice; Daniel Pantaleo, who killed Eric Garner—had not been charged. While the charges against Liang stuck, in the end he was only sentenced to community service and five years of probation.

The reactions varied in the aftermath of Liang's sentencing—no one at the table tried to interrupt; I wet my mouth with more chianti and kept going—but in my view, it's apparent that there are systems in place that make pawns out of all of us as people of color. No one "wins" here except the white people in power who protect their own. Our current "justice system" stratifies and oppresses us the same way Catholic colonizers did the Philippines—a pointed glance from my mother at this, no visible reaction from stepuncle-archbishop.

So I'm voting in November, I answered them finally, in service of the interests of black people, as well as those of the undocumented, the poor, and women, because their interests are mine too.

This was the sparring I did in classrooms, the ideas I'd picked up at school. Regretful that I never got to use these tools at college for fear of retaliation, I began to embrace the discomfort of challenging decorum, of making a scene in public, once I left. The Vassar graduate, says Mary McCarthy, is a yearner and regretter, "poignantly conscious of backsliding." I certainly was.

When I left the school, I left a system that kept me safe, that privileged me even as it denied my peers the same privileges. I had to pass through Taylor Gate for the last time and take off my rose-colored glasses. Outside my bubble, I began to see this country plainly, one built on the dehumanization and destruction of black bodies, on the devaluation and disappearing of yellow lives, on the deportation of and discrimination against brown skin.

To believe that the larger American institution is capable of state violence was relatively easy. Confronting the fact that Vassar harmed my peers, that it accepted me as it rejected those like me in the same breath, was harder. The school had admitted me onto its campus, into its ivory tower, and guided me up its spiral staircases. I had followed, even when I saw the writing on the walls, its hypocrisies exposed. Now, I stopped averting my eyes, saw how performing respectability and overcompetence had opened the doors that led to the paths upward I took in this alleged meritocracy.

As I ascended, I began to realize that the walls of the bucket in which we've been placed were taller than I thought, insurmountable for those of us trapped at the bottom. The ingrained imperialism of America buckets us, places us in tiers, measures our worth based on the colors of our skins, how much money we make, the places we were born, who and how we love, the shapes of our bodies, what we say we are, the ways we say our names.

In Las Vegas, at Vassar, at work, I had chosen to keep quiet, do as I was told, fulfill the myth of the model minority. All it required was allying myself with the dominant culture, even when that meant being passive, standing apart and away from other immigrants and people of color. At the time, that didn't seem so much to ask, considering what I stood to gain. By performing for white audiences, I believed, I would survive.

We all perform in such ways big and small, for audiences who don't understand us. I was at a restaurant with my friend Alanna when a white woman asked if she could touch Alanna's braids. I tensed on my side of the table, but Alanna didn't want to make a scene and said, "Sure." It's not always white people, either. At a dinner party, a black man who was a born-and-bred New Yorker told my friend, also a New Yorker by way of Beijing and Queens, to pick only one place "where he comes from." We tried to explain, in the most cautious words we could find, that, actually, no, he doesn't have to choose.

But in those moments, we sometimes let the comments blow over or change the subject, conscious of the fact that, if we push back, we could easily be written off—as the angry black woman, the ignorant foreigner, the ungrateful immigrant. There are situations and contexts where, to survive, we make allowances. But when we're no longer just surviving, we must learn to stand our ground. To retreat, to keep our heads down, to be quiet only preserves the status quo and keeps us all trapped in the bucket.

The last thing I wanted at that dinner in Rome was to give my family a lecture on politics and racism in American culture. All they did was ask me an honest question, tuned out of US affairs as they were when they had their own strongman president to deal with in the Philippines. Plus, I so rarely see my parents now that one of the greatest gifts is to simply not cause a fight when I do.

But I couldn't help it, angry and fearful as I was at the possibility of harm coming to immigrants, of borders closing, of citizenships denied—all while we, a global family, ate overpriced pasta in a tourist trap with passports in our bags and our humanity unthreatened. How could we make small talk of an issue that puts real lives at stake? It seems frustration and alcohol, as proven at the holiday party with Christian, is my recipe for outbursts of resistance.

My mother shrugged when I apologized to her about my tirade, for getting worked up. "It was fine," she said. She just didn't want me to upset stepuncle-archbishop with my remark about Catholicism. Apparently, her surprise stemmed more from the fact that she hadn't heard me talk like that before. I had come back with a lot of ideas. My mother said, "It was good to hear you speak up."

I've thought a lot about the Ralph Lauren mother's comment at the graduation reception, about Sau Lan Wu and Asian accents, about me speaking English so well. Mainly because I'm petty. But also because I wonder: How could I have better responded to that woman? Perhaps with a dose of her own WASPish condescension: "Professor Wu's team of particle physicists understood her so well that they won a Nobel Prize, but I suppose not everyone is equally intelligent." I hope Mary McCarthy would deem such a riposte sufficiently cutting, worthy of a Vassar Girl.

Years later, I routinely end up back in that reception room. I'm at Vassar a lot these days, for panels and mentorship programs. I'll turn up for anything; any excuse to get away from the city and to pay the library a visit. And I'm good at holding court with the current undergrads. Though it's not yet a commencement address, it's still an opportunity to chat with students, people who—like me—are still learning.

When they ask for advice about facing life after Vassar, I admit that I look to them for inspiration. They're the ones rallying for labor rights in solidarity with campus dining workers, hosting events to counter visiting lecturers making bad faith arguments for hate speech as free speech, and condemning racism in whatever form it takes—by hosting sit-ins at the library where violent antiblack graffiti was written on its doors and by marching in support of Black Lives Matter. They're committed to civil disobedience, kapwa at its best. It's that spirit from which I take my cue.

That's my advice, then. Whenever I return to campus and pass through Taylor Gate, I remind them to do what I didn't at Vassar, what I strive to do now: Keep fighting for your people, for lives both like and unlike your own, and stand not idly by. Come home with a lot of ideas and critique everything you're told. A Vassar Girl, after all, must think for herself.

TO BE ASKED

I MEET HIS gaze, he holds mine, and thus, we say yes.

My heart rate jumps when Theo playfully raises his eyebrows and cocks his head to the exit. They're subtle gestures, nearly invisible in this trendy gym with too much mood lighting. But I'm watching his reflection closely in this house of mirrors, and his intent is unmistakable to me. We've done this before. I'm barely halfway through my cardio, but I turn off my elliptical as Theo returns his weights to the rack. I follow him down the stairs, to the lockers, to the steam room.

In the steam, my right knee leans into Theo's left. His left pinky toe rests on my right foot. We stay there for a minute, maybe five, maybe forty. However long it takes for the crowd in the room to dwindle. Towels around our waists, we rub ourselves; then under our towels go our hands, to start. Sets of eyes—two, three, four—make contact. Silently, they point. Downward, across, to the side. Looking. For now, we work discreetly. This is how we signal to our fellow conspirators, to those who choose to stay.

Once we establish a coalition, whether a pair or pairs or parties, touch becomes bolder. Theo's fingers waltz along my lower back. My hand, hungry palm and digits, rubs his thigh. He works his way down as I work my way up. Towels loosen, fall away. I grasp Theo's cock and he sighs with the steam. He's slick with sweat and vapor. I stroke him slowly and I bend forward so his fingers can open me up. It's a gift, a reward for my patience and duty as leader.

I survey our company. They are all facsimiles of Theo, all whittled from the same white marble, but pedestrian copies carved by amateurs. One taller, some shorter, most softer than him—with a body sculpted in the Pergamene style, all straining muscles and taut flesh, even at his age, twice mine. Today, I'm the only brown boy and the first to remove my towel, the one to bring us to sexual consensus. After months in the steam, I learn this is the norm: it often falls to us, the men of color, to lead the way in our sweltering underworld.

A third man joins us; he was on the elliptical next to mine. A fourth watches, his hand slippery with the conditioner stocked in the showers. A fifth and sixth, now a couple themselves, are by the door. I've always chosen to sit in the back, far from the entrance. When newcomers and locker-room attendants enter, they need about two to five seconds to let their vision acclimate to the fluorescents and the steam. In the space of these two to five seconds, the rest of us must behave ourselves, rewrap towels, put hands where we can see them.

When I'm lucky, I'll finish my cardio and arrive to find I'm the fourth, or sixth, or tenth. The sudden rush of activity, of reorganizing cloth and crotches, is a sign I timed my workout well. When the coalition has begun without me, however, the problem then becomes finding a seat. Cruising in this steam room is a game of musical chairs.

At first, it was tough joining a game where I didn't know the rules. I watched how others played and mimicked their moves in kind. I gathered what friction meant, what lingering touch allowed. To take in as much as I could, I seldom said no to anything—or yes, for that matter. Silence, it seemed, was our golden rule. Sometimes, there were clearer directions, things mouthed and whispered—*suck me*, *fuck me*, *come for me*. Diction, as ever, is a skill. We made tools of exacting lips and tongues. I followed as they led.

Today, our third is a greedy one. His lips go quickly from my nipple to navel to dick. He didn't ask for permission, but I suppose my knee on his gave it. Though he wasn't exactly my type—too many tattoos, bald—I'm already here and his mouth is wet and now I am too. He bobs up and down, the sounds of his throat echoing against the tile in between spurts of steam. I notice that our fifth and sixth have left the room, perhaps for a shower or that other far corner, by the lockers rarely used. Our fourth is still watching, his strokes erratic. He's obviously close. I am too.

To my right, I see Theo. His pinky toe still on my foot. Brow furrowed, breathing shallow. Focused on the finish line. Then he's smiling and so am I. He comes, decorates my wrist as his grunt slides into a moan. Steam floods the room. The heat rises. I tug Theo closer, knees over knees, lips to lips. A bit more stroking and sucking and kissing, and I come into one man's mouth as I taste another's tongue, flavored with notes of creatine and vanilla whey.

———————

I'VE BEEN WITH these men more regularly than with my boyfriends. There's Otto, who I sneak into my shower where he comes just from kissing me. There's Paolo, who only fingers me, his fellow Filipino, when no one else can see. And there's James, who offers to share with me a beautiful cock he's been sucking, who tells me, as we chat by the lockers, that to enter that steam room is to give my consent, to say yes, my first of many.

Of course, I knew that. I'd read the books. I took a course called "Gay Male Literature in America" at Vassar and used Charles Kaiser's *The Gay Metropolis* for thesis reading. I'd heard the stories too. Christian had told me about the gay baths, as well as secluded areas like the Ramble in Central Park and the Meat Rack on Fire Island—wooded areas, in more ways than one. I'd frowned at the 1980 film *Cruising* and devoured HBO's *Looking*—and FX's *Pose*, once it came along, its cast of brown and black gay and trans folks a breath of fresh air among shows featuring mostly white gay men. Also, there was the internet. To cruise, I knew, at its simplest, is to look for sex, to loiter where there are those who seek the same.

Cruising was familiar to me, and I'd long consented to its physics. Grindr was my convenient entry point. No need to attend a steam room or stroll through the woods to find the secluded spots on maps I was never given. Gay sex apps have made cruising grounds of all neighborhoods, mapped whole cities and heartland states. They've rendered gay spaces more accessible and visible.

I got Grindr as a teen in Las Vegas. Upon loading the app for my inaugural cruise, it was a revelation to see neighbors of all races who were queer too, to realize I wasn't the only gay in our gated community. When I first returned with the app to Manila, I was floored. As a kid, my homosexuality was unwelcome here; now, as an adult, my hometown came with invitations written in my mother tongue. In New York, Grindr was how I explored the city, made a flânerie of cruising the arcades of men. This technology opened doors for me. It disrupted the idea that, for much of my life, I was alone.

While I'm grateful for Grindr and Big Tech's optimization of casual sex, the ease of this frictionless habit has made me lazier. A Friday night at home with a bottle of wine, dispatching nudes and messages saying *hey handsome* left and right, too unmotivated to host or travel, is a regular, though hardly thrilling, evening. Which was why I sought a steam room in New York: for the joys of a night with friction. I wanted a taste of that storied kind of cruising, that thrill of the chase, sneaking into back-alley places, being tapped by a secret society that would reassure me I was one of many.

Cruising as a historic tradition has been emblematic of how queer people invent ways of working in between straight lines. To operate invisibly among those unlike us, we developed a wordless art, this queer argot dependent only on eyes and skin, one that linked men with men. When I first read *The Gay Metropolis*, I envied the Eden to which Kaiser bore witness, that of New York before the AIDS crisis. I pictured men cruising fertile streets in their jean cutoffs—in my head, it was always summer for them— reveling in the joys of gay sex, gay touch, gay love, celebrating every day of life in an exhilarating orgy, in all senses of the word: as drunken revelry, as excessive indulgence, as euphoric singing and dancing. I imagined them fleeing the society that condemned them as sissies and fags to join ecstatic fraternities, animated by solidarity between queer bodies, against heteropatriarchy, regardless of color.

Most depictions of gay history in American media make it look like only white men existed in such spaces—like only white gay men existed at all in those days. (See also: the whitewashed narratives of the 1969 Stonewall riots, which bleach from memory the queer working-class people of color present that night, trans activists Marsha P. Johnson and Sylvia Rivera, among them.) But I have to believe that men of copper and bronze moved through those hidden realms too, the plentiful cruising grounds of the '60s and '70s. There were the back rooms of the now-defunct Anvil and International Stud, the Ramble, the piers, the showers at the gym, the iconic Fire Island—and the baths! Oh, the baths!

New York's gay bathhouses were institutions. Equipped with lockers and private beds, steam rooms and saunas, even entire pools, each bathhouse was partly a community center, partly a nightclub, and wholly a sanctuary. Not only did they provide a safe option where men could meet and mate, the baths also leaned into public service. In the East Village, the New St. Marks Baths held a voter registration drive on-site for the 1980 election. On the Upper West Side, the Continental Baths maintained a clinic for STI testing. Many baths promoted sex education and even operated on public holidays like Thanksgiving and Christmas, providing a refuge for gay men shunned by their families on these feast days of togetherness.

But gay bathhouses have waned in New York and in the United States more broadly. The compounding factors: first, public health officials called for the closing of bathhouses in the mid-1980s, ostensibly to prevent the spread of HIV; second, the rise of the internet and hookup apps; and third, the increasing acceptance of homosexuality. Gay baths were "like dirty bookstores and parks: a venue to meet people," as the owner of the North Hollywood Spa, a bathhouse in Los Angeles, explained to the Associated Press in

2014. Nowadays, he said, "You can go to the supermarket" to meet men.

To combat low patronage, some baths have taken to courting the Grindr generation. In Los Angeles, the Melrose Spa began allowing free entry to eighteen- to twenty-five-year-olds on Tuesdays. A young guy who spoke to the AP was complimentary of the place. Compared to meeting a stranger online or drunk at a bar, he said, the baths are less dangerous. He felt safer in this environment, where condoms were provided, the staff screened for sober clientele, and the men adhered to the best practices of the baths. Of all the safeguards in gay bathhouses—and in the steam room I attended—chief among them is this established cruiser's code of conduct and consent.

There's a nonverbal contract you sign when you enter a cruising ground, a place meant specifically to be sexual. Good cruisers express (and heed) consent at every step of the way, accept or refuse the touch and invitations they receive. In these spaces, eye contact, smiles, and nods are intentional. They're ways of saying yes in a realm where speech is, though not discouraged, kept to a minimum.

For the most part, the rulebook to cruising is unwritten. It is, after all, an oral tradition. These days, you can find forums or blogs—like one I love called Bathhouse Blues—that give you a crash course in the theory. But cruising is focused more on learning the practice from experts or in the field. It's an arcane craft, tough without a teacher, even with the help of the internet.

Thankfully, I learned a lot from James. He was black, dark-skinned, and a dancer—proof of it in his elegant fingers, his washboard obliques, and how he'd stretch into a full split on the gym floor. ("All the better to show off my ass, my dear.") He was confident in how he led us to orgiastic unanimity, in how we black and brown men set an example in the steam.

James suggested that, since men of color are the most susceptible to blame should we be caught in a room with everyone in flagrante delicto, we may as well be the leaders in the steam. What better way to go down than while going down? Plausible deniability is a tactic available to all, regardless of race, but it works best for white men, who are deemed most believable when they deny involvement in any and all things, steam room sex among them.

"They're not all bad," James allows. That said, most snitches, at the gym and elsewhere, are white. I now wonder if this was how we gays of color earned access to (and cachet in) these spaces—by putting our bodies on the line.

On the other hand, white men got a free pass. They weren't held to the same standards to which men of color were subject. As illustrated by men's underwear ads, men's magazines, and the profiles of anonymous men on Grindr, white men have the privilege of being inherently desirable. The rest of us have to go to the gym.

Steam is not the great equalizer, nor do the facts of our race, size, gender, and ability exist here in a vacuum. Whenever I saw a man snub a cruiser's overtures, I could only guess why. I had my own reasons whenever I said no: low energy, a lack of time, an unshakeable deference to more conventionally masculine and muscular men, whether white or black or brown. But whenever my touch was declined, it was easy to chalk it up to racism.

You simply can't dwell on refusals, James reminded me, especially when you're cruising and especially when they're white. He understood these racial politics well: Were he fat or old in addition to being a dark-skinned black man, he said, men in the steam room would never have given him the time of day.

"I bet they love you though," James said to me once, as we got dressed by the lockers. I asked what he meant, and he replied, "Well, you're Filipino, right?" I smiled. He slapped my ass with a towel.

Now, having learned my lessons, I agree with James: I don't have the energy to get hung up on what every Chad thinks of me. At the time, I was still learning how to navigate the steam room, studying the customs, picking up the language. No words, just touch, looking.

Since our gym was not an actual gay bathhouse, we had to operate discreetly. Sometimes, we even worked in teams. There was the day James and I were in the steam room's alcove, hidden from sight but vulnerable, as we couldn't watch the entrance. He asked someone to keep an eye out while I blew him. Theo agreed to whistle whenever he saw a shadow approaching through the glass door.

Men here looked out for one another. What gave rise to this solidarity, in my experience, was our unwritten oath as cruisers to respect boundaries. Though we broke the stated rules of the gym against "lewd behavior," we adhered to the codes of our steam room, established by our bygone forefathers. In our age of Grindr and marriage equality (however flawed in its lean toward heteronormativity), the cruising ground, which developed in an era when explicit queer desire was dangerous, might feel anachronistic, obsolete. But to inhabit it is to understand its original intention as a space that honors the queer body and its desires. At its best, a cruising ground is like Atlantis—utopian and ancient.

I could consent to that hallowed ground, choose to enter the steam knowing what to expect. I'd join that room to give my first yes, to be undressed, to let my towel fall away. With my gaze, my touch, my nonverbal cues, I chose whose hands would dance on my skin. And I'd leave that space to reenter another, one bigger and more complex, where fewer obey even the most basic codes of conduct.

Elsewhere, roaming freely, are men who neglect the unwritten rule book of common decency. There was the dude at a friend's party who pinched my ass as I shook it to the music. There was the guy on the subway who placed a hand on my lower back when his knees touched mine in a crowded car. And there was the man at a bar in Manila who wouldn't let me go after our dance. In each instance, a man took a simple gesture as my yes, as if he were my co-conspirator in the steam room. But mere touch, eye contact, or a smile aren't invitations to, say, a groping hand on the crotch at the club. Even in the steam room, they were only save-the-dates.

By the same token, cues like shaking your head or pushing away unwanted hands, which are plenty clear, took on greater power in the steam room. The men who've failed to heed them—at a party, on the subway, at a bar—could learn something from that sultry world or even the Bathhouse Blues blog. When you're rebuffed, "you cannot take it personally," writes the blogger, echoing James's suggestion that I not dwell too much on the motivations of other men. "That is the biggest rule at the baths (although it is still hard for me to digest)."

It's that refusal that gets some men worked up, makes them turn aggressive. On a dance floor in Manila, I tried to move away from a man who kept grabbing my forearm, insisting I stay with him. His hands grew more claw-like with each attempt, his uncut fingernails digging into my skin. I started dancing with someone else, just to get him to go away, hoping my new partner wouldn't repeat the cycle.

The steam room at my gym was largely immune from these attitudes but not entirely. One evening, Otto was there to provide backup when another man wouldn't take my nos for an answer. The man's initial overtures could have been read as mere ignorance. He'd rub my knee, I'd inch away, he'd inch closer. He touched me as he touched himself. I allowed it for a moment, focusing on Otto on the other side of me. I was insistent too when I was first starting out, pushing the limits, seeing how far our rules could bend. But even then, I knew when no meant no. I could read the kind of silence that turned the steam room cold.

So it was hard to argue for the man's innocent ignorance of our codes when he tugged open my towel, grabbed my neck, and forced me to face him. At this, Otto stood from his seat, wedged himself between me and the man, pointed at him, then the door. Looking foolish, the man made his exit. He had entered that space, wanting to be wanted, and, when he was not, chose to assert his dominance over me. After he stormed off, I kissed Otto more fiercely than I ever had before—a gift, a wordless thank you.

I had hoped that queer spaces, whether steam rooms or gay bars or islands on fire, could always be those safe enclaves in a world ruled by the straight hegemony that marginalizes us. That's the romantic ideal. But there are a great many among us who act based on old myths we've yet to let go. Though gay men have been rejected by the patriarchy, we do not exist outside it.

Men are told that we always have agency, that our actions are always ours. That men can't get hard unless we're aroused, and therefore if we have sex, we must have wanted it. That we're so drunk on our own testosterone that we always want sex, anyway. That, if we didn't want it, we could have fought off our assailants, given that "real men" are always dominant. That men who are assaulted, raped, coerced, or abused are not "real men." That men who are weak or timid aren't "real men." That men who are anything but heterosexual and cisgender, men who challenge the seemingly irrefutable pillars of masculinity, are not "real men."

These damaging ideas are so deeply lodged in cultural imaginations that I don't even have to source that paragraph. Queer people are not immune to the same modes of thought and behavior. That's what continued exposure does. It enacts conditioning—not to a bell, but to the beat of a war drum—that I've had to actively unlearn in my own life as a cisgender gay man. For years, I allowed that war drum to dictate my rhythms and my roles unconsciously. I've witnessed myself and others like me bend under the weight of such cultural myths—myths about what it means to be a man, and a gay one at that, even myths about what it means to be Asian and Filipino.

In the steam room, Paolo and I had been eyeing each other for a while by the time we finally hooked up. He was shier than his workout buddy, who had already been my occasional partner. It was only when Paolo and I were completely alone in the steam that he undid his towel, that I blew him, that he fingered me, that he asked for my name.

How nice, I thought, he wants to get to know me. Then Paolo explained that he and his buddy had been calling me "Island Boy." I held my tongue. To have shot back a similar nickname would've been to give in to the colonialism we had both inherited.

In that cruising ground, I could control what could be physically done to my body but not how it was seen. Paolo and his friend had written a narrative for me, one to which I did not consent. This was what James had alluded to, what I looked like to white men—and apparently fellow brown men too. The moniker "Island Boy" was rooted in colonial ideas about my masculinity, the fantasy of an exotic and obsequious body, a "little brown brother." They had positioned me in their minds as a racist sexual stereotype, that of the subservient Asian bottom. And I wasn't sure they were wrong.

READY, WILLING, AND nineteen, I raised my ass into the air. He told me to keep my voice down; his housemates might hear. It hurt. Not in a bad way or a good way. It just hurt. The next day, on the feast of St. Valentine, my friends and I ate heart-shaped pancakes for brunch at the college dining center. I told them I was glad to get it over with.

It wasn't exactly my first time. In high school, my boyfriend tried to top me, but either he was too soft or I was too tight, or maybe we couldn't get the right angle. I tried topping—same issues. We might have just been ill-matched, physically and emotionally. I was disappointed; I really wanted to get fucked, to finally have a sure answer to the question: top or bottom?

Though the first time I bottomed was less than porn-perfect, it gave me assurance that the innate bottomhood I had sensed in myself was true, that being the receptive partner was the right fit. As for whether that was something my body told me or something popular media told my body, it's unclear which came first.

In puberty, I mapped out my sexual future using those prime barometers of the American erotic imagination: internet porn. In the countless videos to be found without ever paying a dime, there was a clear message: Asians get fucked. We were regularly the ones being penetrated, gagged, subdued in the gay porn I found. (I never watched straight porn; I didn't bother pretending.) A majority of the men were East Asian, primarily Chinese or Japanese. The only porn I could find with Filipinos were clips so pixelated, they were probably recorded with a flip phone.

At Vassar, a friend taught me how to download porn on a torrent site. What a torrent it was. There were more videos to choose from, but it was more of the same. White men got to be jocks and twinks and daddies and bears and all the overlaps therein. When black men or oft-searched "Latin papis" were given chances to shine, they were often cast as hypermasculine tops, another manifestation of racialized typecasting. (BBC does not stand for British Broadcasting Corporation.) And even in those waves of smut, the majority of videos that featured Asian men still cast them as bottoms.

There are exceptions that prove the rule, of course—most notably the Asian American porn star Brandon Lee. Just as the name evokes a pan-Asian quality, so do his looks. His face is a transmutable brown canvas on which a viewer might project their fantasies of the exotic Asian. His birth name? Michael Hernandez—he's Filipino. And he's been very successful, crossing over from niche Asian-only porn productions to more mainstream studios, where he would top white men.

I've seen Brandon Lee's work. He's inspiring to watch, in possession of a leading-man quality without the requisite cheese-grater cheekbones. Lee is dominant without being violent. In some videos, he even plays the all-American male—no playing up an accent or language barrier as in most porn with Asian players. And, fuck, he's huge. His cock takes the myth that Asians aren't well endowed and slaps it across the face. There are few like Lee, however; he's such a unicorn that the queer podcast Nancy made Brandon Lee the focus of nearly a whole episode, calling him "the first Asian top."

Purveyors of pop culture and porn also fall back on tired stereotypes of Asian women—that of the compliant Asian woman who lives to serve ("I do nail for you!"), and the eager Asian woman purchased to please ("Me love you long time!"). "For the past decade," writes Maureen O'Connor in *New York* magazine, "seeing women who look like me—Asian women—in sexual contexts has meant seeing women who look like me being abused, dominated, and defiled."

O'Connor interprets the racial dynamics of porn tropes, particularly in cuckold videos, a fetish genre that emasculates a man, the cuck, as he watches his wife get fucked by another man. "White men eroticize their anxiety about black-male sexuality," she says, "by creating humiliation fantasies that involve sexually superior black rivals." I've seen gay cuckold films play out the same racial configurations and anxieties, but I've yet to see any kind of porn where the cuck is Asian. Perhaps because those who care to make cuck videos already see Asian men as emasculated. "Porn is a theater of the id," O'Connor writes, "and America's id is racist."

The common denominator here between her experience and mine is the white psyche's feminization and subordination of Asians. White men assign us supporting roles so they can be the leading men, who get to feel bigger and stronger when they perceive us as smaller and weaker. (This mix of racism and misogyny is the cocktail of choice for men with fragile egos.) Such positioning has become a given in US culture, going well beyond porn. As O'Connor writes, "*Is this how people see me?* I used to wonder, but perhaps the most disturbing realization is that I don't ask that question anymore."

In 2005, two years into my life as a Filipino immigrant in the United States, I watched the film adaptation of *Memoirs of a Geisha*. It swept me up in its melodrama and its portrayal of feminine power. I was twelve, malleable, and in awe of this agency through beauty. At the time, I had few models after whom to shape my Asian identity in America. One other choice was Jackie Chan, a masculine action star. He found strength in physical force, while geisha survived on aesthetics and relationships. It was an easy decision for a young gay boy who loved to wear his mother's silk robes when she wasn't looking.

As an adult, I realized how much racism went into creating *Memoirs of a Geisha*. Not only were Chinese actresses cast to play Japanese characters, but it was a film directed by a white man, based on a novel by another white man. Rob Marshall and Arthur Golden created a camp fantasia on racist themes—on screen and on page, respectively—based on a Western framework of love, a Cinderella story transposed into an exotified Oriental world. The protagonist is a rags-to-riches archetype, saved from poverty by a man's love, won through her performance of femininity. In this performance, she resembles the lotus blossom.

The archetype of the lotus blossom is simultaneously virginal and sexual. Her carnality, her "exotic" femininity, is tamed and made pure by her willingness to be reformed by the man she loves. She is elevated from her destitute Oriental conditions, rescued from objectification by her own culture, because she is loved and saved by the white man.

Consider *Miss Saigon*. Kim is our lotus blossom, working at a brothel during the Vietnam War until she's rescued by the white man who loves her, an American GI named Chris. She is the lone virginal figure among a cadre of hypersexualized women—calling to mind the trope of the Asian dragon lady—who seduce the other GIs, selling to the highest bidders. I watched all this play out as a teenager; my high school did the show when I was a freshman. There is no *Miss Saigon, Junior* edition, so my classmates of all races sang songs of Asian sex workers in wartime, of how they longed, "in a strong GI's embrace," to "flee this life, flee this place." I, on the other hand, was the token male Asian extra, adding "Man at Payphone" and "Man Driving Rickshaw" to my acting résumé.

I was never given lead roles in high school, so I fantasized them for myself. I'd imagine playing the titular role in *M. Butterfly*, the play by David Henry Hwang, where French civil servant René Gallimard (a white man, of course) falls in love with the singer Song Liling, oblivious to the fact that women characters in Chinese opera were played by men.

In hindsight, perhaps that was the least damaging fantasy I've ever indulged in. Hwang's play problematizes Oriental stereotypes, as well as conceptions of how we perform gender, race, and femininity. In *M. Butterfly*, Gallimard projects a fantasy onto Song and himself: he and Song, whom he presumes to be a woman, as the two romantic leads in the Puccini opera *Madama Butterfly*—the faithful Butterfly and the swashbuckling Lieutenant Pinkerton. In a 1988 afterword to his play, Hwang describes how it was easy to believe in the play he wrote because "the neo-Colonialist notion that good elements of a native society, like a good woman, desire submission to the masculine West speaks precisely to the heart of our foreign policy blunders in Asia and elsewhere."

As with the US in Vietnam, a white man thinks he can save the East and its people as he belittles them, as he ravishes his lotus blossom. But there's a welcome twist in *M. Butterfly*. Gallimard's fantasy is upended when it's revealed Song is a spy for the Chinese government. Gallimard had it backward all along: Song was the dominant Pinkerton and he the submissive Butterfly. In the end, he shares the same fate as her and dies by ritual suicide.

To manipulate Gallimard, Song weaponized his sexuality, but his primary tools were the white man's own delusions. He danced the perfect dance of an Asian woman, and the myth was enough for the Frenchman. "I am an Oriental," testifies Song, when asked if Gallimard ever knew he was a man. "And being an Oriental, I could never be completely a man." As I became acquainted with my bottomhood, I was excited by the idea of weaponizing sexuality, playing into the stereotypes forced onto female Asian bodies. Only when another Filipino clocked my performance did I ever think it might not be the right role for me.

I leveraged my body when I first came to New York. I used Grindr to place me in queen beds with park views, transmuted the desire of others into my own validation as a dairy queen seeking the approval of whiteness. I had watched enough bodies like mine on various screens to know that this was the role I was expected to play. Long before Paolo saw through the steam and through me to the caricature I had become, I had submitted to this sexualized racist trope.

If this is how I am seen, I thought, then let me allow it, that it may be my choice, that I may imbue it with my narrative as a bottom who can take it. With only a teaspoon of self-awareness, I perpetuated a stereotype that seemed to empower me at first glance but in reality made me subservient to powers that dehumanized me. I heard the war drums, could not ignore their rhythm, and so I chose to dance.

———

AT THE MOVIES with Theo, I felt I was being watched. It was summertime in Chelsea, and the boys of the neighborhood were out with their tank tops and jean shorts and adventurous eyes. I could feel pairs of them landing on me. Downward, across, to the side. Looking.

We were in line for popcorn, when I saw a man staring at me from across the lobby. He was smiling; I assumed we knew each other. I was trying to place him—steam room? Twitter?—when he turned to his friend and whispered something, eyes never leaving me. Theo put an arm around my waist, and the two gay guys laughed.

Theo's nickname in my group chat was Salt and Paprika; he was a front-row-at-the-Tom-Ford-show kind of gorgeous, with strawberry blond hair going gray at his temples.

It was not lost on me that whenever I went out with Theo, or another older white man, I could be seen as an Asian stereotype—a mail-order island boy with his white sugar daddy. I could rarely be sure, of course. But moments like this—those eyes, that laugh—affirmed the possibility, however plausibly deniable, that I was moving through a space reduced, seen only as a stereotype.

I've adopted that gaze too, whenever I people-watched in Manila at Café Havana. It's popular with tourists and expats, but locals know it as a place where visiting white men pick up Filipina sex workers. We call the men AFAMs, "A Foreigner Assigned in Manila," and as all those who work in Manila service industries know, AFAMs tip well.

Pairings of brown women and white men are charged with fraught racial and gender dynamics that too easily create power imbalances. American GIs intermingled with local Filipinas during the American colonial period—and still do so today, given all the US military facilities still operating in the Philippines. At Café Havana, I'm sometimes reminded of my Filipino American friends with Filipina mothers and white fathers. I tell myself to not project my own colonial mentality onto them; just because an Asian woman marries a white man doesn't mean she's the perfect submissive wife of his fantasies. But I sometimes wonder if her husband knows that.

I wonder too if Theo or Otto or Christian—any of the white men I've kissed or slept with—were rice queens, seeing me through the same colonial lens. And as Paolo reminded me, it wasn't only the white men I should have worried about; we as people of color can get too comfortable with the colonial gaze, the stereotypes imposed upon us. I certainly did, making use of what I'd seen Asian bodies do on my screens. I felt I could wield these roles for my own gain, neutralizing their harm. I would learn the hard way that they could be a double-edged sword.

To perform the Asian feminine seemed to draw more audiences, could be parlayed into adoration and validation from white men. As a gay Asian man—already neutered, positioned opposite to masculinity, and made a bottom without question—I thought it a subversion to leverage those constraints placed on Asian bodies. But constraints are still constraints. Not only did I perpetuate stereotypes, I did nothing to challenge or undo them. When Paolo either called me out on my performance or revealed his own absorption of these myths, in naming me "Island Boy," I had to confront the fact I'd been letting others dictate who I was.

Eventually, I began to demur whenever Theo asked me to be seen in public with him. I'd think of those eyes at the movie theater in Chelsea and I'd make up some excuse, still uneasy about being in a configuration that could be written off as a PG-13 Pornhub video. Soon we fizzled out.

It was a shame, but I knew it couldn't last. Krutika had pushed me to think about how comfortable I was with the considerable power discrepancy between myself and Theo, now that I was beginning to understand our racial dynamics: "How comfortable are you with a white man always paying for you?" Whether or not Theo saw me as a body to colonize, I remained too conditioned to see him as my colonizer, my white savior. I didn't want to submit to my own colonial mentality.

I did consent to Theo. I consented to the movies and popcorn, to takeout from his favorite Italian place, to paying for our Seamless when I could afford it, to espresso and conversations in the morning, to kisses in the shower, to a *Hamilton* sing-along as we got dressed for work—and, of course, to sex. When I dropped by Theo's apartment once after a work event, he undid my tie and asked to be bound to his bedposts. I slipped out of my jacket, and we pulled three more ties from his closet. I was excited by how, as I exercised my control over him, he retained his.

Sexual role-play and kinks, I've found, are like the steam room. We give that first yes and consent to a contract wherein the terms are agreed upon by all parties: what to do, how to do it, how far to go. As we did in the steam, Theo and I gave a yes or a no at every step of our play as it escalated. He asked me if I could go get a fifth tie from the rack, and I happily obliged.

"I have a question," Theo said. He kissed my cheek and whispered in my ear, "Do you want to fuck me?" How novel it was to be asked to top. I gave him an enthusiastic yes.

By being more honest in bed, I learned to establish sexual guidelines with men I occasionally called daddy—Theo, naturally, among them. My friends had told me stories where they were called daddy (or even mommy) without warning, which only killed the mood. I made sure to ask about names, characters, and limits before indulging in the types of role-play I first saw in porn and in my head, e.g., daddy-and-boy language or president-and-first-gentleman scenarios (I am a simple man!). This should be the approach to play of all kinds. (I'm less into worshipful island fantasias, but whatever floats your boat.) As in the steam room, all must consent.

After a year of stomaching the gym's exorbitant monthly fee, I left the steam room. Theo and I kissed elsewhere—at his apartment, at the movies—but then we lost contact too. I've lost Otto and Paolo to the throngs of the city as well, but I'm in touch with James on Twitter; we've just never mustered the follow-through to travel ten miles and cross borough lines to get together. The gym and steam room were convenient that way. They provided a ready pool of men, horny after lifting weights, swollen and ready.

I look back with nostalgia on that year in the steam, on my own "cruising of yore." I felt attractive there, developing an appreciation for my body, this battle-scarred thing that could give and receive pleasure. I leaned into the hungry palms and digits making a ballroom of my body, drew confidence from being wanted by these men. (I know steam rooms—and hookup apps—aren't sustainable sources of self-worth, but I took it where I could get it.) This confidence was most potent whenever I took the role of leader, initiating our game and bringing us to sexual consensus.

I loved conducting our orchestra and the symphony we played—the hisses of steam and our stifled little deaths.

I came to wield this power beyond the steam room too. It may not have defended me from racism and colonial imaginations, whether in our steamy underworld or in the world above, but it reminded me to not let the motives of white men affect my self-esteem or dwell on moments when I heard no. I learned that I could say no. Like most men in this cruising ground, I did my best to honor our queer brotherhood, our common goals and common codes—how we touched, how we looked, and how we said yes. Perhaps this was what I liked best about my steam room: the fact I could consent to it and my consent mattered.

Of course, there's more to cruising and the baths than a now-extinct steam room in a gym in Lower Manhattan, more to colonized desire between gay men. Racism persists, and it'd be a lie to say steam rooms eliminate the complicated intersections of race and queer sex. But, for me at least, they were certainly warped in the steam, bending under the newfound weight of the air.

SHARED HISTORIES

RIGHT AFTER MY first year of college, I wrote a novel based on my first year of college—naturally.

Though most events in the three-hundred-page manuscript aligned with reality, I took some dramatic liberties. The fall semester's circus-themed party did not, in fact, feature student dancers in leopard prints writhing around in cages. But I did see Adam leave the party with another man, a buff Asian dude who maybe played rugby, as depicted in the scene where "an irrational jealousy suddenly invaded my chest and rooted me to the spot." Adam had just turned me down the week before, and it was gutting to see the man I thought was the love of my life choose what looked like an upgraded version of me: more muscular and masculine, sportier and relaxed, less desperate to take his name.

Later, novel-Matt confronts novel-Adam at another party. "I fought for you," he says, "for something I thought we had. Every dance, every party, every time we were together." Reader, we were only a month into our freshman year.

The manuscript is both a quippy romantic comedy and a personal documentary. It's tempting to edit it, to recontextualize the past, to add new information, or to rewrite my history entirely. But the point of it is to capture who I was at the time, what I knew and the limits of my imagination. It's nice to see how I've grown when I revisit its pages, or those of my old drafts of fan fictions and plays—which I've saved to the cloud or external hard drives. They're time capsules, living archives that illustrate how a life is an accumulation of tokens. But my archival workhorses are the more passive recorders of my life: social media like Twitter, Instagram, Facebook; office suites like calendars and emails; text messages. They act as my primary diaries, mementos I take with me on our twenty-first-century march toward climate death.

Though I do my best to not delete any part of those archives, they can be lost. Hard drives dropped, cloud log-ins forgotten, phones updated and wiped can erase whole swathes of my history. It's a bummer to lose those mementos and instead rely on my own memory, that choosy old thing. The more I return to the threads it keeps, the more they seem to fray.

Some memories I lose on purpose. Cleaning up is necessary. There's only so much space, so much to carry at every import. Digital hoarding is easy enough, but the clutter can get in the way; what's the point of keeping fifty-three near-identical selfies when I have the perfect fifty-fourth?

When I back up my phone, there's a selectivity to the process, picking what gets trashed or archived, weighing what I keep. Inevitably, my digital archives come to resemble my natural memory, imperfect and partial.

I don't remember how parts of that three-hundred-page manuscript disappeared. It's missing pages, maybe a whole chapter, about Adam. The material about how we met, how we broke up, and how he kept cropping up in my life—it's all in there, in black and white. But there's nothing about the complicated *during*, memories I still have that let me think of him with fondness. I recall writing them, but did I never save them? Or did I lose them in a transfer? Maybe I deliberately erased them. It's possible, given my habit of deleting memories with men I've kissed.

When I broke up with Stephen, I got rid of everything. I wiped our text message history clean. I removed the photos of him I'd saved on my hard drives. The ones on my Instagram too; he did the same before we blocked each other. We forfeited our relationship and our friendship on Facebook. We never moved in together, only briefly considered it, but the digital cleanup felt like a domestic dividing of the things. After I drunk-dialed him on my birthday, I deleted his number too. Our smartphones keep us always at each other's fingertips, however passively. They never close doors, only leave them ajar. With Stephen, I had to slam them shut and call a locksmith.

This was my inelegant coping mechanism. I couldn't bear to see what no longer existed between us. I was a heartbroken editor, a biased historian looking to rewrite the past, to hide evidence of the fact Stephen and I had once made each other happy. Though effective in the painful aftermath, this did me no favors in the long run. After the wounds healed and the scabs fell away, I had no proof of our history, nor a way to evaluate how much I'd grown since.

I turned to secondary sources. Some time after the breakup, I texted my friends, asking if they still had the pictures of Stephen and me that I'd shared so freely in our early days, filled as I was with hubris and nearly wedded bliss. My friends had told me to be careful then—told me to be careful now. I explained this was a test. If I could see us together, as much of an *us* as we ever were, without any pang of guilt or remorse, then I'd know I was OK.

And I was. I recovered screenshots of our swooning texts, a photo of Stephen and me at the park where he'd meet me for lunch, the collage of selfies I made on the night Stephen and I broke my bed. He was a beautiful boy, really, with a crooked smile and steel-blue eyes, Episcopalian tattoos and perfectly manicured stubble. I felt no regret, only a fondness for what we had—an incandescent romance of First Real Boyfriends, a light bulb that had burnt out.

It took longer to recover from the chapter of Adam, one that extended past what was missing from my manuscript. We were never in a relationship, not exactly, but we had an off-and-on whatevership through college. I was his backup, invited into his bed whenever his official boyfriend wasn't using it. Adam loved him, it was clear to me then—loved us both, said Adam, when he visited me in Brooklyn two years after graduation.

He apologized for all the times he hurt me, all the memories I'd erased from our texts, Facebook messages, photo albums: the Thanksgiving when Adam was on a break with his boyfriend and we slept together without *sleeping together*; the following summer when his boyfriend thought Coney Island was too far, so he called me ("Wanna do the beach, babe?"); our regular dates over the summer they were broken up—seeing *Frances Ha* at the IFC Center, eating at the Thai place we loved on Prince, dancing at The Woods, kissing on Christopher Street, having sex in my stifling sublet at 151st; and all the times he asked to put a stop to us, to meet me for coffee, to "clear the air," to start again though I knew how we'd end.

I had deleted us, happy or sad, at every turn, with every update of my phone or laptop or archive. This romantic revisionism left significant gaps on my end of our shared history. Adam's, however, was intact. Over dinner during his visit, Adam showed me his phone's archives, all preserved in amber, down to our very first online exchange. We met in the Vassar College Class of 2014 Facebook group, where we overeager high school seniors got to pick our roommates before move-in day. I asked Adam if he would be mine—*i love making espresso too!! we could take turns pulling shots every morning ;)*—but he turned down my proposal. He wanted his roommate to be someone different from him, he told me, in my bed, "not someone I'd fall in love with."

I'd given myself emotional lobotomies to pretend I hadn't wasted my time and tears. I deleted all my mementos of Adam, of our complicated *during*, and in doing so, I played myself. I modified my memories so often that I couldn't learn from my past, dooming myself to repeat the same beats, same mistakes. Of course, these mementos and other records—my tweets, Instagram stories, and Facebook statuses—are not memories in and of themselves. They are sites of memory, useful data points in how I re-*call* and re-*collect* my past. Historians rely on documents and artifacts. My friends have planners and little leather Moleskines. I have technology to guide me down memory lane.

I vaguely recall my first time having sex, but checking the events of that day on my Google Cal (February 13, 2011) helps me reconstruct the night, bringing the man, the party, and the vodka into clearer focus. Harder to retrieve are memories from my youth in Manila, before coming to Las Vegas. So I pull from pictures: a precocious boy corralling his cousins; a fey first-grader striking a pose with his hands on his hips; a cross-eyed toddler in an itchy barong Tagalog at his very first wedding. The stories I'm told secondhand become the stories I tell myself.

Memory can be like a garbled game of telephone. I'm fuzzy on the details of the holiday party where I called Christian a racist and threw up in a cab. So I had to rely on Krutika's own pickled recollection the next day. Sometimes, in our retellings, we remember the evening differently, reordering the sequence of events. Time stamps on Instagram posts and apologetic text messages can help pin down facts, but those guideposts can only do so much. There's room to play in the gaps in between.

Whether drunk or sober, our brains are imperfect archivists. This fallibility of memory is well exploited in court. Defense attorneys and prosecutors alike can discredit testimony by casting doubt on its veracity. When Dr. Christine Blasey Ford testified to the Senate Judiciary Committee that then US Supreme Court nominee Brett Kavanaugh sexually assaulted her when they were teenagers, she could not recall the exact date of the assault or how she got home afterward. As seems almost inevitable when the memory in question is of a sexual assault, this was taken by some as proof that all her memories from that night were unreliable, inadmissible.

Dr. Ford, a psychology professor, explained how memory works, how the hippocampus—a part of the brain that processes memory—traps trauma, holding tightly onto that event, but lets go of less visceral details. She described her strongest memory from that night: "Indelible in the hippocampus is the laughter, the uproarious laughter between the two [men], and their having fun at my expense."

She spoke on the morning of September 27, I remember. It was my twenty-seventh birthday. I'd been celebrating in Manila, in a time zone twelve hours into the future. As I stayed up late that night, getting news updates and birthday greetings from the US through Twitter, I thought about my life thus far, about my own moments I can't—and would rather—forget.

There was that night in New York, when I met a man through Grindr in Hell's Kitchen, when he—well, I don't know what to call it exactly. Technically, it was what I wanted. I said yes. I did not say no. I got drunk on happy hour drinks, but I think I was sober when I asked him to stop. He didn't seem to hear me, just kept up his jackhammer pace. He came at the back of my throat and kicked me out. Across the street at Starbucks, I bought an iced latté to wash the taste of him from my mouth. But certain memories never leave our bodies, even when we wish to be exorcised of them and the pain they carry.

After Dr. Ford's testimony, the prosecutor who questioned her on behalf of the committee's Republican majority claimed her account was inconsistent. The trauma she had experienced, the very thing to which she bore witness, was used to frame her as an unreliable narrator of her own story. Less than two weeks later, Kavanaugh was sworn in to the Supreme Court. As ever, those in power got to assert their own version of history.

———

MY FIRST US history class was in the seventh grade. I studied, among many things, the Thirteen Colonies, the American Revolutionary and Civil Wars, the country's manifest destiny, its involvement in the two World Wars. It was my first encounter with this history that had only partially overlapped with mine. In Manila, the United States began to appear in my araling panlipunan classes when they collaborated with Filipinos in ousting Spain from Las Islas Filipinas, only to purchase and annex us as the Philippine Islands, their new Asian colony, at the end of the Spanish-American War in 1898.

President McKinley, when he claimed us as a protectorate at the dawn of the American empire, declared Filipinos were "unfit for self-government." America had no choice, he said, "but to take them all, and to educate the Filipinos, and uplift and civilize and Christianize them." We'd been Christianized by Spain for centuries, but the Americans overwrote our past with their own stories, stories we would come to share.

From then on, the US shared top billing in our Filipino history lessons. They gladly assisted our revolution against the Spanish but squashed our rebellion when we resisted them, our new colonizers. In the Philippine-American War, US troops were told by their generals to "kill every native in sight," a soldier wrote in a letter home to New York. He said, "I am probably growing hard-hearted, for I am in my glory when I can sight my gun on some dark skin and pull the trigger." In retaliation for the death of American men at the hands of locals in the town of Balangiga, General Jacob H. Smith demanded, "I want no prisoners. I wish you to kill and burn, the more you kill and burn the better it will please me." He wanted every "native" over the age of ten shot on sight. By 1902, as many as one million Filipinos died in the three-year war.

The United States decreed the islands an unincorporated territory and supplanted the First Philippine Republic with a military government. Then they established a common-wealth to "prepare us for independence" by July 4, 1946 (a very purposefully chosen date). The Philippines eventually did become an independent republic, after being dragged into World War II. Just ten hours after its 1941 attack on Pearl Harbor in Hawaii, the Imperial Japanese Navy bombed the Clark Air Base in Pampanga, roughly fifty-five miles north of Manila. In the capital, Japan overwhelmed Filipino and American defenders and occupied the Phil-ippines until the war's end in 1945. During Japanese oc-cupation, another estimated one million died—about ten thousand of them during the Bataan Death March, a forc-ible transfer of Filipino and American prisoners of war.

It was one of the few events addressed by history class-rooms in both the Philippines and the United States. My teachers in the US, in covering the Death March, lamented their countrymen's deaths at the hands of the Japanese. They also taught General Douglas MacArthur's "dramatic" escape from the islands in 1942 as they fell to the Japa-nese, as well as his "triumphant" return two years later, in a unit they called the Liberation of the Philippines. In both episodes of American Philippine history, white men were written as victims, saviors, and literal comeback kids, either succumbing to, saving, or defeating a nation in the "Far East"—one dangerous, another helpless.

Beyond that, my American classmates and I were made to study the events happening on these greater American shores. Nothing about the Asian colony it owned nor its people—nothing of the pensionados who immigrated from the Philippines for an education in the US; nor the Filipino farm laborers in California who sparked the Delano grape strikes; nor the soldiers shafted by the Rescission Act of 1946, which annulled the pledge of money and US citizenship to Filipinos who fought in World War II. Nothing at all of the anti-Filipino sentiment we faced on this land that claimed to protect us: how antimiscegenation laws were modified specifically to discriminate against "Malays"; how quotas limited our immigration to the American mainland (though not to plantations in Hawaii); how our communities were attacked and bombed, at the dawn of a new century, when we persisted and built homes for ourselves.

I studied the history of Filipino America outside school, had to collect its disparate fragments and piece it together because the culture at large didn't care to remember us. This forgetting is a predominant theme in the scope of Asian American histories. The Chinese Exclusion Act, Japanese American internment during World War II, US involvement in Vietnam and the following refugee crisis—my teenage textbooks made footnotes of these events, centered their chapters instead on America's victories, its generals and politicians, and ignored whole lands and peoples used as props in the game of American imperialism.

There's only so much that can be covered in a semester or a year, I know that, and so much we shouldn't forget. While some of my classmates extended their education through Korean and Chinese schools in Las Vegas, I had no access to Filipino schooling. It's a recent development in the US (the Filipino School in San Diego, California, was established in 2015; the Filipino School of New York & New Jersey in 2008) and limited to areas where Filipinos have reached critical mass. These programs are run as after-school classes or summer camps, which can make attendance prohibitive, especially to the immigrant families who might need it most. We're asked to pay in time and tuition to learn about ourselves.

Thus, we're left with the footnotes, relegated to the literal margins, in the texts where we learn from "our" pasts. Asian Americans are "invisible minorities" (is that why we're the "model" to emulate?), our people's traumas "forgotten wars." American educations hail the United States as exceptional—rebellious, righteous, and great. As a revolutionary country with a manifest destiny, the events that bear witness to the violence of American imperialism are omitted in the history taught in schools. Cultural memory is selective, especially with the stories we're told to "never forget."

It's an Americanism so clichéd that it's now a meme. There are variations, but in essence, it's this: a photo collage captioned "America tells us," with two images opposite each other—the first, a picture of the burning Twin Towers, with the text "Never forget"; the second, a picture of an enslaved black man scarred by a whip, with the text "Get over it." In some versions, the image of the slave is replaced with one representing Native American genocide or Japanese American internment; in other iterations, in addition to 9/11, we're reminded to "never forget" the Holocaust or the sinking of the *Titanic*. It's a blunt articulation of the way American culture privileges the remembering of white deaths, white suffering, and is all too eager to forget the historical and continued violent oppression of people of color—especially in cases where the US is the oppressor.

Selective forgetting and historical revisionism are, ironically, well-chronicled tactics. In ancient Rome, the Roman Senate scrubbed from memory those they believed had brought dishonor to the Roman state in a practice known as damnatio memoriae, literally "condemnation of memory." The emperor Domitian was so condemned: coins and statues bearing his face were destroyed, his arches torn down, and his existence deleted from public records. The Senate's historians were tasked with recasting Domitian as a tyrannical autocrat. (Today's scholars document his ruthlessness but also consider him a foundational architect of the Roman Empire's peaceful second century.) In the Twelve Latin Panegyrics, Pliny the Younger recalls the catharsis in destroying objects with Domitian's likeness: "How delightful it was, to smash to pieces those arrogant faces, to raise our swords against them, to cut them ferociously with our axes, as if blood and pain would follow our blows."

This sentiment was echoed when a colossal bust of the former Philippine president Ferdinand Marcos was destroyed with explosives. The year was 2002, a decade and a half after the end of his dictatorship. Responsibility for the bust's destruction was claimed by the New People's Army, the armed wing of the Communist Party of the Philippines. In their statement, they called the Marcos monument "a mockery of justice and a betrayal of the will of the people" and declared, "Let the ruins be an ugly reminder that the Marcoses have yet to pay for their crimes." Others believed the bust framed Marcos as a cautionary tale. A local archbishop shook his head at the loss of "a monument to evil, warning people never to become what this man was." Among Filipinos, Marcos is never forgotten, though the ways he's remembered and represented vary.

One such representation is the musical *Here Lies Love*, which centers on his wife, Imelda Marcos. It was running in New York when Stephen and I, still giddy boyfriends, went to see it. We walked into a space made to look like a '70s dance club in Manila. Stephen bought us cocktails, infused with tamarind and calamansi. He loved the tart drinks and puckered his lips against mine. I was elated to share with Stephen my history, my culture, even my food. I was learning to appreciate my Filipinoness, called myself lucky to love a white man doing the same.

The immersive experience of *Here Lies Love* was brought to life by a predominantly white production team; the costumer Clint Ramos was the lone Filipino among them. The score was a disco "poperetta" composed by two white men: Fatboy Slim and David Byrne of the Talking Heads. The set consisted of moving platforms and walkways that shifted with each scene, enveloping the audience in the story: that of the ascension of the Marcos family to the presidency, their bloody rule under martial law, and their expulsion from the country during the People Power Revolution. The cast of actors—majority Asian, many Filipino—ushered us through the space as it changed, taught us to dance to the songs, and, never breaking character, asked us to vote for Marcos.

With all its instruction and coercion, the flashy production reflected how it must have felt to live in the gilded Marcos era, a decadent period of which Imelda was the patron saint. She entertained heads of state with lavish celebrations, a diplomatic ace in Marcos's campaign to turn Manila into a global city. The economic boom of the '70s pulled the wool over the public's eyes, belied the administration's crony capitalism, like a mirrored disco ball that dazzles and distracts before exploding in a violent rain. A note in the program for *Here Lies Love* said, "Ferdinand Marcos led a brutal and murderous regime and his wife was in many ways its leader."

I weighed the worth of this asterisked note, and the musical as a whole, while the actors performed my Philippine history lessons: Marcos declaring martial law under Proclamation No. 1081, the assassination of his political rival Ninoy Aquino, and the crowds protesting in People Power. What could a postscript, or even fake explosions, staged gunfire, and well-rehearsed screams tell the predominantly non-Filipino audience about what had happened in my birth country? How could they even come close to understanding what brought me to tears, what still lived in my body—not as my firsthand experience, but as my psychic inheritance—and what we remember: the historical traumas that do not, cannot, leave a people?

My people have made their own attempts to recast our traumas. In 2016, two years after I saw *Here Lies Love*, Marcos's body was moved from his home province of Ilocos Norte. It was brought to Manila and buried at the Libingan ng mga Bayani, literally "cemetery of heroes." The transfer was ordered by Rodrigo Duterte, who had won the presidential election that year and was fulfilling a campaign promise. (He has claimed that the Marcos family made financial contributions to his election campaign. They deny this but admit to having campaigned for him in Ilocos Norte.)

Duterte attempted to justify the burial by saying he was following precedent—Philippine presidents have the privilege of being memorialized as heroes—and positioned it as an opportunity for nationwide healing, a step forward and away from the dark past. Protestors, many of them families of those tortured or killed during the Marcos regime, considered it a negation of their history and the atrocities of his presidency and petitioned to stop the burial. But the Supreme Court voted to allow it, with nine in favor and five opposed—and one abstention—under the logic that Duterte's order didn't violate any laws.

Chief Justice Maria Lourdes Sereno was opposed. She described Marcos's burial as the antithesis of symbolic reparation for his administration's victims. It was also a misuse of public funds, given that Marcos reportedly plundered up to $10 billion during his dictatorship, the majority of which remains unrecovered. Sereno criticized the revisionism enacted by Marcos's apologists, who downplayed the burial's symbolism and how it would be remembered in the future. In her dissent, Sereno wrote, "That is the peculiar power of symbols in the public landscape—they are not only carriers of meaning, but are repositories of public memory and, ultimately, history."

Sereno was also critical of Duterte's drug war and his declaration of martial law in the region of Mindanao. Eventually, she was ousted by Duterte's appointees in the Supreme Court, in 2018. The Human Rights Watch called her removal an affront to constitutional checks and balances, a concentration of power "in the hands of Duterte and his allies, posing the greatest danger to democracy in the Philippines since the Marcos dictatorship."

IN MIDDLE SCHOOL, one of my teachers spent over half the school year on the Civil War and its aftermath—the Reconstruction. I was fresh from Manila and eager to cover something else. My adopted country's less-studied colonial crimes seemed more relevant to my life, could show me how my birth country's history overlapped with that of my new classmates. I believed that the Confederacy and its mission to expand the institution of slavery lay buried firmly in the past.

Some classmates had different priorities too. Like the white kids who were taught at home that the Confederacy fought the war to defend and preserve a more "genteel" way of life. Our teacher, a black woman, worked to impress on us how the subjugation of black people lived—*lives*—on. It was from her that I learned the disgraceful fact that there remain extant memorials to the Confederacy, endorsements of white supremacy meant to intimidate Black Americans.

The Southern Poverty Law Center reports that at least 1,700 such symbols still exist in the United States, as of 2018. They're most common in former Confederate states: Virginia, Texas, and Georgia each have about 200 (the exact numbers vary as more are identified and removed over time). But you'll find them in Union states as well; there are streets named after Confederate generals in Brooklyn, New York, and in San Diego, California, a cemetery plot owned by an organization called the Daughters of the Confederacy features a monument dedicated to the "Confederate Veterans and Their Wives Herein Buried." In 1926, a ten-ton granite memorial was erected in a cemetery in Seattle, Washington—a state that didn't exist during the Civil War. Inscribed in the stone: "In Memory of The United Confederate Veterans / erected by Robert E. Lee / Chapter Number 885 / United Daughters of the Confederacy." Nevertheless, it seems, white women persisted.

For as long as they've existed in the US, Confederate memorials have been removed from public spaces in isolated instances. Local communities have become more vocal in advocating for their removal since June 2015, when a white supremacist opened gunfire at the Emanuel African Methodist Episcopal Church in Charleston, South Carolina, killing nine Black Americans. Since then, 114 Confederate symbols have been removed, reports the Southern Poverty Law Center, "including 48 monuments and three flags, and name changes for 35 schools and one college, and 10 roads."

Among those symbols was the one taken down by black activist Bree Newsome. Ten days after the Charleston shooting, Newsome climbed the flagpole in front of the South Carolina State House and removed the Confederate battle flag. There are videos of her, high in the air, clutching the flag in her hand. Newsome shouts to the crowd below, to the world: "You come against me with hatred, oppression, and violence. I come against you in the name of God. This flag comes down today."

Earlier that week, *The Atlantic* had published an article by two history professors wary of "sanitizing the commemorative landscape." Ethan J. Kytle and Blain Roberts write: "Confederate and proslavery memorials embody, even perpetuate, deeply flawed narratives of the Old South and the Civil War. Yet they also reveal essential truths about the time during which they were erected." They propose an additive, rather than subtractive, method: building more monuments to black freedom—like the statue of Denmark Vesey, the alleged leader of a slave uprising and an early member of the Emanuel African Methodist Episcopal Church, installed in Charleston in 2014—and amending Confederate statues with plaques, putting them in a historical context.

That recontextualization is a two-way street. At the 2017 white supremacist rally Unite the Right in Charlottesville, Virginia, self-identified neo-Nazis, neo-Confederates, and Klansmen, among others, protested the removal of a statue of Robert E. Lee, a commander of the Confederate States Army. In the rally's stated goal to unify the white nationalist movement in the US, this symbol of the Confederacy was endowed with another layer of meaning, made part of another myth. As Eleanor Harvey, a scholar of the Civil War and a curator at the Smithsonian, told *National Geographic*, "If white nationalists and neo-Nazis are now claiming this as part of their heritage, they have essentially co-opted those images and those statues beyond any capacity to neutralize them again."

In 2019, two years after the Charlottesville rally turned violent and left a counterprotester dead, a state judge ruled that Confederate monuments are protected by state laws. Some parties—including the City of Charlottesville itself, which had planned to remove the Robert E. Lee statue in 2017, thus sparking the rally—read such images as symbols of white supremacy. But the judge writes, "others see them as brilliant military tacticians or complex leaders in a difficult time." Objectively, he says, they are war memorials in and of themselves; how they are viewed is up to the viewer. The ruling echoes the Philippine Supreme Court's verdict on the Marcos burial: commemorations do not violate any existing laws and are therefore permitted, even when they seem to sanction those who held intents and ideologies reprehensible—even outright violent—to some in the contemporary public.

From Marcos's bust and burial place among heroes in the Philippines, to figures of the Confederacy still standing across the United States, these sites of memory live at the intersections of historical truths and the stories that survive them. Whether we're told to "get over it" or "never forget," we're reminded of the power of personal and public memories. To control how things are remembered is to control history and, in turn, to control ongoing narratives.

Through damnatio memoriae, the ancient Romans weaponized oblivion. They understood the significance of memory, the disgrace of being erased. This was the fate to which, I was afraid, my people were condemned. Because I never saw substantial coverage of Filipino Americans in my texts and classes growing up in the US, never learned about my past in this land, I feared I'd have no future. That seemed to be my nondestiny, according to what I was—and wasn't—taught in history books.

Our histories, both remembered and forgotten, repeat themselves. In the late nineteenth and early twentieth centuries, the US passed several exclusionary acts to restrict immigration from Asia; now we have travel bans to and from predominantly Muslim countries. We had Japanese American internment camps; now we have Immigrations and Customs Enforcement encampments filled with children from Central America, separated from their parents at our country's southern border. We had Jim Crow laws; now we have the rampant police brutality against Black Americans and the prison-industrial complex. These are not mistakes unintentionally repeated because we've been too careless to consult our history. These are extensions of the same campaign to shape our society for the comfort of white communities and psyches. These are the tactics of empire.

Imperialism reconstructs the pasts of its subjects, supplants them with narratives that fit their agendas. Before my homeland became Las Islas Filipinas, its pre-Hispanic society had its own faiths and social systems. The Spanish replaced them with Catholicism and colorist hierarchies (that we still haven't unlearned), while American cartoonists drew Filipinos as unwashed barbarians, doubly invalidating the histories of their new subjects and a rival empire. The colonized are not permitted records, archives of their own, that exist outside the scope of their colonizers' stories. They insist on writing our stories for us. This means the most accessible records of the Philippine-American War are from white perspectives that glorified violence against bodies unlike theirs. In these histories, my people are targets, objects, inhuman. I understand the desire to forget.

But worse still is oblivion. To give in to the condemnation of memory, the whitewashing of cultural and social narratives, would be, as Chief Justice Sereno wrote in her dissent to the hero's burial of Marcos, to take a myopic and shortsighted view of history, "to disregard historical truths and legal principles that persist after death." We must choose to remember, not just out of respect for our shared histories, but also for our entwined futures—and, more urgently, our present that is occurring, our past that is repeating.

There is no perfect solution to the question of memorials to tyrants and traitors. Whether in Roman, Filipino, or American society, there are cases to be made both for the dismantling of such public symbols of trauma and for their preservation as evidence of atrocious histories. (For what it's worth, I say get rid of all Confederate memorials, put them in a museum of shame, and install images of black freedom where mementos of racism once stood.) That we're having this debate at all is a sign of progress, an acknowledgment of these events, issues, and challenges to our morals. To honor that progress, we must insist on remembering.

Let us remember it all. Let us recount the chapters of history untold, diminished, purposefully lost. Let not our memories fail us, nor our names endure oblivion, nor our records remain partial and our scholarships half true. Rather than forget, let us carry the weight of the past. When I came to the United States, I was given a thorough education in the dominant American narratives. I cannot remember everything I was taught, but I can remember what I was not.

Indelible in my hippocampus is the silence, the deliberate silence of a cultural narrative that allowed my people and peers little to no room to speak and the possibility of going forever unheard, invisible, without a place in America's story.

THE LAST TIME I saw the bust of Ferdinand Marcos was on a road trip with my father's side of the family. It was during one of our usual Ortile vacations, the kind I took before moving to the United States: a weekend in a beach town in La Union, then a week at my grandfather's country house in the mountains of Baguio. To get between the two, we'd drive along the Aspiras–Palispis Highway, formerly known as Marcos Highway, and pass his ovoid likeness, a landmark that told my cousins and me we had less than an hour left to our house.

Marcos's face was still intact when I last took that trip. The explosion happened just about four months before I immigrated to the US. When I heard that the bust had been reduced to ruins, I didn't know that the New People's Army, an officially designated terrorist group, claimed responsibility. At the age of eleven, I did know that the monument to Marcos made Mom and Tatay feel bad—so if it couldn't make them or the other people he hurt feel bad anymore, then its loss was a good thing.

I've yet to take another Ortile vacation to La Union or Baguio; my cousins lament the bitch of a drive to the countryside. But I've seen the ruins of the Marcos head in pictures online. All that's left of the bust are the criss-crossing concrete pillars and beams that held up his face, resembling the skeletal steel globe at the foot of a bad hotel in New York's Columbus Circle.

The remains of the Marcos landmark are poorly reviewed on Google Maps. "It is a good reminder of the hardships our country went through under the dictatorship," writes one reviewer, who gave it a one-star rating. "But I still believe it should have been blasted away [entirely]."

Before my mother and I moved to Las Vegas, we had a one-month stopover in San Francisco, where her parents lived. I only ever visited them in San Francisco as a kid and so never fully clocked the monument that towered in the middle of Union Square. I just thought it was a pretty statue of Nike, the goddess of victory. On a visit as an adult, I realized it was the Dewey Memorial, built to commemorate Admiral George Dewey's success in the Battle of Manila Bay during the Spanish-American War.

The inscriptions on the column describe how Dewey and his fleet, "undaunted by the danger," overwhelmed the Spanish warships and "held the city in subjection until the arrival of troops from America." There was nothing of the American promise to liberate the Filipinos from the Spanish Empire, nor the subsequent purchase of—or war against—the Philippines to create an American colony. For a moment, I longed to attempt the New People's Army's method of turning a monument into a ruin, into a reminder of crimes still unpaid.

But I had other plans. I was in town for the wedding of my college friend Noah. At the reception, I admitted that I was also meeting up with Adam, who lived in the Bay Area. My friends, as always, told me to be careful, and I explained this was another test. If I could spend time with Adam, figure out the *us* we are now after the *us* of our past, without any pang of guilt or regret, then I'd know I was OK.

And I was. At a café in Oakland, we hugged and kissed familiar stubbly cheeks. The rush of seeing Adam was familiar but calmer, more assured about our complicated history—the full extent of which is a private one that only we know, subject to the ways our hearts are inclined to remember it. It must have hurt too much to re-read those pages chronicling him, the ones missing from my manuscript, that I intentionally lost them, even though I wrote them. At least my memory has outlived my records, thus far and for now.

As Adam and I walked around Lake Merritt, zoomed through the park on electric scooters, what I could still remember, the best and worst of us, held no terrible power over me. I could make new memories with him, however few, and save him from oblivion, now that I—we—have moved on.

In my latest re-read of my freshman novelization, I thought about filling in the gaps. Instead, I went back through the whole thing, considering my characterization of Adam. I don't think I ever made him out to be a villain. If anything, I exaggerated the objective significance of our interest in each other. The facts: boy likes boy, boy likes boy back, the timing isn't right.

Adam's more complete archive might give him a different view of our shared history. But that was how I remembered it, had chosen to put it to paper. Adam and I fought often, on this we can agree. I remember, during a fight, one of our first, Adam said, "Don't put this in your book." Even at our worst, he always believed in me, that one day there'd be a book. "Just write about all the times we were happy."

I understand the impulse to delete, to paint a rosier picture. But memory is already so fallible as it is. To forget records, rewrite memories, and negate our histories would be to deny our ability to remember and to learn, the growth of which we're capable. So, I'd say to Adam, to write all the times we were happy is to write all the times we were together.

On the night he stayed with me in Brooklyn, we took a selfie: my head on his chest, his hand on mine, both looking at the camera. In the photo, Adam and I look surprised, astonished by where we found ourselves six years from where we began. In the weeks following his stay, I considered deleting the photo. I was afraid I'd fall into old habits. (I did; I made it my phone's wallpaper for a day.) I buried the picture in my archives instead, with my digital clutter collecting dust in the cloud.

Years later, on a stroll down memory lane, I came upon that memorial, one that has since lost its charge. It exists now as a happy souvenir of our whatevership, among the drafts and texts and signposts telling me how far I have come and have yet to go. It's a gift to be reminded of that. I'm fortunate to have that history, to carry the weight of all the times we were together.

BALIKBAYAN

Stuck on a train underneath Manhattan, running late for an appointment, I was struck by the sense I'd forgotten something vital. I went through my bag, just to check. It was all there: sunglasses, gum, lotion, cologne, the pages that were becoming my book—save for the most essential thing. My heart clenched. I didn't have my passport. And now I was too far from home to go back for it.

Blue and incontestable, I had carried it with me always, to be safe. I'd even renewed it three years before, in the fall of 2016. Though it was then still years from expiring, the recent election's outcome had scared me. I didn't know what would happen to the US State Department in the next four—or eight—years, so I got a passport to last me the next ten. But it didn't do me any good sitting on my desk at my apartment, next to my hard drive and a photo of me with my mother. I was so used to always having it that I took it for granted, that irrefutable proof of my American citizenship.

They might still let me through, I hoped. I pressed on, emerged from the subway at Bryant Park, and walked up Fifth Avenue. At the Philippine Consulate General, they pointed me to the basement, a holding room with fluorescent lights and stale air. There was no one in line, so I went to the clerk processing dual citizenship applications and explained the situation.

My petition required proof I was a former natural-born citizen of the Philippines. I offered two supporting documents: my birth certificate, reprinted by the Philippine Statistics Authority, and my old Filipino passport. In the latter half of 2007, the Department of Foreign Affairs began to issue them in brown, but mine was printed earlier that year. It's the old color, a deep jungle green, and expired. Two years after its printing, it was invalidated; I had to give up Filipino citizenship to become an American.

To prove my "naturalization or acquisition of foreign citizenship," I needed my US passport. Without it, I only had a secondary document, which my mother had told me to bring, just in case: her certificate of naturalization. It's light green and printed on parchment. It resembles a college diploma, with cursive script and gold-foil accents, as if commemorating an education in Americanness. Glued to it is a photo of my mother, taken before her chemotherapy for breast cancer. In the picture, her hair is shoulder-length and brown, the rich color of acacia.

I handed my mother's certificate to the clerk. "Nakalimutan ko po yung US passport ko sa bahay," I told him. Since this document of naturalization wasn't mine, not exactly, I thought it might be insufficient: "Pwede po itong gamitin?"

"Kelan birthday mo?" said the clerk.

September 27, 1991, I answered. I was one day shy of seventeen when my mother took the oath of allegiance on, as the certificate reads, "September 26, 2008." Had I been eighteen at the time, I would've had to jump through the same hoops as my mother did—US civics test, interview, and all. But because I was her underage ward, the privilege of citizenship was granted to me by extension. I became an American passively.

Without a naturalization certificate of my own, I relied on my US passport to prove my citizenship. To find myself without it at the consulate, as I attempted to reclaim my identity as a Filipino citizen, left me feeling vulnerable. I had only a tenuous claim to being American.

The clerk inspected my documents, cross-checking names and dates. Satisfied, he said, "Pwede yan." He didn't smile, not quite, when I sighed with relief and he put my petition through. But his expression was reassuring, supportive. We were compatriots.

I gave him the requisite three passport photos and fifty dollars in cash, then signed the application form. Come back at three o'clock, he told me, to take the oath of allegiance to the Philippines. "Salamat po," I thanked him. He replied, in English, "Welcome."

NINE MONTHS BEFORE I became a dual citizen, in September 2018, I flew to the Philippines on a fourfold mission. First, to retrieve those documents: my old Filipino passport and my birth certificate. Second, to celebrate my birthday: I hadn't been in Manila for it since I moved to the US, so I thought it fitting to be home for my twenty-seventh on September 27. Third, to be there for my father's birthday: his was two days before mine and we were treating the Ortile clan to lunch for a joint party. Fourth—and most important to me—to visit my country on a trip where, for the first time, I could dictate the terms.

Previously, my pilgrimages home had been part of the deal my parents brokered on my behalf. Take him to the United States for a better education and a better life, my father had agreed, then send him to the Philippines, as often as possible, to see his cousins, his grandmother, and me. I have done this from the age of fourteen, crossing the Pacific almost every year for my scheduled quality time with the Ortiles.

In my memory, these trips were mostly uneventful. I was never there for a "vacation." I was there to be in the presence of my father. Reading the LiveJournal I kept in those years, the highlights of these visits involved the rest of the Ortile family—raucous family meals, road trips to the cooler elevations of mountainous Baguio, long weekends at the waterfront resorts of Tagaytay. On our own, my father and I kept to our quiet routines.

When I stayed with him on my visits, whether in my childhood home or in the apartment he rented as a bachelor, he'd give me his bed and sleep instead on a floor futon ("It's actually better for my back," he said) and remind the doormen—or, rather, the gatemen—who I was, that I was his son and should be looked after. We would hit our regular beats: quiet afternoons watching TV, quiet meals at restaurants, quiet car rides while stuck in traffic. Since he couldn't always take time off from work, he'd sometimes leave me at his apartment, in front of the air conditioner and his desktop computer. I'd spend the day online, surfing and reading and role-playing on a Harry Potter message board with my internet friends—as if I were back in Las Vegas, waiting for my mother to come home from work.

My teenage summers crossing the Pacific largely resembled the routines of my US-born peers with divorced parents. As was the custom of our breed, we'd shuttle between two homes, keep two beds and two closets, a go-bag and a commute. Mine just happened to be a seventeen-hour flight with a stopover in Korea.

Classmates told me how much better it was once their parents separated; no more broken dishes or frosty silences, no more screaming or bruises. I agreed; no more witnessing "heated discussions" or shouting matches, no more attempts to run away or to hide in closets. I couldn't stand it when my parents were in the same room, the tension and threat of danger palpable whenever they breathed the same air. I had long wished for a buffer between my mother and my father. When we moved to America, my wish came true—I got a buffer the size of the Pacific.

These summer trips were dutiful attempts to maintain good relations with a man around whom I wasn't sure how to act. In other words, we were your typical dad and gay teenage son. Though my father has always loved me—I know that—our relationship was strained after years of comments like "stand up straight like a man." His demands that I "man up" echoed the bullying I faced at my all-boys school in Manila, from classmates who told me I was going to hell for being a "sissy," a "bakla," a "girl." As a young gay boy, I counted my father among my tormentors, people who would rather I weren't myself.

Whenever I visited him, I was evasive and watchful, once again that baby gay in front of the television, watching MTV in the late '90s, looking over my shoulder while I studied choreography by the Spice Girls. If my father ever caught me feeling my Posh Spice fantasy, I had my excuses ready: "It's for a class project," "Victoria's just very beautiful," etc. Not only did I love the ladies of Spiceworld, I imprinted on *Sex and the City*, *Will & Grace*, *The Nanny*, the keystones of my bridge to New York. Before I even understood that America was part of my mother's plans for me, I looked westward in the songs and scripts that would influence my adulthood. That these models belonged to the realms of the feminine and queer only solidified the notion that, for my emerging identity as a gay boy to flourish, I'd have to leave my father's house, my father's land.

Each time I left the Philippines for the US, I was always happy to leave behind my father's criticisms, if not necessarily my father himself. Our conversations on my pilgrimages home were stilted, superficial. When he asked, "How are things in Las Vegas?," I gave diplomatic answers— polite but vague. I told him, "Thanks for asking. Mom is keeping herself busy while I'm away," when she was on a wine tour in Napa Valley with my stepfather, and, "No, I'm too focused on my studies to be dating anyone," when I was making out with a boy from a rival high school in the back of his Mustang. I obscured from him my life in the US, didn't want to paint too detailed a picture of my American life that was easier without my father and better with my mother.

She and I were your typical mom and gay teenage son. Both new immigrants in the States, with my stepfather still living in Manila, we only had each other. She was my best friend, the first person I told I was gay, at thirteen. I sought her counsel in the face of adversity, as I faced new teenage tormentors, patronizing teachers, and homophobic priests. Confused and hurt at how efficiently people in America could hate, I was still that three-year-old boy at his uncle's wedding, running to his mother whenever he felt uncomfortable and hurt. I felt safe coming out to her, felt safe coming to her for everything, knowing she would do all she could to protect and care for me.

So, on my inaugural trip to the Philippines from the US as a Filipino American, it was difficult to be far away from my mother, to put the Pacific Ocean between us for the first time. On top of that, returning to the place I'd left behind was unnerving. Upon seeing Manila again, I felt much like I would on my first holiday back in Las Vegas as a freshman in college, over Vassar's winter break. Whether the dim and cramped apartment where I grew up, or the backwoods desert I despised, I was returning to places I had longed to escape, only to find that they seemingly had not changed since I last saw them. It was as if the progress and accomplishments of my life were imagined, dreams from which I'd suddenly woken up.

Each trip, I would recover from the jet lag and wake up to my past, preserved in amber. It all reified my parents' custody agreement, which country would belong to whom: The US was where I'd grow up fast, make plans for my future, and (as my mother taught me) literally mood board a life, willing it to arrive; the Philippines would remain in my past, a fossilized life I'd left behind.

My motherland became my fatherland. In my commitment to keeping my parents separated, I cleaved not only my family, but myself as well, into two parts, along the international date line. I thought the things that make me who I am—my father and my mother, my Philippines and my America—were facets of my life I couldn't ever conjoin. It was an impossible idea, I believed, to be a son and citizen of both.

The US government held the same belief. For the first several years of our life in Las Vegas, we were classified as "permanent aliens" in America—not quite visiting, not quite living. To "naturalize" us both, my mother took an oath. She gave up "all allegiance and fidelity to any foreign prince, potentate, State, or sovereignty," renouncing her—our—birth country. After a few more words—and a "so help me God" for good measure—a government clerk gave my mother a piece of paper. It had her name and picture, brown and smiling. She was now American, the clerk told her, "like the rest of us."

That oath was not mine to take, not officially. I had no say in the matter, just as when the choice to come to the US was made for me by my mother. My father, I'm told, didn't put up a fight; one less fight, thankfully, for my parents to have. As a kid and teenager, I could only engage with them in isolation, separately. I have always felt torn between the two, as though I can only belong to one—one country and one parent—at a time.

This was how I became an ambassador. I traveled overseas and upheld their custody agreement, negotiating with one party while maintaining allegiance to the other, brokering my family's peace—and peace of mind. I don't want to frame my transpacific obligations as filial duty; there exist too many platitudes about Asian families and the attendant piety, about "how we do it in the East," often delivered as Orientalist generalizations. But, in this case, I have to say, the house slipper fits.

In Las Vegas, maybe in 2007 or so, I asked my mother if I really had to visit my father. Each return to Manila was a return to a place where I had to subtract parts of myself, to posture again in a certain way. I was doing the same in the US, buying into the myth of the model minority and tailoring myself to the double standards by which white America measured its immigrants. In doing so, I was awarded laurels and pinned with medals. They suited me. I was loath to take off this costume and wear again my barong Tagalog, itchy and ill-fitting as it was. In the States, with my mother, I was inking the lines of who I wanted to become. In the Philippines, with my father, I reverted again into a pencil sketch.

But these visits are part of the deal, said my mother. He pays for the tickets, she told me, and, after all, he's still your father. It was important to have him—and our home country—in my life, especially now that we lived far away, now that I was a balikbayan.

To translate literally: balik means "to return" and bayan means "country." It's a word that refers to a Filipino abroad who comes home—whether for a visit or an indefinite period of time. It's a moniker you can't ever take off. You're always a balikbayan; when you return to the Philippines, you'll always have left it.

———

BEFORE I SOUGHT dual citizenship, before I prematurely renewed my US passport, I took a trip to Manila for Christmas and stuck around to ring in the new year. A week into 2016, I met up with a friend at a bar called Today x Future. Locals abbreviated it to simply "Future," but I liked the whole name—the idea that you could multiply the present by what might come tomorrow.

Google Maps said the bar was a stone's throw from where I was staying over the holidays. My friend had invited me to meet her there at around midnight. I called an Uber at eleven, anticipating the city's notoriously heavy traffic. But the ride took all of fifteen minutes, the Escalade cruising down wide open streets. The city had changed, it seemed, since I had last come home.

When I got to Future, the crowd was spilling over onto the porch and the empty street, cigarettes and bottles of Red Horse at their lips. Inside, I linked up with acquaintances I knew from Twitter, danced with them to strains of both Carly Rae Jepsen and Sarah Geronimo, English and Tagalog sparkling on our tongues.

I was on my third bottle of San Miguel Light when I noticed him. "With the tattoos and the leather?" my friend asked. I nodded, and she smirked. "Sabi na nga ba."

He was taller than me in his boots, broad-shouldered, and bespectacled. He wore a leather bracelet that partially covered the tattoos on his muscled forearms. The designs were bold and geometric, calling to mind the tribal tattoos of the Kalinga people in the north, done in patterns said to ward off enemies.

"Felipe, this is Matt."

He knew who I was, he said. He'd read my essay about a man I called Nate, about mistaking familiarity for knowledge and sliding into a relationship. Sure enough, there was a DM from Felipe in my Twitter inbox, a kind and polite note about my body of work to which I had replied "thank you." We had overlapped elsewhere too—we'd both attended the same all-boys school; I was in the first grade while he was in the seventh. I teased him about the age difference. He teased me back: "Don't you like older men?" Felipe had read me, it was true.

It was getting sweaty inside, so we went to get some air. I asked Felipe if I could try on his leather bracelet. He unclasped it from his arm and wrapped it around mine. It dangled like a tennis bracelet around my wrist, the way Gareth's watch did whenever I tried it on as he slept. Felipe had made it himself, he explained; leatherwork was one of his trades. He also made bags, belts, purses, suspenders—anything with a strap.

"And harnesses?" I asked.

Felipe smiled. "Yes, and harnesses."

He insisted that I keep the bracelet. It reminds me of the spiked one I bought in Las Vegas to get a boy to like me back. At home in Manila, a man gave me leather to get me to like him back, when I already did.

From the street, we heard the DJ throw it back to a song by the Spice Girls. Cigarettes were put out, beers were downed. I grabbed Felipe's wrist and pulled him inside, onto the dance floor, the most packed it had been all night. As we fell into pace with the music, I began the usual motions: I pressed my body against his and danced with my back to his solid chest. He reciprocated, his breath warm at the nape of my neck, his beard grazing ticklish skin. My ass dipped at each of the downbeats, and I could feel his crotch level with my lower back. Across the dance floor, our mutual friend winked at me and Felipe, proud of her job well done. I looked at Felipe and mouthed along to the song: "Who do you think you are?"

Felipe moved his hips with mine, quickly matched my tempo. He baited me, skimming his fingers along my torso until I closed the gap between his chest and my shoulders. Then he tugged at my belt to turn me around. His hands on my waist, our faces drew closer as my thumbs massaged his neck. The dance floor was hot, and he melted into my touch. We kissed, grinning with boozy lips, as our past soundtracked our present.

Later, he hailed us a cab. I couldn't remember my address but was fortunately sober enough to direct the driver down the tricky side streets to my temporary home. Felipe was respectful: he didn't insist on spending the night and suggested instead an evening for dinner and drinks. Then he kissed me deeply, outside the gate to the residential complex, for all the nightwatch to see, under the canopy of Christmas lights that would stay up until June.

The spare key gave me a bit of trouble. With a push and a turn, I stumbled into the townhouse, my shoes clacking on the new marble foyer. I switched into house slippers and went up the stairs. It was dark, with only the faint red light of the altar to the Sacred Heart to guide me. At the second-floor landing, I nearly knocked over a figure of the baby Jesus in his manger. I crept along the walls into the guest bedroom, down the hall from where my mother and stepfather were, I hoped, fast asleep.

MY MOTHER MOVED back to the Philippines in my final year of college, in 2013. This was always part of her plan, I had believed: after taking me to the United States for a better education, that "better life," she'd return to my stepfather in Manila. There, she'd become a philanthropic doctor's wife, brighten up his home, make it theirs, and, with Social Security dollars against the Philippine peso, live well and generously.

"No, anak," my mother told me when I asked her to fact-check my memory. "That wasn't it. Not exactly."

Her actual plan, she said, had been to stay in the US. My stepfather, who had been making the same transpacific commute as me, would have joined her full-time and retired there—whether in Las Vegas or otherwise, they never got to figure out. After she lost her pharma job in the recession, my mother got a gig in the Clark County elections office. There was a growing population of Filipinos in Nevada, and she was hired to translate voting materials into Tagalog. It was a civic-minded job that paid, she said, but it was not enough, not the right fit. America was not the right fit either, not anymore, for her or my stepfather.

Why live in Las Vegas, they said, and pay a mortgage on a home worth less than when we bought it, when we have a home in Manila, one long paid for in full? Why not return to the place where my stepfather could continue the medical practice he loved, where he and my mother could invest in their own health-care business, where they could donate to charities, build communities, and serve folks in a country where no one questioned their right to belong? They already had roots in the Philippines, a land that had nourished them from the start. The choice was a no-brainer. It wasn't only a matter of convenience. It was one of survival.

I had filled in the blanks with a more typical story, the kind of fable we as Filipinos in the United States often heard—one where immigrants who got the job done earned the mobility to return to the Philippines, to become permanent balikbayans, to live like kings in a country to which they'd always had a right. Not all Filipinos living and working abroad can hope to move back with a small fortune in foreign money, of course, or even to visit the Philippines frequently, but it was a popular plan among our privileged set.

Many of my parents' peers scaled the ladder in the US and, upon returning to Manila, branded themselves as American imports, leveraged the dollar-to-peso conversion and their stateside cachet. I thought my mother had planned to do the same. I was wrong—especially about the

Social Security part. Since she was laid off in the recession, she did not finish the requisite decade of employment in the US that would have made her eligible for Social Security benefits. For all my mother's fortune and bootstrapping, it was not her lot, in the end, to reap those American rewards.

Still, my mother thrived upon returning to Manila. She was living with her husband full-time and seeing her peers and old friends. She and my stepfather renovated their townhouse for a fresh start. Their wellness consulting business took off. Life was very good to them—apart from the coupled diagnoses of his-and-hers cancers in 2015.

My stepfather got his news that summer, around the Fourth of July. When my mother called to tell me, I was at a company party in the Hamptons, distracted by the chardonnay and the bliss that would soon run out. I was too flippant, noting that prostate cancer, especially when localized, is very curable. But that was beside the point; she was upset. I called later that week to apologize and, upon hearing my stepfather's levity, laugh-sobbed into my phone. It hit me then that this man we loved, who could make my mother and me smile even when we didn't want to, was mortal and in danger.

In the end, his prostatectomy was a breeze compared to the treatment my mother was to face. He'd been cancer-free for a month when my mother rang me again in September, over Labor Day weekend. I ignored her calls that morning, actually; I was still in bed with a handsome novelist who bought me drinks at the bar across the street from his apartment. On the sidewalk in Crown Heights, still wearing last night's contact lenses, I called my mother back. Her voice was calmer than it had been when she called about my stepfather. I skipped a heartbeat as she said the words for which I could never be ready: "I have breast cancer."

On the way home, hungover and in shock, I missed my subway stop. I got off at the next station, walked into a church, lit a candle, and said a prayer. I had never stepped into Saint Ann's before, had only ever passed it on the way to my dentist. Still, conditioned as I was like Pavlov's dog, being in church, any church, made me feel as if my mother were beside me.

By the time December arrived, I visited them in Manila, my stepfather was fit, not looking a day over seventy, and my mother was in the middle of chemo, looking like my grandmother. This was all old hat to her, in a way. This cancer had come for her own mother, her aunts, and her cousins before her. Women in our family had faced this genetic bequest with grace, lived with the emperor of maladies for as long as they could. Every one of them was a Manahan—a name that translates loosely to "inheritance." They had no choice but to be brave.

As my mother lay in a hospital bed, IV in her arm and scarf around her scalp, I sat beside her, with an open computer and an overflowing inbox. It was Christmastime. The chemo ward at the Cardinal Santos Medical Center was lit with unforgiving fluorescents, but the walls were festooned with tinsel. Patients seated in recliners were hooked up to bags of clear fluids. All were accompanied by their friends, their families, each group resembling a Nativity scene, pious and grateful.

The hospital staff had given my mother a private alcove with a curtain. She was being treated at the hospital where my stepfather taught and practiced, with the best oncologists and nurses taking care of them gratis. It was my mother's third round of chemo, and by now, everything had its place: purse within reach here, snacks and water over there, rosary for Mom here, iPad for Dad there, Wi-Fi hot spot at full-batt and ready to go.

When it was time for my mother's daily prayers, I took the opportunity to catch up on work, to send emails with too many exclamation points to colleagues who were currently asleep. I was the editor of the website's popular Philippine edition, making time for it and for free, as well as a glorified assistant, training new hires how to make animated gifs. I was a "cultural fit"—driven and indoctrinated, willing to do labor above my pay grade. Though my bosses loved me, I had just narrowly avoided becoming a casualty in another one of the company's massive reorganizations. I needed to prove I was reliable, I thought, even while on vacation halfway around the world.

Finally, I reached inbox zero, and my mother finished her prayers. She smiled at me. "You seem stressed," she said, not unkindly.

I'd told her about my career's sudden zigs, how my home life with my roommates took a downward zag. I was living with people I loved, but our friendships were souring for reasons I couldn't yet parse. Work provided little reprieve. Not only was there little stability at the office, I'd been striking out with my queries to literary agents. I told my mother less about my romantic failures—and certainly not about how I'd accused a man of racism at a holiday party just weeks before—but she knew enough to gather that I felt unloved in New York. I was spinning wheels, going nowhere and starting to wonder if America, as my mother had felt, was no longer the right fit.

On my phone calls home, she had half-jokingly suggested that I return to Manila, too. There was a sound logic to it. From the American perspective, it was the millennial safety-net option; one of my parents' guest rooms could easily become my bedroom, and I'd save on rent. In the Philippine context, it was a natural postgraduation step. Most young Filipinos don't move out of their family's homes until they marry—and sometimes not even then. Better, they say, to live with people you love. Now, I considered living with the people I loved, becoming a permanent balikbayan. I felt severed from my family; we lived on opposite ends of the earth. I didn't know how much time we had left together on this earth at all. And did I want to spend that time, however long or short, with that ocean between us?

"What if I moved back?" I told my mother. She looked at me, confused, as she put away her prayer rosary, careful not to let it snag on her IV tube. "Back here," I continued, "to Manila, like you've been saying."

"You have your book," she replied, in a tone that said *the pope is Catholic.* I might give up on it, I said, this silly little pipe dream. I wasn't even sure if it would sell, if anyone would read it at all.

She would read it, my mother said, and I was bolstered by this guaranteed audience of one.

I was struggling with the book, I told her. The problem with writing about your history is that you need to reconnect with it. My memory was patchy and scarred, heavy with the load of what I'd faced as a queer brown immigrant kid. At twenty-four years old, I had been smithed against the American anvil for over a decade. In those years, I willingly subtracted parts of my Filipino self, tossing them off for the laurels, the merits, the tailored Americana. How far I'd come from where my mother and I began—maybe too far.

She put her hand on mine. "Do you remember," she said, "the first time you wore your barong Tagalog?"

Yes, at my uncle's wedding—she in her pearls and me in my Filipino clothing. After we took a picture together, my mother helped me take off my barong when its scratchy fabric was irritating my skin. But the reprieve was only needed temporarily. She reminded me, "You got used to it." I wore it again once it was time to go home.

My mother had always been the one to guide me to my future, my dreams, that "better life." On that day, she became the guide to my past as well. My mother walked alongside me as I revisited memories of our lives in Manila and in Las Vegas—over phone calls, Viber text messages, FaceTime over breakfast and breakfast-for-dinner. Twelve hours apart, we spent time together, studied our past together, Pacific Ocean be damned.

She has never lost faith in me, in my words. It was only right that she helped me find them. As our shared history came more clearly into focus, so did the country I'd been so impatient to leave and leave behind. To return to my motherland, I turned to my mother.

———

AFTER FUTURE, FELIPE and I went on our date at the Maginhawa Food Park. We were in Quezon City, the part of Metro Manila where I grew up. I was surprised to see this corner of it, a strip of bars and restos that resembled Bed-Stuy in Brooklyn, or Williamsburg before it became a mall. People in their twenties and thirties were splitting sisig bowls, toasting their beer bottles, tossing heads back in full-throated laughter, their dewy brown skin gleaming under fairy lights.

My prior visits to the Philippines had only ever been to see my family, the narrow world of my childhood. Maybe my hometown had always been like this. "Bago ba 'to?" I asked Felipe. He replied, "Everything looks new to a balikbayan."

As we walked to the food park, we were heckled by a man from across the street. "Oooh! Lovers!" he called at us. Felipe and I laughed. He had clocked us so easily, unassuming as we were in t-shirts and jeans. It must have been my gait, or his leather bag, or the way we looked at each other. I was surprised but not threatened by the remark. It almost seemed good-natured.

"Tayo ba?" I asked Felipe if the man had meant us. But there was no one else on the street. His pinky caught mine as he said, "Lovers na ba?" It was a joke: *Are we getting ahead of ourselves?*

I told this story to my cousins, an enthralled audience, over cocktails at the Palace Pool Club. Now that I was visiting as an adult, those of us who were of legal drinking age could go out to bars and nightclubs. Our cabana was fully stocked with pulutan—nachos, mini-pizzas, and mozzarella sticks, the usual fare of our youth together. As we downed shots of tequila and dipped our feet into a swimming pool flashing with neon lights, one of us remarked how far we'd come, a far cry from the inflatable wading pools we shared as Ortile children in our grandmother's garden.

With my cousins, I was taking up new routines, going to new places, having candid conversations, no longer opaque or evasive in my words and stories. How easily I could share with them my romances, here in Manila and in New York, and how eager they were to listen. I must have been eager to share as well, as I could feel in my cheeks my elation to simply be with them, with those who shared my name.

I wanted to feel the same kind of openness with my father. We'd had some tender moments when I was growing up in Manila: he cooked for me, shared music with me, taught me about jazz, the planets, and mint-marinated lamb. But the more I leaned into my authentic self, the more he seemed to bristle, to want to correct me. At least he expressed fewer critiques of my femininity during my pilgrimages home. He refrained, for example, from criticizing my taste in books when I picked up *The Devil Wears Prada*.

As he paid for it at the register, he said, "You read stuff like this?" His tone was, it sounded, uncertain. He didn't understand me, someone so different from him, so easily letting go of his father and this country. When I was a kid, I didn't share much of myself with my father, believing it was necessary to protect us both. Now, returning to the Philippines as an adult, a gay man who had already done much of his growing up without his father, I felt I could make space for him in my life while protecting who I am. So I took a risk. I came out to him—sort of.

I met my father for dinner, just the two of us. Over vegetarian sisig (his heart) and cans of calamansi juice (my hangover), he asked how my mother was doing. Rather than give a vague answer, I told the truth. Chemo has been rough, I said, telling him how much I admired her strength as the doctors fried every cell in her body in their attempt to destroy a few.

"Your mother has always been resilient," he said simply. I didn't say anything for a moment, only smiled. My father was being honest. I wanted to repay him in kind.

He wanted to hear how I was building my life as an adult in the US. Work has been unstable, I told him, explaining the frustrating instability of the New York media world. I talked about my book, how it didn't seem to be going anywhere, not the query letters nor the proposals, none of them and not yet. On top of that, things had been tense with my roommates; I was worried they would kick me out. My father listened. His nods were attentive, careful. At the mention of my roommates and our strained friendships, he said, "May I offer some advice, my son?"

Permission granted, not that he needed it.

"Sometimes, the roles people play in your life . . . They change. You learn to let them go."

We fell silent, a familiar dynamic between us. I sipped my calamansi juice as he took another helping of tofu sisig. Other than this moment, tonight had been different, perhaps signaling a new pace to our relationship. I wasn't sure what had changed, encouraged my candor. Maybe it was that I began to let go of the memory of my father who didn't understand me, welcoming into my life my father who was willing to try.

Finally, he broke the silence. "Are you taking care of yourself?"

Trying, I told him. I mentioned that I had started going to therapy. I had him and my mother to thank, I joked, trying to lighten the mood by blaming them equally. He didn't say anything. I also have a regular doctor now, I said.

My father was running a hospital at the time; I knew he would approve of my finally having a PCP.

"My doctor specializes in travel medicine," I said. Then, in what is probably the most passive coming-out in history, I added, "As well as gay men's health, so he's the perfect doctor for me." Another attentive nod. If he was following, he didn't make a fuss. Maybe he wasn't surprised. I'd always let my father assume a lot.

"Are you?" I said. "Taking care of yourself?"

Trying, he told me. His health was important too, especially now that he had a daughter on the way. I'd recently met his very pregnant girlfriend and felt my half-sister kick against my hand. She would arrive a couple of weeks after I flew back to New York, so I wouldn't meet her until around her second birthday. When my father sends me photos of her (reclining on a king bed, riding a miniature horse, stunting for the camera in a tiny wrap dress), he says she takes after me: "She knows how to pose." I had assumed we got it from our mothers. Now I wonder if our father had those genes to pass down too.

At the end of dinner, I paid the bill. My father offered to drive me back to my mother's, but I insisted on calling a car for myself. I was making a statement: as I reconnect with him now, I do so as an adult.

And I did feel very adult on my last morning in Manila, sitting at a café, poring over the daily broadsheets, and sharing a leisurely breakfast with Felipe before he went to work. ("It's fine," he said, kissing my neck as I handed him the *Inquirer*. "I have a good reason to be late.") He was blazered, cuffed in new leather, and eye-catchingly beautiful; I noticed at least two other people in line for coffee checking out this man I would have been proud to call my boyfriend.

"Dito ka dapat," Felipe said, reminding me that I belong here in the Philippines. Between our courtship, short but genuine, and our kisses, long and earnest, he had a very good point.

Felipe showed me what my being in the country could look like beyond the domains of my family, how I could express my queer life in my homeland. Here was a man who might help me navigate coming home, guide me through the places I believed I'd forgotten, the places I thought I'd known so well. Felipe could even be a bridge between my romantic and familial worlds: he offered to check in on my mother while I was away in New York, to visit her after chemotherapy treatments. Of all his gifts—the leather bracelet, a video of him playing guitar and singing a song we loved, a blue rose still pressed in one of my notebooks, kisses in broad daylight—this was by far the most generous.

I didn't take him up on it. I didn't let him in, not on that first night, not on the final morning. I was still hesitant to let my worlds collide, too conscious of the fact that, here in Manila, I was staying in my mother's and stepfather's home, which I instinctively kept separate and guarded from other areas of my life.

When one of my cousins came to pick me up at the townhouse for our night out at the Palace Pool Club, he asked if he could see my mother, his aunt, and share well wishes as she went through chemo. She's asleep, I lied. I was too terrified of what would happen if another Ortile entered my mother's territory.

I had long promised that the two halves of me, my mother's side and my father's side, would never touch again, if I could help it. So long as the idea of becoming a permanent balikbayan was hypothetical, I could imagine a seamless return, a life without worry. But what would it really be like to come home and replant my roots when it was such a hassle to keep my parents apart whenever I visited the Philippines?

In 2008, when my mother and I were in Manila for her second wedding to my stepfather, I carefully arranged to be shuttled from one household to another without my parents' having to share the same space. At the end of my three weeks with my father, I arranged for us to have lunch at a mall, where he left me with my suitcases. After an hour of buffer time, my mother found me at the same mall for an afternoon merienda and took me and my suitcases to my stepfather's, where we were staying until after the wedding. I'd planned this transfer with Swiss precision, a museum object organizing his own loan via armored van. I was sixteen going on seventeen and, as the song goes, "timid and shy and scared."

I was the same at my graduation in 2014, at twenty-two going on twenty-three. When my father asked about watching me get my college diploma in New York, I told him not to come. My mother and father's terrible marriage conditioned me to think that if my parents ever breathed the same air, it would combust. For the two of them to stand on my campus—the one place that felt truly mine, that I didn't have to share with them—even the mere idea of it made me panic. Once again, I thought I had to choose between my parents. My mother and stepfather had already bought their tickets, booked a hotel, raised me during the years in which I climbed and clawed my way to Vassar. At twenty-two, I made the same choice I would have made at twelve, had it been mine to make.

Time possesses a magic, I know that. But when it comes to my family, I find it hard to believe that time can work its alchemy, its ways of changing things. What can it do to temper my parents' innate opposition, like poles that repel? I obey the laws of their physics, obliged by nature to keep them apart, even now that they share the Philippines again. Before coming to the States, I had to share our country with my two parents. To return now would mean sharing it with three, taking up again that tricky balancing act—a life of being loaned between competing institutions. My therapist has suggested I might be exaggerating, martyring myself, doing needless work. Why am I so sure, she asked, that my parents can't be civil, share space for the sake of their son? I am sure of this because they can barely share their son.

I visited Manila again in February 2018, for only ten days, to celebrate the birthdays of my mother and stepfather, a week apart. When I told her I'd like to see my father and the Ortiles while I was on this side of the Pacific, she scowled. She had paid for my ticket, she reminded me, and I was staying with her, in her guest room. This wasn't like my pilgrimages in the old days, paid for entirely by my father, conducted under his roof. Time together was costly. My mother wanted her money's worth.

I paid for the ticket too, I told her. She covered my flight in; I bought my flight out. And what difference did one afternoon with the Ortiles make, if she and my stepfather were going to be busy that day anyway? Would she rather I spend that time alone at the mall, spending for spending's sake, or at the townhouse sitting in front of the computer, as I did the rest of the calendar year? While her time with me was limited, so was my time with my father. I reminded her of what she'd told me, as a teen, when I didn't want to visit him: he's still my father and it's important to have him in my life. She was the one who had told me that I shouldn't give up my name.

Presented with her own arguments, my mother relented. I was given a day to see my father, to say hello to my ex-tended family, and to meet my half-sister for the first time. For the rest of the ride home, we sat silently in the car—my mother and me in the back, my stepfather up front, and their driver steering—stuck in a smoggy traffic jam on EDSA, as I willed this old life of mine to move forward, inch by exhausting inch. Even as I hope to share my life with my parents, it's this ambient resentment, the aftershocks of trauma, that prevent me from ever sharing a room with both of them at the same time, let alone a country.

On that one day with the Ortiles, I showed up unannounced at a family gathering. (There were four February birthdays among the cousins, so the timing was opportune.) My cousins were gleefully surprised, immediately pulled me aside to pour me a glass of wine and catch me up on their lives and the petty family dramas that I'd missed. I pulled another bottle from the cellar, as I had my own news to share with them. We would be here awhile.

That's how it works when you're a balikbayan: you always have to keep up. My people in Manila make it relatively easy. Whenever they get wind that I've touched down at Ninoy Aquino International Airport, the Viber group chats come alive with notifications. *Matt, you're home!* they exclaim. *We have to do dinner; we need to get coffee; you've got to see this new mall; I need to introduce you to who I'm dating; we must tell you how, contrary to what you thought as that kid from Quezon City, this world keeps on turning without you.* In this way, I'm stuck at the margins of even the Ortile family, an electron orbiting the nucleus.

As a balikbayan, you're not an outsider, but you are rarely a primary witness to the weddings, the debutante balls, the graduations, the births, the deaths, all the major and minor events in the lives of the people you love. Nor are they privy to yours. So you catch up, as best you can, when you can— and, in the meantime, keep in touch, building bridges that span oceans.

When the party ended, my cousins asked when I would be back; one day was not enough. Picking up on what I'd divulged, tipsy on wine from our favorite Santi's deli, they told me, "Kuya, come home na lang."

I hesitated, not knowing what to say. How could I come home when my parents made it so stressful? As long as I share a space or a country with them, there will always be tension to navigate. It's ever present on my family visits, guaranteed in my future, whether I return for good or "split my time" as a global bicoastal.

Was there a different way of being a balikbayan? Rather than taking pilgrimages and playing the emotional diplomat in the service of an expired custody agreement, what if I could set the terms of how the Philippines fits into my life, how I fit into the Philippines? The logical solution would be to plan my own itineraries, foot my own bills, find my own temporary roofs whenever I was in Manila—to try on that adult life for a while, what I glimpsed on my evenings with Felipe, where everything seemed new.

So, to my cousins, I promised I would visit for my birthday, as well as their uncle's—my father's. September was a mere seven months away. I would have more vacation days by then, more freedom to work remotely, and enough cash to pay for my tickets, to make my way back to Manila.

When I told my mother about this upcoming birthday trip, she insisted she at least pay for my lodging. I kindly and firmly refused. She was hurt, but I explained: "I want to do this for me." I was not trying to avoid debt, financial or emotional. I was simply willing to pay what I felt I owed myself—some time and space to come home on my own.

Before I returned to New York, I reached out to Felipe and asked if he could meet up. I wanted to remind myself of what a life in the Philippines could look like, one where its terms were dictated by no one but me, where I could be myself: queer and out and in the arms of a man who was respectful and adoring and sexy in great and equal measure.

But Felipe was busy. There were work trips and deadlines—and a man too, I assumed. Bad timing, he said, I'm sorry, my fault. It was mine, I assured him. I hadn't told him I was coming, hadn't told him much of anything at all in the two years since we first met. As inviting as it was, the prospect of Felipe was daunting. Knowing the foolishness of writing someone into your life too quickly, I'd shied away at his generosity, his thoughtfulness, our terrifying potential.

Is there room in his calendar, I asked him, in about seven months? I offered to buy us drinks. In the Philippines, when it's your birthday, you pay for everyone else. I almost laughed when Felipe said his late September was looking pretty bad; "We'll be entering Q4." But he'll make it work, he told me, especially for a balikbayan.

Don't worry, I said, it won't be the only time I'm back. That's the comfort to be found in the word "balikbayan," in its inverse: as someone who will always have left the country, I'm also someone who will always return.

FUTURE WAS HOT, in the bar and on the street. September, I'd forgotten, was typhoon season. The day's rain still hung in the air; were it any more humid, our cigarettes would've refused to light. I bought a pair of Red Horses and found him at a table on the front porch. We toasted our sweating bottles. Felipe greeted me: "Happy birthday, kiddo."

Thank you, I said. I was glad we could catch up, however briefly. We had planned to meet earlier on this trip, but a flood had forced us to rain-check. It was tricky, given his schedule; mine I had kept flexible for my first week in town, by renting an Airbnb. It was a one-bedroom in the financial district, in a high-rise with a gym, a pool, and central air. In the mornings, I woke up in a king bed, jet-lagged and alone.

I hadn't remembered to pack the leather bracelet, let alone wear it. Felipe didn't ask about it either. We were slow to start. I teased and prodded and flirted, but he seemed exhausted. With work, with clients, with boys— me among them, I imagined. He was distracted, his eyes on some elsewhere beyond my right ear. Our halting conversation left Future's regulars plenty of openings to cut in and say hello to Felipe. He made introductions; most gave me a perfunctory "nice to meet you" and I echoed the sentiment. I was thankful for the diversions, excuses to scroll through Twitter, to count faves and retweets from faces more familiar. We were with his people, not mine.

I don't recall much of that hour or two we spent together. As with past dates that I wish had gone better, I remember only the moods and impressions, the feeling that I failed—not just Felipe but myself. I had promised him I would be in touch when I left him after that visit in 2015—after our first dance, our first date, our first breakfast together. But our firsts had turned out to be our lasts. It was presumptuous of me to think we might slide into our old groove, rekindle something extinguished by my neglect or unreadiness. I'd forgotten that people change over time, that they learn to let us go.

"Low-batt na phone ko," I said, so I called it an early night and a ride home. See you later, I told him, and Felipe mirrored my good-bye: sincere, neither hopeful nor hopeless. I kissed him on the cheek. My hands lingered too longingly on the muscles where his neck met his shoulders, those perfect traps. Across the street, I rolled down the car window to blow him a kiss, why not. But he'd already returned to his people.

In the backseat, I checked my notifications. There were invitations on Grindr waiting for me, none too appealing: "Place ko bro," "Bj kita," and the universal "Where u?" I switched over to my music, listened to the Spice Girls song that had played during my first kiss with Felipe. Over and over, to that discotheque beat, the Girls demanded, "Who do you think you are?"

I stepped out of the car and went up to the guardhouse. The nightwatch waved me in, now familiar with my face and habits. They joked about my unexpected return—"Sir, ang aga ng uwi ninyo! One a.m. pa lang!"—and let me past the gates with a salute. Our front door unlocked easily with my copy of the key. I quietly went up the stairs, the faint glow of the Sacred Heart lighting my ascent to my old room, across the landing from my mother and stepfather.

After my week at the Airbnb, it was time to check into my parents' townhouse for an eight-night stay. The plan had been to exercise my autonomy, free from the whims and guiles of my parents, and live, however briefly, in my hometown as an independent adult. One week all by myself to go out, have sex, do some writing, and visit the Ortiles without worry over territories and trespassing.

But I hadn't factored in jet lag. After lunches with friends and cousins, shopping trips, and afternoon delights, I'd return to my apartment and risk a nap, only to wake up four hours past dinnertime. For a night out at the clubs, this worked well enough, but most of my after-midnights were spent on the couch with a Chickenjoy meal (two-piece and rice; thigh part and extra gravy) from the twenty-four-hour Jollibee nearby. I'd eat it and watch TV, whatever movie Starworld was playing at that hour, until my melatonin pills kicked in, usually at around four in the morning.

This lethargy paired decently with the wet season. I couldn't go out at all whenever the rain turned torrential, so I got to share the more quotidian schedule of local Filipinos, free from the packed itineraries that families put together for visiting balikbayans. Plagued as Manila was with typhoons at this time of year, I had strategically picked September to prevent possible storms within my family.

As planned, when my father's birthday arrived on the twenty-fifth, I was still in my Airbnb and free to arrange my schedule as I saw fit. We had lunch; my little half-sister chose the venue: "Ja'bee!" For our joint birthday party a few days prior, my father and I had paid for the whole Ortile clan's hot pot feast. Now I bought us our Chickenjoy meals, sodas, and desserts. A break from Filipino birthday tradition, I offered, as my gift to my father. He graciously accepted but insisted on at least paying for our afternoon merienda.

To give him and his girlfriend some time to breathe, I took their daughter to a nearby kids' play area. I was mistaken for her dad, a fair assumption—she was two and I was turning twenty-seven. We still had our futures ahead of us. I hoped hers would be less tense and fearful than my past. As far as I could tell, her mother and our father parented well together. Their daughter was curious, friendly, unafraid. She pulled off her tiny hat and put it on my head. Grabbing at my phone, she said, "Kuya, picture!"

At the end of the day, my father offered to drop me off at my apartment. No need, I said, the roads are so bad right now, anyway. Pero malapit lang, he told me, it's right around the corner. I checked Google Maps. I hadn't realized when I booked the Airbnb: to walk from my place to his would take only ten minutes. (Forty minutes in a car, given Manila traffic on a weekday rush hour.)

The next day, I transferred to my mother and stepfather's place—no feeling like a museum loan this time;

these hand-offs have been downgraded to nonevents thanks to ride-hailing apps. I let my mother, healthy and smiling, plan my second week in Manila—dinners, Sunday mass, the works. I woke up as a twenty-seven-year-old in her home as my gift to her on my birthday, to keep up with Filipino tradition. I gave her that sacred domesticity, the kind my American peers give their families on Thanksgiving, Passover, Ramadan. Some parents draw satisfaction from the mere fact that their children, regardless of age, are under their roof. My mother is one of them, and I wanted to keep her happy.

As smoothly as my two-week stay went, I was ready to fly back to the States by the end of it. I wanted to return to the things I'd started there: my new job as an editor at a literary magazine—as well as my first book, which I had sold a few weeks before my birthday. I was feeling that familiar sensation of changing energy, potential turning kinetic, wonderfully terrifying all the same. "New York is your home, at least for now," my mother assured me. "And we will always be here in Manila to also welcome you home."

There were people waiting to welcome me in the States too, where I've come to build a chosen family that I don't want to live without. From the Philippines, I was flying to San Francisco for a college friend's fall wedding. His save-the-date had appeared in my inbox seven months earlier, on my February trip to see my family. The grooms were pictured cuddling, perched on a pile of coastal rocks. Noah was smiling toothily, arms around his betrothed, and my heart expanded against my ribcage. I immediately replied with maybe twenty exclamation points—I'd be there. I had flown halfway around the world for my parents; for my friends, with whom I'd grown just as much, I could at least make it to California.

And back to New York as well; we had birthdays to celebrate, vacations to take, houses to warm, writing dates to keep, drinks to postpone and rain-check and finally have and wish we had done this sooner. We're a fortunate group, committed to making it work and privileged enough to stay. The city's tempo can be overwhelming, but I've found its downbeat, those moments that tell me, yes, I know this song. I dance to it with my friends, the people I love, who make me feel loved, who help me face that terrifying potential as it becomes electric.

There's that potential in Manila too. It used to be my fallback plan, the kind my mother and stepfather had to put together when America was no longer the right fit. I am luckier, thanks to them, able to fit both the US and the Philippines into my life. Now, I'm figuring out how my families and my countries can coexist in my present as I learn to set my personal boundaries. I'm letting more of those circles touch while accepting there are parts that cannot, for now or forever.

I presumed too much about what it would be like to live full-time here again as a balikbayan, how easy it would be to match the pace of my beloved hometown. But I could fine-tune this new habit, sharing the Philippines with my parents; being shared by them, by my two countries, now that I didn't have to choose—now that I realized I never had to—now that I was finally becoming a dual citizen.

My to-do list on this fourfold mission: Celebrate my birthday, check. Celebrate my father's birthday, check. Do both on my own terms with no one getting hurt, check—thank goodness. One last task, accomplished by my mother: gather what I need to apply for dual citizenship.

From her safety deposit box, she retrieved the two documents and added a third, giving them to me in a bright yellow folder. They were immaculately kept, irrefutable proof of who I am and always have been: my Filipino passport, my birth certificate, and my mother's certificate of naturalization—just in case.

I SHOWED UP for my oath taking at three o'clock sharp. This being the Philippine consulate, we began at three-thirty. We gathered in a semicircle in front of a bust of the national hero and activist writer José Rizal. With my right hand raised and a written oath in my left, I solemnly swore to obey and defend the laws promulgated by the Philippines, as did fourteen other Filipinos beside me. I faltered, wary of affirming the supremacy of any one state or institution, as they recited, "I recognize and accept the supreme authority of the Philippines." But I caught up for the final flourish: "So help me God."

I didn't feel particularly changed by making it official. Most benefits to regaining my Filipino citizenship weren't immediately actionable. For example, I could vote in the next election; the vice consul reminded us that, though the midterm elections had passed, we'd be eligible to vote for a new president soon at the end of his six-year term. I could also own property in the Philippines now; this was the main draw for my mother, who was revising her will and wanted to ensure, as she called it, "an organized exit." As for me, I wanted the option to work in Manila—or as the consulate put it, "the right to engage in business and commerce as a Filipino." I also needed the freedom to enter the Philippines and stay indefinitely; I was permitted only thirty visa-free days in the country as a US citizen. I left the consulate that day wondering if I might sense the shift in my legal personhood once the Department of Foreign Affairs issued my Filipino passport, which would take months to be processed, printed, and sent to me.

Ironically, having dual citizenship forces me to keep choosing between my two countries. If I were to visit, say, the temple complex at Angkor Wat, upon arriving at the airport in Siem Reap, I'd have to decide how to get through customs: with my Philippine passport or my US one. In that case, I'd cross the Cambodian border as a Filipino; we can enter visa-free at no cost while those with US passports must pay for a tourist visa. The inverse situation is more common; according to the Passport Index, my blue US passport grants me visa-free entry into 117 countries, whereas my brown Philippine passport can only say the same for 35.

While the US passport may be more powerful, the United States is also less welcoming. It grants visa-free entry to only five passports: those from Canada, the Bahamas, and the three sovereign states in free association with the US—the Marshall Islands, Micronesia, and Palau. Meanwhile, Spanish, Japanese, and Singaporean citizens, to name a few, all have passports more powerful than those of US citizens. Yet they're required to apply for travel authorization with US Customs and Border Protection when visiting the States. It's no wonder that this land, even when we are deemed worthy and granted entry, can make us feel unwelcome. It all begins before we even cross its borders.

Three months after my dual citizenship ceremony, I went to the consulate and picked up my Philippine passport— clean and unmarked with stamps, not yet a history of the borders I've crossed. I got to use it when I flew to Manila in September 2019. Upon arrival at the airport, I went up to the immigration counter and presented my two passports: one brown, one blue.

I didn't feel any different, as I practiced an old habit, returning to one of my homes, my homeland. What I did feel was the familiarity of passing through the crowds, the air filled with crisp Tagalog and English tinged with various accents, from Australian, to Singaporean, to Filipino. I went through my routine, swapping the SIM card in my phone for a Filipino number, texting my mother and stepfather and father that I had landed, and speaking to an immigration officer whose brown face resembled mine.

"Salamat," I thanked her. I got that habitual reply, in our English made Filipino, "Welcome."

In my heart, though I was late to realize it, I've been a dual citizen this whole time. What else do you call someone who's spent their life straddling two borders? Someone juggling two parents and two places that gave them life? Someone disentangling all the comforts and crises of being an immigrant in the world? Well, I suppose, a balikbayan.

TO LIVE ALONE

I<small>T</small> <small>HAPPENED WHEN</small> the pies became a habit.

Every Sunday evening, after camping at a café in Park Slope with my unsold book proposal and doubt, I'd go to the bakery. Bountiful goods awaited within: beautifully risen cakes, pastries gleaming with egg wash, cookies crispy and chewy and in-between. I was always happy to sample anything on offer, but I quickly stopped pretending to survey the wares before ordering "a mini pecan pie to go, please."

Likewise, the shopkeepers stopped asking if I wanted a bag. They'd watch me through their front window as I left, cradling in my hands a little box containing the single personal pie. (I didn't dare put it in my backpack and risk the delicate thing getting crushed between the same yellowing books, the same incomplete pages, the same dried-out pens.)

En route home, I'd get excited about the prospect of having the pie for dessert and, as a result, become eager to cook a dinner for one, worthy of the pie as finale: maybe a roasted chicken breast, pan-fried asparagus, some mushrooms and quinoa—or, better yet, risotto. In my studio apartment, rather than order takeout or skip dinner altogether, I would prepare my meal with care. I cook without recipes, which are often scaled to feed a couple or a family and, as such, less accommodating to single chefs.

That's what I loved about my personal pies, my treats for one. I relished them, languidly devoured them, maybe with a demitasse of espresso or a scoop of ice cream—both, on decadent days. A pie was my reward, if the writing was good that day; two were a pick-me-up, if it was not. This was my little luxury, my self-care, my "me-time." Whatever the name, this habit made me feel good, like I was eating joy.

But then, one Sunday, pie in hand, the crying happened. The day's writing had been good, and yet, walking home, I stopped in the middle of the sidewalk to weep. A family of four broke around me, reconnected their hands after they'd passed. I perched on a stoop for a moment to get out of the way and regain some composure. Here was a grandfather shuffling along as a set of cherub-cheeked toddlers orbited him. There was a young couple laughing; she'd accidentally hit him with her braids and now she was kissing his cheek better. I almost texted my friends in our group chat—*help i'm crying and i don't know why*—but stopped myself. Maybe Park Slope was just especially Park Slope that day, and I was taking it personally.

Or maybe it was a delayed reaction to the day before, when I grabbed a bite to eat at Le Pain Quotidien, that chain of quasi-French café bistros owned by Belgians. "Dining alone?" a staffer asked. She seated me at a long communal table next to an old man. He ate a croque monsieur with a fork and knife, slowly, gingerly. He was either working against arthritis or savoring the Gruyère cheese, maybe both. A bite, some chewing. The lipless line across his wrinkled face curved into a smile.

I caught myself pitying him, hoping he was not alone in the world, wishing he had people to love him—a partner, a family—and, therefore, a happy life. This was foolish of me. I was perpetuating the dichotomy that otherwise raised my hackles, that aloneness is to sadness as togetherness is to happiness. That day, I believed the old man's aloneness was different from mine: I'm alone, for now, yes, but I have friends to see in an hour, a Broadway show to attend. We shared lives, a commute back into Brooklyn, a neighborhood, a group text.

That poor old man, I thought, how alone and sad he must be.

His eyes met mine, and I looked back down at my menu. Then, he leaned over and said, as if conspiring, "The croque monsieur is very good."

Maybe I cried on the sidewalk in Park Slope because the loneliness I had seen in the old man was mine. The judgment I cast on him was rebounding onto me, uncovering my anxiety. The pies, my routine, were they actually a rut? Had I fooled myself into thinking that these tiny pleasures, these silly little tarts filled with nuts, were self-care? Did I only eat joy because I was starved for it? What if the shop-keepers at the bakery thought the same of me? "That poor little boy. How alone and sad he must be."

It was probably the seasonal affective disorder too. Or the compounding daily despair of that big wig's first full year in the Oval Office. Or that I was overwhelmed by the apparent need to keep waking up every day, whether for sixty more years or—depending on how quickly we let the climate crisis unfold—just ten or twenty. Or the fact that I had just consciously uncoupled with another romantic prospect; he wanted kids and I had lied, told him I was 90 percent sure I didn't, when really the figure is closer to 99 percent. We agreed to part ways, and we're amicable today, but still. Endings are always sad.

I was living my life as best I could, and it was a good life—in possession of a home, citizenship, employment, enough cash to afford a seven-dollar baked good once a week. But whatever the cause for my tears, it chipped away at my love affair with pastries. As good as my pie habit felt, I had to wonder if it was only a Band-Aid. A pie is not a date. A pie is not a partner. A pie is not a family. I was weighing myself by that long-standing measure of prosperity and protection: the degree to which one is not alone.

It's par for the course to feel lonely in a place like New York, a city of over eight million people. Just as there are so many opportunities to fall in love, there are even more chances to fail at it, to miss the mark, to be rejected, to

be ignored and unseen altogether. And I had been indoctrinated by American culture to believe that social bonds
like marriage and a biological family are the pinnacle of
personal happiness, friendships are consolation prizes, and
singledom is a life unfulfilled.

With that mind-set, my personal pie wasn't delightful
because it was the right fit for my life. It was pitiful by virtue of being a pie for one.

———————

IN HER BOOK *The Lonely City*, Olivia Laing writes that
loneliness "feels like being hungry: like being hungry when
everyone around you is readying for a feast." Laing, a British transplant, arrived in New York feeling untethered and
alone. She navigated the city by researching the lives and
works of artists who had grappled with loneliness there,
seeking proof that others who lived alone endured the same
piercing sadness. Laing describes it as a sensation of being
exposed. Loneliness can feel like what's private has been
made public, as if your belly button has come undone and
your liver, lungs, and beating heart have spilled onto the
sidewalk.

The loneliness that struck me that day, as I cried into
a pie, resembled the painful desolation I had confronted
two years prior as I turned twenty-four. I had already been
feeling alone—sad that I didn't have a boyfriend and dearly
missing my family in the Philippines. Then, in a series of

blows, my parents were diagnosed with cancer, my friendships with my roommates began to deteriorate, and my job at the website began to seem less certain, at risk for termination. As I entered my midtwenties in New York, I felt endangered, helpless, and abandoned.

My roommates were two friends from college, people I'd grown close to after graduating and moving to Manhattan. Our apartment leases were up for renewal at roughly the same time, so we decided to become Brooklyners and split a tiny three-bedroom. Better, it's said, to live with people you love. My roommates hoped that living together would mean built-in socializing, guaranteed community. But between my active nightlife and a job that demanded nonstop perkiness, I needed the apartment to be a space where I could recharge by myself, take a breather, stand still.

When I did have the energy to be with my roommates, I was often the third or fifth wheel with them and their boyfriends. Insecure and jealous by nature, I felt left out. When things took a turn for the worse at work, I started staying in my bedroom more frequently. When I didn't know how to handle the distance from my parents after their cancer diagnoses, I began to lock my door. Between my personal stressors, my hermitage, and my roommates' unwavering sociability with their lovers and each other, the air in our apartment turned combustible. Any tiny spark of friction would have set the house ablaze.

Even when sharing a home, I was lonely. Previously, I had shared in their joy. Now, they feasted as I scrounged.

I was unwilling to reach out precisely because I felt un-loved. "This is what's so terrifying about being lonely," Laing writes, "the instinctive sense that it is literally repul-sive, inhibiting contact at just the moment contact is most required." Spare them the contagion, I thought, this pox on our house. And so, my loneliness waxed. A rising tide of depression pulled me under.

In *The Lonely City*, Laing finds some remedy to loneli-ness by finding her reflections in art. That is art's power, she writes, how it provides connections between people who might never meet, never know each other, but enrich each other's lives regardless. She sees herself in Edward Hop-per's paintings, in the solitary women he framed within windows, emphasizing the public gaze of others. For my part, I find reflections in the public itself, in those wander-ing alongside me in our lonely city.

I spent my twenty-fourth birthday alone. I walked around my neighborhood, Brooklyn Bridge Park, as well as both Villages—West and East. So cramped for solitude in my home, I relished my own company that day. In a restau-rant, at church, and on park benches, I witnessed others doing the same: eating, praying, staring up at the sky, lan-guidly devouring the time they could devote to themselves. It was nourishing to see people content—happy, even—without being attached at the hip to a partner or a family, especially when I had neither in this city.

As I read a book at a crowded café, a woman asked if she could join me. Sure, I said. We finished our stories in silence, watched each other's stuff while we went to the bathroom.

It was a comfort to be reminded that I was not alone in my aloneness. Even in seemingly superficial interactions, I could find connections and togetherness. I drew confidence from this knowledge as I began twenty-four and from the privileges I had despite my loneliness: that I had a place to call home at all, that my job could be saved, that I was only a seventeen-hour flight away from my parents in Manila.

To assuage my loneliness, I turned to the family I have in New York, friends like Mia and Sarah, who lived two train stops away. When they first moved in together, into their apartment in Park Slope, I had tried to give them space to savor their domestic bliss. But they insisted on cooking dinners for three, on listening to me talk about my parents and my work and my roommates, on telling me, "We are your sisters. You always have a home with us."

When my roommates left the apartment to celebrate Thanksgiving with their families, my family arrived at my doorstep with six bottles of wine and a chicken big enough for three. I injured myself an hour into cooking, and my sisters took care of the rest. Mia rubbed the bird with butter and tarragon, Sarah baked two pies (one pumpkin, one pecan), and we toasted to the holiday, to the rewarming of a home that had been feeling so cold.

I would have moved out of the apartment that winter, but I didn't have the money. I didn't have it the following spring either, when my roommates announced that they were re-signing the lease without me. My parents, whom I had briefed on my living situation when I visited them at Christmas, sent me money to help cover the exorbitant fees of real estate in New York. By then, my mother's chemotherapy was done and paid for, so they had cash to spare when I needed it. Through Craigslist, I found a cheap studio apartment. The bathroom was old, the street was noisy, and the commute to work was terrible. But I could live alone there, could recharge and reset in a peaceful kind of aloneness, in solitude.

Mia and Sarah encouraged me to throw a housewarming, then gifted me a golden candelabra, warmth and light, when I did. I invited my core group chat too: Alexis welcomed me to the neighborhood and offered to hold on to a spare copy of my keys; Alanna brought a plate of cheese and Lactaid for us both; Anna came all the way from Queens and was one of the last to leave, laughing and sharing secrets until well past midnight. Krutika admired my decorating, the life I gave this box the color of old canvas, and said, "I want you to make me a home."

I host friends at my apartment more often than I host dates or men from Grindr. Out-of-towners now visit so often that I put together amenity kits for my guests—toothbrushes and face masks included. And Krutika loves to come over, sending Seamless orders and bottles of malbec to my place before she gets off work, even though we have to sit on my bed because I don't have space for a couch. At the housewarming, I took a picture with me and at least thirty of my friends, proof I could fit so many people into my home and share this sanctuary I made for myself.

Still, the stinging desolation comes and goes—for me, for many of us. I was in my second year of living alone when I began my pie habit, when I saw my reflection in the old man at dinner with his croque monsieur. We were alone together. Yet a high tide of self-doubt made me project onto him my painful loneliness. The next day, I cried over my personal pecan pie because, for a moment, I lost faith in my contentment and my methods of self-care. On that ordinary Sunday, I did not think loving myself was enough.

When I first saw the old man, he appeared to be already halfway through his meal. In front of him was a neatly sliced half croque monsieur, sitting as primly on his plate as he on his chair. But then a server came by, with the other half wrapped up to-go. She addressed him by name, handed him the bag, and, after an affectionate shoulder squeeze, kept on moving.

He had a habit too, it seemed, whether it was an everyday rhythm or a little luxury, self-care, "me-time." I didn't know his story, where his partner or family or friends were, if he had them, but it was evident that he wasn't completely alone in our lonely city. He brought me into his world too, suggested that I have what he was having. The croque monsieur was delicious, he was right, and I thanked him for sharing. That had been the lesson of my twenty-fourth birthday, that aloneness can mean solitude or peace. Being alone with others can mean turning to your neighbor and looking out for them, asking them to look after you.

Yes, loneliness can hurt deeply. Now, when it comes, I try to reverse the instinct to shy away from contact, to shield myself from the world. I tell myself that loneliness is a reminder to seek the support of others, friendship, and affection—whether romantic or not. It nudges me to meet my friends for coffee or ask them for a hug, to call my parents when they wake up and tell them I love them. (One thing the news cycle is good for: there is no shortage of reminders to reach out to the people you love in our world that seems to be falling apart by the day.)

I am lucky to have people I can lean on in my life. By nurturing those relationships, the loneliness wanes and the tides do not rush in, cyclical though they be. Loneliness is inevitable. The best we can do is to understand our own loneliness, to be ready when it comes. After all, as Laing writes, "loneliness, longing, does not mean one has failed, but simply that one is alive."

THIS IS HOW I remember the 2016 election: Going to my polling place early that morning with a hot coffee, chatting with my neighbors, sharing warmth in the November chill. High-fiving our security officers as I walked into the newsroom, drinking more and more gin at my desk as the night wore on, sitting with my colleagues as we called

Pennsylvania red and, at two o'clock in the morning, decided it was over, finished, done.

I remember getting a text from Mia, at work in another newsroom, staring at the same map flush an angry scarlet: *kuya what the fuck?* Telling her, my mother, my stepfather how scared I was. Answering my father, who messaged me asking if this was "good news" for America: *no Tatay, not for my America*

And I remember coming home to my empty apartment. Texting my friends in the group chat before falling asleep, texting them the next morning, hungover, asking if we all had the same bad dream. Meeting the group at Alexis's for dinner, splitting bottles of wine. Holding hands, crying, laughing because we had to. I remember feeling helpless, outraged, but strangely, mercifully, as alienating as the election results were, not feeling alone.

When I ask others about what they remember from that night, many of them tell me how grateful they are they didn't have to face the news by themselves: "My wife was with me at the bar, thank goodness." "We let the kids stay up to watch history, but we're in the wrong time line." "I don't know what I would've done had I been alone." They ask me what I remember, and I say that, though I'd had no boyfriend or husband to hold me nor any little ones to protect, I wasn't alone either. My family does not look like theirs, bound by biology or law. Mine is joined by choice.

A "chosen family" is exactly what it says on the tin: a family you choose for yourself, rather than the one you're raised in. Also phrased as a family of choice, rather than a family of origin, a chosen family is a historically queer concept. By definition, it's a queer idea about what a family is—or can be. It offers an alternative to the "traditional" model of genetic ties, of a nuclear family with two parents and one or more children. Most often, we build chosen families when we are rejected, or merely tolerated, by our relatives because of our queerness, or when our bonds and partnerships are not recognized by the law, or when we finally find people who reflect us in some way, have walked the paths we have.

It's telling that chosen-family models are also common among veterans of war and within twelve-step communities. We wade through trauma together. Immigrants coalesce into chosen families too; separated from our homelands, we're drawn to those who resemble us—just as I was first drawn to Mia at Vassar, leaping into her arms, calling her "kapatid," as we exchanged phone numbers on the quad. We grew up in that ivory tower together, all the while each other's lifelines to home. Building a chosen family is combating oppression and loneliness, turning to others to survive.

Weeks after my pie-and-cry in Park Slope, I attended a queer dinner hosted by a friend and his now-husband. I got his invitation via Twitter DM; he'd seen my tweets complaining about my lack of platonic gay male friends in New York and messaged me, "You should join us for Communion." It was a monthly affair, he said. This made me anxious when I arrived at their doorstep with a bottle of merlot on a cold November night, about a year after the election.

As a satellite friend, I was wary of passing through this new solar system of strangers. But my trepidation evaporated when I was welcomed with open arms and attentive faces, invited to tell my story, given permission to be as vulnerable and alive as I needed to be. Each month, I joined this rotating cast of queer creatives—varied in histories but alike in our solidarity as queer people, as people of color, as both—and sat with them at a communal table, partaking in a scrumptious feast, eating joy together.

At one of these dinners, over a year later, the cohosts announced their engagement to us. The din of our cheers nearly shattered the wineglasses. Soon after, we were dancing at their backyard wedding, a Communion for the ages. As they shared their vows and made their toasts, I counted myself privileged and loved, happy to celebrate the partnership of my queer brothers, to thank them for the sanctuary they hosted at every full moon, to be held among their chosen family.

Through these dinners, I began to see my core set of friends in a new light. With them, I had daily communion in our group chat. ThriveOps, we called it, a space dedicated to celebrating our wins and sitting with our losses. We all met as colleagues at the website, where we were bound by shared experiences both delightful and dreadful, and remained friends as each of us left for new jobs.

It is difficult to remember a life before my beloveds. Once, we were reminiscing in the group chat about how we first met. I recalled how Alexis and I started work on the same day; how I was intimidated by Alanna at first; how Anna realized a childhood friend of hers was a good friend of Mia's, my sister, and so we decided we were family too. I met Krutika early on in my tenure at work. We quickly established a habit of trading memes on Slack and piercing the newsroom silence with our Disney villain cackles, but she didn't become my person until I found her hiding in a conference room, distraught and crying. I listened to her, held her hands, and told her, "You don't have to go through this alone." In the group chat, Krutika's response: *i feel like i hugged Matt once in the office and suddenly he was everywhere*

Chosen family is defined by care and mutual support, the kind of compassion and grand acts and little gestures that nourish us as individuals, whether together or alone. When he came to live alone, Alexander Chee writes in his essay "The Rosary" that "I was a mess, a disaster in need of a reckoning." He moves into a small garden apartment in Brooklyn after having a vision of vibrant roses blooming in the backyard, at first miserable and neglected. So he makes the soil fertile—cow manure, seaweed, the remains of gutted fish—for the roses he brings home, which come to thrive under his protection.

Even when he leaves them alone—for a wedding, a family visit, a residency at a writers' colony—they are valiant, perhaps grateful too for some solitude, respite from their gardener's overeager pruning. Chee comes home to the rosary to find his wards jubilant, mightier than when he left them, drinking up the sun and air and nourishment in this Eden he has made. The roses are his role models, he says, growing even faster, stronger, after they are cut back. In the once-empty garden, Chee saw his reflection, filled with potential, and dreamed of a vibrant future for them both. He planted a rosary, a prayer. He nourished that plot and made a garden grow, one that gifted him with beauty and inspiration, one that nurtured him in return. As much as he made a sanctuary for his roses, he also made one for himself.

Before the backyard evolved into the rosary, it was filled with the dead roots and the fallen limbs of trees; they had been poisoned by the landlord for threatening the building's foundations. With time and nourishment, Chee gave the salted earth new life and his roses room to spread out, to breathe. One of his roses first comes to him in a too-small pot. He undoes the knotted ball of its roots and replants it in his rosary. Despite the late-season transplant, the migrant rose blooms for its caretaker in thanks, grateful for the chance to take root. Chee took time to make his garden fertile, made it a place where outsiders could thrive too.

What I love most about Chee's rosary, my group chat, and Communion, is that they are testaments to what happens when you make space for roots. In these stories, I see the power of nurture, of a land detoxified with compassion. With my chosen family, I am more certain of my place in America, assured that I can and I must claim space in this country. They're my talismans against loneliness in a nation that insists I don't belong, don't have roots.

The night after the 2016 election, in Alexis's apartment, I remember thinking we would survive this. As vulnerable as we were as queer people of color, we were fortunate too—with our protections as citizens, as young able-bodied people with jobs, however poorly we were paid to watch the world burn, to write words that described the burning. We were and are lucky, still, to have one another. This fact has been made more apparent by the years that have followed, in which so many families have been subject to increased violence—kept apart by discriminatory travel bans, deported from their homes, forcibly separated at the border, teargassed as they fled their homelands to seek safety. All this while my chosen family has remained whole, has escaped physical threats, protected by the presumed sanctuary of our city.

New York is considered a sanctuary city. The term simply refers to a city, county, or state with sanctuary policies that limit cooperation with national immigration authorities. The stipulations of such ordinances and laws can vary between jurisdictions, making it difficult to give the phrase any real legal definition. So the term "sanctuary city" is something of a misnomer, implying more inclusive protections than its policies offer in reality.

Consider an undocumented immigrant, one with no criminal record, held in jail overnight by police for, say, driving without a license. That person's information is added to a database shared with Immigration and Customs Enforcement. ICE can then send the local police a detainer request to hold that person in jail for an extra forty-eight hours past when they're due to be released so ICE agents can get to the jail and deport that person. In a state like Texas, with explicit antisanctuary laws, the police would be legally required to cooperate with ICE and honor the detainer request. However, a state like California has perhaps the strongest sanctuary policies in the US; in 2017, California governor Jerry Brown signed a bill that limits how state and local law enforcement can cooperate with federal immigration authorities.

In most other situations, the police must choose: either comply with the detainer request or not—recognizing that imprisoning people who have not been given due process (or, in some cases, who have not been charged with a crime at all) is unconstitutional, that enabling ICE's rampant abuses is acting with cruelty toward living, breathing human beings.

Sanctuary policies do not make cities and states total safe havens. Their primary intention, ostensibly, is to encourage undocumented residents to report crimes to their local police without fear of deportation. But once that undocumented immigrant driving without a license is released by the police, there is nothing stopping ICE from finding and deporting them, whether on the streets of San Francisco, at their place of work in Portland, or in their home in New York.

When government policies cannot protect us, we find ways to protect one another. I've witnessed a rising discourse and practice revolving around daily exercises in solidarity, in New York and online. When ICE increased the prevalence of their checkpoints and scheduled raids, I saw people tip off immigrants and their allies on Twitter about locations of ICE activity. (I witnessed the backlash to these warnings too, from people who cautioned that anyone, particularly fear-mongering trolls, can spread misinformation.) I've seen my friends remind each other to not call the police, especially in predominantly black communities, or to swipe people into the subway behind you, when you have the opportunity and the money. It's the least we can do, we tell ourselves, these quotidian gestures of allyship with the more vulnerable in our communities, given that we're living under a presidential administration blatantly pursuing hateful aims and goading a country that's historically been anti-immigrant, anti-poor, anti-trans, anti-black—among many other things.

"We don't need more allies," Vincent reminded me once. "What we need are more co-conspirators." We were texting about the politics of solidarity—a casual conversation between two Vassar Girls—and he made a fair point. Much more needs to be done to create true public sanctuary.

Rather than trying to only survive under an oppressive system, better to take it apart and create something better in its place. We need visionaries, Vincent said, who help us build something different: a country without forced deportations, without walled borders, without law enforcement agencies that purport to protect us when, in truth, they'd rather cleanse this land and poison our roots.

Small gestures of solidarity and allyship are not enough, but they're not nothing. Sharing a "know your rights" post on social media can feel like facile activism against the violence of immigration law, but it might reach someone in your online neighborhood who will read it ("You have the right to not open the door. / Tiene derecho a no abrir la puerta.") and know not to answer ICE when they come knocking. The MTA still gets their $2.75 when you swipe someone into the subway, but at least that person gets to go home safely to their family. It is terrible and demoralizing that we live in a country that is hunting down its own residents, that we have to do these things at all, that it's literally the least we can do.

Vincent is right—we must do more than "the least we can do," must work toward a future without violent institutions that capitalize off the bodies they break. While we do, we must resist the American drive to prioritize nuclear families at the expense of the community and act instead in the spirit of kapwa, of radical togetherness with others.

———

FOR A SHORT time, I didn't have anyone to call in case of emergencies. As a teen, my emergency contact was my mother. If anything happened to me in Las Vegas, she was in town. If anything happened to me at college in New York, she was at least in the country. As a student, it made sense to have a parent be the person a hospital calls if, for example, I'm hit by a car because I was busy checking out a hot guy while crossing the street. But as adults, it's expected that your in-case-of-emergency person will be a spouse or partner—because who else will be there for you no matter what? Some single people still put down their folks as their contact, but when my parents moved back to the Philippines, I just had to hope that I'd never need to call on them, on anyone.

When Krutika moved into her one-bedroom, she had one concern: What if I hurt myself and I can't call for help? I had expressed this fear myself, though in half-earnest, half-joke form: I was afraid of dying alone in my studio apartment. Death is inevitable, but I can't schedule it or throw it on my Google Cal, can't get a haircut for the big day. Get me high and I will worry: Who will look for me when I am dead? When I am missing, when I don't show up to work for days, when I don't post on Twitter or Instagram for weeks on end, who will consider it an emergency? Who will call 911 or bang down doors, praying that I am safe?

Krutika and I developed a system. *Check in*, we would text each other, *R u alive?* We kid, but we always respond. *Lmfao no* might mean, I'm drowning in work. *Nah bitch* could translate to, I am sad at the state of the world today and I need to be sad for a bit. An actual *yes* indicates things are going smoothly, often surprisingly so. Thrivelets, we call them, mini-thrives: A job interview that went well. An essay accepted by a magazine. A nice chat with a parent.

A date. Between the constant grind of our millennial lives and the omnipresent sense of doom hanging over the post-2016 era, simply finding ourselves content is something to celebrate. *Yes*, we say, *I am alive*.

I don't think too hard about the potential for dramatic irony should one of us one day ask if the other is alive and never get a reply. Sometimes, I text Krutika, *Check in I'm dying*. Usually I'm referring to my emotional distress; rarely am I in the way of any real danger or bodily harm. *I'm dying*, I texted her once, and then, *I'm at the doctor's*. Translation: I'm having a bad day and I am at the clinic for my yearly physical exam. Her response: *wait do you have an actual medical emergency right now bc i'm at the theater about to walk into Cursed Child with my parents if this is real pls call 911*

These days, Krutika is my emergency contact. On forms I haven't updated since Mia and Sarah left New York, Mia is my sister and Sarah's my sister-in-law—after all, we've spent enough Thanksgivings and Christmases, enough years and tears, together. Thankfully, I have never had a dire enough medical crisis to see what would happen if any of my in-case-of-emergency people were actually called upon, but should it ever come to pass, I'd feel no hesitation at proclaiming Mia, for example, my sister. It's not a stretch: we share the same black hair, the same brown skin, the same values, the same queer, Filipino spirit. We've grown up together and, as such, are siblings.

My chosen family complements the peace I draw from living by myself. They alleviate my loneliness on days when

I am too alive, too exposed. They give me space to yell and cry when I have yelled at the news and cried over a job and broken my heart too eagerly against the bodies of other men. Their gift is the same as the rosary's. Chee names this lesson, the teaching of his roses: "You can lose more than you thought possible and still grow back, stronger than anyone imagined."

Like him, I have found myself in need of a reckoning. When I first came to New York, I felt untethered, uprooted from the Philippines and unrooted in America. Galvanized by a vision of dinners and community, I built a dining table out of wood and steel, something over which I could break bread with those I love. I've carried it and them with me ever since, building a family along the way. They are my garden, my sanctuary.

Loneliness reminds us that we need others to survive, that to live alone must not be to live in isolation. My chosen family roots me in the United States. When I'm in the Philippines, I feel homesick for them, longing to share my birthplace with them as we have shared New York. I am thankful that they've helped me to build a home in the US, to persist even when the poison in this land sickens me, rejects me, tells me to go back to where I came from.

We are living in a racist and xenophobic chapter in American history—not the first such chapter, only the most recent of many. This presidential administration sows division and mistrust, provoking the worst in us—our fear and our hatred—and salting the earth, leaving people to die. We must fight this poison and detoxify our land. Make space for others. Check in. Break bread together in communion. Stand with our communities—our families, whether of origin or choice, and our neighbors, those pushed to the edges of society as well as the folks next door—in the spirit of kapwa. Inspire in each other the bravery to not bend to the will of those that reject us, to put down the roots we need to survive, to wake up every day in this place where we've come to live.

Part and parcel of living is that loneliness. In moments of self-doubt or fear, I think of the resilience that loneliness teaches, the solitude aloneness grants. This lonely city teaches the importance of befriending yourself. It reminds me to be kind to my body and mind, my spirit and heart—even as they tumble out of me and onto the sidewalk every now and then.

On that ordinary Sunday in Park Slope, I cried over a pie. I almost texted my friends, but I didn't for now; I knew what I had to do on my own. I paused and caught my breath. I walked past Mia and Sarah's apartment and took the train home to my studio. I sat in my bed for one and ate the pie. It was good—delicious, actually. A thrivelet it remained, despite the tears, a little something I could celebrate on my own.

Yes, I assured myself, *I am alive*.

THE GROOM WILL KEEP HIS NAME

His mother gave a toast at the wedding. Of course, we said, save the best for last. She was charming, a high school teacher beloved by her students. Though she was the clear favorite, teachers, in turn, aren't supposed to have favorites. "But could you blame me," his mother said, gesturing to the head table. The whole dining room laughed and clapped in agreement. I smiled at her, already wiping my tears.

"In all seriousness," she went on, "what a gift it is to have a student become like family, to care for one like your own son—only to have him become your son-in-law." She didn't do the matchmaking, but what a happy coincidence this day was. A pause, then gathered breath. "If I had to pick anyone for my boy, it would be my best student; and if I were to pick a man for him, it would be my son."

I grinned, and I could taste salt at the corners of my mouth. Vincent let go of my hand, dabbed at his tears with a dinner napkin. He was careful not to smudge his makeup. He leaned over to me and murmured, "J'ai promis de ne pas pleurer." But there he was, crying nonetheless. I put an arm around Vincent's shoulders, tall as he was, and I kissed him on the cheek. Here was a love so special it could bring wedding tears from even the most unbelieving of Frenchmen.

She raised her glass and we followed suit. "To Noah and Evan!"

Noah was our friend from college. After a semester abroad in Sydney, he came home the summer after junior year to be with family in California. And there, at his mother's kitchen table, was the love of his life, helping his old high school teacher grade final exams. Evan had just finished undergrad, so he was free to visit Noah at Vassar when we were seniors. They made a balanced pair, equal parts acerbic and easy to laugh, both generous with their friends. We knew it even then. Noah loved Evan so fully. How lucky were we that Noah loved us just the same.

Four years later, on a hike, Evan got down on one knee. Marriage wasn't on Noah's mind, and he mistook the gesture for something else. A wedding guest told us the story at the cocktail hour. "Evan was proposing, of course!" she said with a laugh. "What else would he be doing on his knees!"

It was a perfect wedding. Early October, a miraculously sunny day in San Francisco. We celebrated at the northern end of the city, high on a hill. The ocean view was magnificent, the breeze was lovely, and there was an aerobatic demonstration by US Navy jets. We took our seats as the procession commenced. Down the aisle came the grooms, wearing matching suits in a handsome slate gray, as Adele sang, over the speakers, "Make You Feel My Love."

Then came my favorite part: the vows. Noah and Evan reified the choices they made on that fateful hike, now declaring their mutual adoration and commitment in front of—and with the help of—their family (Noah's brother was his best man; his sister-in-law the officiant). Just the month before, I watched two other friends, both writers, make their poetic promises about all the dreams they have left to live together. And within the year, I would witness two more friends, a pair of queer men, affirm their partnership in the eyes of the law and make known to us, their chosen family, a devotion no borders could divide.

On a cliffside by the ocean, Noah clasped Evan's hands in his and told him, "I love you." I sniffled into my handkerchief. Vincent squeezed my shoulder and said, "Save the tears for the toasts."

It doesn't take much to make me cry at weddings. I admire anyone who makes a public declaration of love, cares for someone who does the same in return. The first time I cried at vows was at my mother's wedding to my stepfather in 2005, at their civil ceremony in Las Vegas. Before her father, her brother, new friends and old, my mother promised to the man she loved her lasting affection, her full companionship, and her unwavering faithfulness. My stepfather mirrored her in kind. I sobbed as they exchanged wedding rings, the ones they still wear today, the ones that inspired their vows.

For their rings, my parents went to Cartier, bought a pair from the jeweler's Trinity collection. Each ring is a set of three interlaced bands, in three different golds that represent the three components to a lasting marriage: rose for love, white for friendship, and yellow for fidelity. They made this marketing lore a canonical element of their narrative at their next wedding in 2008, the one in the Philippines.

The reception in Manila included live performances. My stepfather and I sang songs dedicated to my mother; two ballroom dance instructors (a requirement at any Filipino wedding) did an interpretive dance. This was how we told the story of my parents' romance—an epic spanning years and thousands of miles. To the rapt audience, my stepfather described the love, friendship, and fidelity that sustained them across vast seas and faraway lands, a microphone in his hand as his wedding ring gleamed in the spotlight.

He once lost his ring on a trip abroad. My parents were traveling for a conference when, packing up their hotel room, he noticed his bare left ring finger. My mother mentioned the loss to me when I called. My stepfather was heartbroken over it, sad to lose this material object that represented them. But they'd already been through so much, my mother said, been married thrice over. (The third was a church wedding, at last, in 2013.) It's not the end of the world to lose a wedding ring, she said, especially after all they've been through.

Side by side, my parents have faced daunting foes: the Pacific Ocean, the emperor of maladies, US Citizenship and Immigration Services. When my stepfather applied for permanent residency, their many weddings and many pictures came in handy. He was a shutterbug, good at photographing our quotidian lives together: holidays at home, opening nights for my shows, visiting and hosting relatives, celebrating birthdays and straight-A report cards and my acceptance into Vassar.

They brought albums and scrapbooks to their interviews, documents to certify an authentic shared history. Once, flipping through the photos, an immigration officer admired our countertops in dark granite, in a house that was too big for just the three of us. "I love that kitchen island," the officer said, as my mother recalled it, before diving right in: "So, how long have you known your husband?"

This is what I am at liberty to say: for most of my life, my mother and my father have been, as I like to call it, emotionally widowed. So when she introduced me to my stepfather, who flew from Manila to visit us in Las Vegas for the first time, and she called him "my good friend," I saw through her fib. Her poker face was too amorous, gave away how wholly she loved him. When she "came out" to me about their relationship, she was nervous about how I'd react. I told her I loved him because it was clear he loved her too.

As much as their three weddings were for themselves, my parents were also proving the solidity of their union to the US and Philippine governments, to the Catholic Church, to their peers and family. It brought home the idea that, in the eyes of certain authorities, a wedding is evidence, a form of validation. To gain permission to live in this country, they were cross-examined, asked to provide evidence of their love, a romance reduced to data points. Sometimes, I resent the song and dance my parents have had to perform, when they've already proven their love time and time again.

For years, I've had the privilege of witnessing the love and mutual support between my mother and stepfather. Theirs is a marriage of equals. Each a whole person, a formidable unit together. They're each other's biggest cheerleaders and loving carers. She knows what he won't eat; he knows what she'll drink. He reminds her to breathe when her blood simmers; she reminds him to be patient when things don't go as planned—even when these moments are often concurrent. They're exemplary of the love, friendship, and fidelity they promised, of the vows they make to each other every day. I want a life-changing partnership like theirs. Not exactly, but something like it.

To replace my stepfather's missing wedding ring, I sent them to a Cartier near their hotel. They went and got the same Trinity ring, a copy. That night, my stepfather found the original. It had slipped off his finger and into his suitcase. They returned the new ring, and Cartier gave them a refund. At dinner, she passed him the salt shaker, saying he needed to bloat his fingers. My parents, as they do, laughed through it.

At Noah and Evan's wedding, Noah had to jam the ring onto Evan's finger. (Later at the reception, he teased his husband, "It used to fit.") With one more blessing, the grooms celebrated their union with a kiss. We clapped as they returned to the grand maison behind us for photographs on the leather couches, under glittering chandeliers. The rest of the crowd followed the wedding party into the reception rooms. Vincent and I hung back in the garden to admire the view.

I want a wedding like this, I told him, a destined love like theirs. Not exactly, but something like it. My heart drummed against my sternum. The San Francisco Bay gleamed before us, a vista of pearly white boats, shimmering waters, and—"fittingly," said Vincent—the maximum security prison at Alcatraz.

———

I SHOULD NOT want to get married. I should not buy into the wedding industry's ritualization of capitalism. I should not long for a legal status rooted in the patriarchal subjugation and ownership of women. I should not wish to go through this rite of passage that promises a vision of idealized love, nor seek validation from cultural and social authorities by participating in said rite, a legal right that such authorities have denied queer people. I should not support a marriage equality movement that has historically excluded trans and queer people of color, that trades on heteronormative respectability politics and hinges my worth as a queer person on how closely I resemble the straight majority. I should not at all aspire to a wedding so fabulous, a marriage so conventional, nor a love so Instagrammable.

Nevertheless, I do.

I used to dream of my wedding announcement in the *New York Times*: "A June wedding," they would have called it, "a Pride month event, if there ever was one." The location: Vassar's campus, regardless of my fiancé's alma mater. Some days, I pictured it on Graduation Hill—an elevated stage, two thousand seats, and all—overlooking Sunset Lake at twilight. Other days, I dreamt of a more intimate affair in the school's library, my beloved Gothic fortress. There, the ceremony would have taken place in the central tower, with the seventeenth-century tapestries hanging high above, depicting the myth of Cupid and Psyche. Against the backdrop of a story in which a mortal is redeemed by sacred marriage, I would have wed my betrothed and taken his name.

"During the procession," the *Times* would have said, "the New York City Gay Men's Chorus sang 'Ten Minutes Ago' from Rodgers and Hammerstein's *Cinderella*." To update the lyrics, the choir would have changed the pronouns, swapping out "her" for "him," singing how I had found my angel at last. My groom and I would have walked down the aisle arm-in-arm, our matching suits black Givenchy, my shoes red-heeled Louboutin. After making vows that could have won Pulitzers, we would have exchanged our Cartier rings. For our first dance, we would have swayed to the jazz standard "That's All," as sung by

Judy Garland by way of 3-D hologram. Veuve Clicquot would have flowed freely. The cake would have been vanilla and wrapped in a coffee mousse. Would that have tasted good? In my fantasy it did.

These dream nuptials were shaped by the wedding-industrial complex, a symptom of the disease that is late-stage capitalism. This fantasy was just that, a fantasy: juvenile, ostentatious, and financially irresponsible. It was a fantasy I kept mostly to myself, to my daydreams. There was no shoebox in my closet in Las Vegas, nothing that contained clippings from *Brides* magazine or Vows, the *Times* wedding section. Though my Pinterest account did have a wedding mood board, which I've since archived. Most of the pins were photos of the library at Vassar and other weddings organized by the Dewey decimal system. There were white columns, white flowers, white linens. Everything and everyone white. Even then, my subconscious projected onto Pinterest my desire for a white married name, for a wedding that made me and my groom "Misters Ford," "Messrs. Hughes," or "Mr. and Mr. Jones."

In my less colonialist daydreams, it's not the Judy Garland hologram who sings at my wedding, but the Broadway legend, pride of the Philippines, and living Disney princess Lea Salonga. She'd require a hefty fee, I'm sure, so I inevitably imagine a future self where I become or marry rich. There's an aspect of futurity to the conjugal myth, as Roland Barthes writes in his essay "Conjugals" in *Mythologies*. Weddings are always positioned as an event to come, ahead of us. The invitations, the registries, the saving of dates. There's a sense of future planning and, thus, possibility. I've had many visions for my perfect wedding. Uniform among them is the assumption I will have one.

In "Conjugals," Barthes also describes the "mythological virtues" of what he sees as the two kinds of marriage: one he calls "the grand wedding," the other "the love match." Both are public spectacles that reinforce the positions of the upper-middle class and the lower-middle class ("aristocratic or bourgeois" and "petit-bourgeois," respectively).

The grand wedding requires a spectating crowd. It must be witnessed, held in the public square, where "money is burned, and with it the assembly is blinded." Barthes makes an example of a war hero's son's wedding in Paris in the '50s: "a consumption of riches" where "all the high offices of the bourgeois theater" are present, from both military and government, adorned with "uniforms and dress suits, steel and decorations (of the Legion of Honor)." The grand wedding insists it is only natural that a bourgeois affair be so fantastic, when the true spectacle, in reality, is the amount of wealth and power such extravagance necessitates.

The love match, on the other hand, Barthes witnesses in the marriage of Miss France '53 to her childhood friend. The beauty queen surrenders "ephemeral fame" for "the anonymity of minor comfort" in the suburbs with a humble electrician, conjuring the image of "the happy hearth." This happiness sustains the millions who belong to the petit bourgeoisie and affirms "it is not wise to leave one's condition, it is glorious to return to it." Such a union brings the spectacle home to the masses, who then feast on it, leaving them content with their station. "Love-stronger-than-glory," as Barthes describes, "renews the morale of the social status quo."

Both are myths that reinforce preexisting class positions, and Barthes saw them exemplified best by celebrity and society weddings. I imagine he would have made similar observations if he read the wedding announcements in the *New York Times*. The wedding section was first printed in the paper's inaugural issue in September 1851, and the *Times* itself admits that, for a long time, the section was exclusive to privileged society figures from prominent families. For over a century and a half, it has made news out of which bloodlines will proliferate and which fortunes have coalesced, which daughters have been traded and which names they will take—or, sometimes, keep.

The Vows section began to modernize in the 1990s and the 2000s, insists the *Times*, when the section expanded "to include people with more diversity in sexual orientation, race, socioeconomic background and age." But even as a kid in those decades, who aspired to all things New York and devoured Vows, it was clear to me which boxes must be ticked for a couple to join those ranks: an undergrad degree from a prestigious institution like an Ivy (League preferred, "Little" or "Hidden" acceptable), a doctorate to match, an impressive career path, and an even more impressive family member who can foot the wedding bill.

Naturally, I've looked into submitting to Vows. Submissions—though, "applications" might be a more accurate word—must provide names, addresses, jobs, postsecondary education, "noteworthy awards" like a Fulbright or a Rhodes, charitable activities, and the residences and careers of the couple's parents, even if they're dead. You're also asked to share how you met; readers like "a unique meeting story" or "a surprising coupling." But the more pedigreed your family and decorated your résumé, the more likely you'll catch the eye of the Vows editors, gatekeepers to the wealthy white women's sports pages. It wasn't a hard lesson to internalize as a teenager, reading the *Times* at my local Borders bookstore. I sought approval from the authorities that governed my life as a young immigrant—school, white peers, straight society. To be validated, I would have to grow up to be a merited citizen, an especially model minority, who gets to marry—like everyone else.

These days, it's true that Vows is more racially diverse—and queerer too. In 2019, the paper covered the wedding of Gigi Gorgeous, the trans YouTuber slash model, and Nats Getty, the gay designer slash oil heiress. Nats proposed to Gigi by helicoptering her from Paris to Vaux-le-Vicomte, the château that directly inspired Versailles. In the candlelit gardens, Nats asked for Gigi's hand in marriage with a tender speech about true love. On Gigi's YouTube channel, the video "The Proposal" has over one million views. The Vows article describes the couple's struggles with infertility, the star-studded guest list, and California governor

Gavin Newsom's toast to his goddaughter, Nats, and her new wife.

Months before that, the *Times* ran 1,500 words dedicated to a gay male couple: one spouse is a chief executive of a tech company who immigrated from Georgia in the former Soviet Union, the other a Harvard-educated doctor and son of a Taiwanese immigrant. (The article's URL on the *Times* website says the couple "wanted-love-and-to-live-american-dream.") They spent $300,000 to conceive two children via egg donors and surrogates. The couple had a ceremony in Bora Bora in the South Pacific with twenty-three guests. They had another wedding in San Francisco weeks later, where they carried grainy sonograms of their two babies, present with their daddies "in spirit."

Though these couples are queer, they also greatly resemble the more normative couples in Vows: wealthy, pedigreed, educated, and keen on becoming parents. It's as if they all come from the same atelier, designed under the same house aesthetics, motifs, and values. They are spectacles that reinforce class ideals and divides, as Barthes might posit, myths spun by the bourgeoisie that glorify the haute and placate the petit. The queer love match of the doctor and the tech exec is sanctified by their pursuit of a nuclear family, projecting the image of a happy hearth. The grand wedding of Nats and Gigi burns the oil money and blinds the audience with "a complete fairy-tale engagement," a tale little kids of all genders have learned to want.

These marriages seem to manifest another conjugal myth: that of the grand love. In each, we witness not love-greater-than-glory, as in Barthes's myth of the love match, but a love match *deserving* of glory, as in the grand wedding. Never mind that these couples have the bank statements to fund their fairy tales; let us believe love is what foots the bill. It's common in today's Vows section to find romances that inspire readers, stories where love conquers all, whether adversity, borders, or social stigma. That was the literal song and dance we told at my parents' second wedding, valorizing a grand love that withstood the tests of distance and time. This new myth seems to say: If you work or spend or love hard enough, you will get your happy ending. What comes after, in act two, is up to you.

That said, my parents' marriage—anyone's marriage, in Vows or not—is at once simpler and more complicated than myth. They got married to address the unsexy logistics of sharing a life: estates and wills, power of attorney, immigration and citizenship. "Pragmatism," Noah said, was one of the reasons he got married. Given the laws under which we love, there are still legal benefits afforded to married couples that unmarried couples can't access. Noah told me, "The phrase 'my husband' has proven shockingly useful in social and medical situations." I imagined for a moment how reassuring it must be to write on a medical form or on travel insurance or on the back of a passport: "In case of emergency, call my husband."

At Noah's wedding, I pressed Vincent about his views on marriage. Did he really think it a prison? "It's historically been a tool of social control," he said, pouring wine for both of us. Marriage makes living with one partner socially and economically easier, he allowed, but it's an archaic system wherein women become property, wealth is hoarded, and class hierarchies go unchallenged. (Vincent studied Barthes too, in the original French.) He swirled his wine, admiring its legs. "Marriage elevates the model of the nuclear family as superior to the chosen families in which you and I have found belonging, especially as queer foreigners of color." He took a sip from his glass. "Isn't that why you hate being single?"

I asked Vincent if he would ever get married. He's not entirely opposed to the idea, but his marriage would "not be about homonormativity and emulating straight people." It would be informed by his commitment to a world without violence—"including the violence of monogamy mythology," he said—and the freedom to create his own family structures. He produced from his pocket a pill bottle of Truvada and took one with his rosé. "Marriage must have ties that support self, family, and community," Vincent said. He gave me a small blue tablet as well. "Never ties that bind."

As a gay man, this is the balancing act I take into account in deciding if marriage is right for me: how to subvert an outdated institution while leveraging its benefits to align it with my personal and political values. My married friends have wrestled with this too, have found ways to make it work for them. Some arrangements are private to the couple in their marriage, some an open couple might share with others, at their discretion. The wedding, then, is the opportunity to make the public statements, to define the context and terms of a marriage before a spectating crowd.

Friends have personalized the more traditional elements of weddings—their gift registries, who walks down the aisle, and who "gives away" the bride. There was the registry that had us donate to queer community centers of the couple's choosing; there was the processional where the grooms' mothers walked with them; and there was the bride who walked alone to meet her partner at the church altar.

I know gay couples who have wed in religious ceremonies, but most of my queer peers have eschewed them entirely. My neighbors, a poet and a journalist, married at a botanical garden in their hometown. Then there were the two grooms who held their wedding in a friend's backyard. They did all the cooking, just as they do for Communion— their regular dinner parties where many of us, their guests, first met. Whether to reduce costs, buck religious conservatism, or align with personal beliefs, weddings today vary in styles and customs, are made-to-measure affairs for the celebrating couple.

This trend isn't exclusive to queer people. The straights have been doing interfaith ceremonies for longer than we've been able to do faith-based ceremonies at all. It follows that they've long been remixing and discarding traditions: jumping the broom one moment, then smashing the glass the next; posing for photographs in her white dress and his kurta, or his tuxedo and her cheongsam (or his kurta and her cheongsam). So it might be naïve of me to think that queers gave the straights permission to also fuck with their weddings and marriages, that we have led the way in this regard—as we've done in most things.

At Noah's wedding, as Vincent and I took a breather from tearing up the dance floor, we both agreed that a wedding is an opportunity ("an excuse," he said) to throw a party for those whom you count as family, to celebrate who you love, and to declare how you love. I think that's why all my married friends chose to write their own vows. In the promises in the backyard, the poetry in the garden, the commitments Noah and Evan pledged before the people they loved most, they got to define love, friendship, and fidelity in their own words, on their own terms.

It's the vows I get stuck on, when I picture my future wedding now. I suppose that's because I don't have a man to dream them for, to dream them with. In my old fantasy nuptials, with the chorus and the castle, I never thought about what the vows would signify, other than our brilliant ways with words. But every other facet of the event signified an aspect of my personal lore. The choir of gay men and Judy Garland indicated that I'm a friend of Dorothy's. The location honored my sense of belonging at Vassar, a privileged white institution that showered me with money and nepotism as a young adult. The Louboutins and Givenchy, the Veuve and Cartier, they represented my frivolous materialism and basic Francophilia. The processional music described how I made a habit of falling in love after only ten minutes. (I used to think this an endearing feature, as opposed to a design flaw.)

In my fantasy, the Cupid and Psyche tapestries were more incidental—at first. But the more I consider it, the more embarrassed I am that the allegory was fitting. In the myth, the mortal Psyche fails the trials set for her by the goddess Venus and is rescued from her fate by Cupid's love for her. Only by wedding a god and marrying into Olympus does she achieve her happy ending and find belonging, too outcast as she was among her fellow mortals. (That said, her difference lay in her otherworldly beauty—wish I could relate!)

This was the kind of grand love I wanted: redemptive, life saving. I was a young immigrant in white America—too foreign, too queer, too brown—and dreaming of salvation through idealized love.

I CAME OUT to my mother when I was thirteen, a year after our move to the United States. The car didn't swerve off the road or crash into a lamppost. She didn't even blink. She said she knew and that mothers always know. That memory came up at dinner ten years later, over the weekend of my college graduation. My mother admitted that, when I first came out, "Natakot ako para sa'yo."

She feared for me, having witnessed the kind of violence queer people face. She thought of her gay peers, who experienced such intense social intolerance that they internalized that homophobia. Carrying such deep self-hatred, she saw how they could not love themselves enough to love others. My mother brought me to the US not only for a better education but also, she hoped, so that I might come to love myself more easily here, in an allegedly more progressive society than our de facto theocracy in the Philippines.

We were at Sunday mass in Las Vegas, in the summer of 2008, when a priest gave a homophobic homily, speaking against the legalization of same-sex marriages in nearby California. It was the same familiar message, condemning homosexuality as a sin and sentencing such sinners to hell. My ears grew hot. My mother walked out of the church with me in the middle of the service. She assured me that she loved me and all facets of my identity, told me that God did too, that He loved all His creations. I appreciated her support, always have. Still, the hateful priest underscored the fact that, as a gay man, I would face hate on all sides of the Pacific.

I was an alien in America already. As a Filipino immigrant, there were barriers in my way—the culture, the language—and those ready to remind me I was unwelcome in this land. To come out, as early as I did, meant I'd be walking this doubly dangerous path as a visibly queer brown foreigner while navigating the usual slings and arrows of middle school and high school. Kids who were white and black and brown—all straight, as far as I could tell—named me and my conflagration of differences, calling me a "wetback" (not quite), a "chink" (almost), a "faggot" (bingo!). They couldn't always get it right, but they knew I was unlike them. "Ortile" was nonwhite, unpronounceable, unidentifiable in the United States. I needed a new name, one that would offer camouflage, let me blend in with my surroundings.

Since I couldn't change my queerness, my skin, or my name—not yet—I kept my head down. I played the model minority, my nose diligently in books and my strange name consistently on the honor roll. By my college graduation, I made my mother proud. I wore my Americana and posed with her for pictures on the Vassar lawn, finishing school with honors and a job at a popular website waiting for me in New York. The next day, she and my stepfather helped me move into the city. Though I would be far from my mother, she found consolation in the fact that I succeeded in making it to this city I so admired, would be surrounded by my gay peers and more open-minded people, with the freedom to love myself and to love others as I wished.

Would she come to my wedding, I asked her, and take another trip to Vassar for the ceremony? Of course, she said, we'll be there. She was no longer afraid for me: "Natakot ako dahil mahal kita. Gusto ko lang na masaya ka." I love you too, I replied, and assured her I would keep achieving, would find that happiness, that man to love.

I made a habit of speaking into the world the inevitability of my wedding. It would happen, I promised my mother. I would find a grand love, just as she had. My marriage would offer the final proof that my mother's fears for her gay son were unfounded, that she didn't have to worry about me. At the same time, it would prove, to myself and to America, that I belonged here, had played this game by the rules and won.

I was still that gay teenager of the 2000s, with the Human Rights Campaign sticker on his three-ring binder, signing online petitions in favor of marriage equality so he and others like him could emulate straight monogamous couples. My political stance was still, "I'm just like you."

That was the unofficial slogan of the nationwide campaign for marriage equality, which has dominated public discourse around the rights of queer people for the past twenty years. It's partly due to the outsized influence of LGBTQ advocacy organizations like the Human Rights Campaign, whose boards of directors and staff of primarily white gay cisgender men get to steer the conversation. This overemphasis on marriage equality makes the fight for LGBTQ rights look like a single-issue kind of activism to someone outside queer spaces and even to those within them. As a teen with a NOH8 profile picture on MySpace, I naïvely thought that equality for gay people like me simply meant having the freedom to marry the love of my life—once I met him.

"The pursuit of marriage equality makes some sense," Lisa Duggan writes in the journal the Scholar & Feminist Online. She lists certain benefits: equal rights under law, access to private health care, and "inclusion in the elementary structures of kinship recognition." The institution of marriage does not provide full equality, Duggan writes, nor does it provide universal health care or, as Vincent reminded me at Noah's wedding, "expansively reimagined forms of kinship that reflect our actual lives." That we now have the federal freedom to marry is a net-plus, certainly. After years of being denied basic rights, it's meaningful that we get to be recognized as fully human, to have our partnerships recognized as real, even if just by a bureaucracy. We get to visit our partners at the hospital, to share insurance benefits, to be in Vows, to have the fairy-tale engagement, to build the nuclear family—but at what cost?

Our activism has focused so much on this battlefront that we've lost sight of other urgent gaps in the laws that protect queer people in our society. As of this writing, of the 50 states in the US, only 21 prohibit housing discrimination based on both sexual orientation and gender identity; only 19 ban insurance exclusions for transgender health care; only 17 have laws that protect queer kids from conversion therapy, recognizing it as a form of abuse. And there is nothing in Title VII, the federal law that prohibits employment discrimination, that explicitly forbids

discrimination based on sexual orientation or gender identity. (A generous reading of Title VII may ban such forms
of discrimination, but as of this writing, we are waiting to
hear from Justice Brett Kavanaugh and the other eight jus-
tices on the Supreme Court on three cases that may limit
such a reading of the law.) It is distressing to lack legal protections in those situations when we, in our lives as queer
people, are more likely to need a job, a home, and health
care that affirms rather than denies our identities, than we
are to get married.

A focus on marriage equality narrows our activism and
places the institution on a pedestal. It privileges queer relationships that adhere to the traditional nuclear family
structure and ignores queer lives and families that don't fit
that model. When the Supreme Court ruled that bans on
same-sex marriages violate the Constitution, Justice An-
thony Kennedy wrote ardently, perhaps too much so, about
the valors of marriage: "No union is more profound than
marriage, for it embodies the highest ideals of love, fidelity,
devotion, sacrifice, and family. In forming a marital union,
two people become something greater than once they were."
What then of loving partnerships and chosen families without legal recognition? What then about single people, who
are apparently lesser than married couples?

I wasn't aware of these criticisms as an impressionable
teenager in Las Vegas, not yet. They weren't relevant in
the life I envisioned for myself. With my Human Rights
Campaign stickers, NOH8 profile picture, and an "It Gets

Better" video on my personal YouTube channel, I wanted to appeal to the majority, to play the gay best friend on a primetime sitcom. To a certain extent, I found sanctuary as a queer kid at a performing arts high school, but I was still measuring myself by how closely I resembled my straight white peers, they who had the right to marry, who could have their weddings—everything and everyone white—and the 2.5 kids, the white picket fence, and the Chevy in the driveway. Equality as a queer person, I believed, meant being able to live a life that resembled the lives of straight people. I wanted their rights and protections rather than my own.

It's no wonder I so easily bought into this sort of attitude, this homonormativity. It closely resembles the Asian model minority myth, which proposes the idealized image of boot-strapping Asian Americans who aspire to whiteness and are thus deemed unthreatening by white Americans. Within these two frameworks, both animated by a deference to the dominant group, those who prioritize assimilation are rewarded, deemed worthier than other minorities of rights and privileges, thereby inhibiting solidarity with those who don't follow the same path. Still unsure as a gay teen how to create spaces for myself and my kin, I sought belonging from those who could elevate me from my subaltern station. Total assimilation into America was my goal. My name stood in my way.

In the US, Ortile was symbolic of all that marked me as undesirable, rejectable, Other. The weight of my difference grew so heavy, so quickly that I asked my mother if I could drop Ortile too, as she had in 2005, the year she divorced my father and then married my stepfather in Las Vegas. As I saw it, marriage offered an opportunity to be freed of your trauma. My mother seemed relieved to finally be married to my stepfather, to at last shed the name that represented so much pain in her past. I wanted the same salvation.

My mother denied my request, told me that I'd be glad one day she did, "and besides, the paperwork is too complicated." So I devised other ways to rebrand myself, testing out personas online and onstage with little success. The ultimate rebranding—foolproof, I was sure—would be to take a new name through my own marriage. I might never have a career as an actor, I thought, but I'm sure I'll find someone to love me.

In middle school, my first crush was on a white boy with the surname Jones. I feel comfortable using his real surname because it's the most generic whitebread name imaginable (good luck googling him!). That blandness made him appealing to me. There would be no mispronouncing "Matthew Jones" over the phone, no misspellings on important documents, nothing to ridicule. A name like that, I believed, would free me of the baggage the name Ortile carried, strip me of my foreignness, and validate me with a sort of cultural green card wedding.

Jones was straight, so that was a dead-end. As I moved on to high school and college, I assured myself that there would be other names to take—names equally legible, infinitely more exciting, and actually belonging to gay men. With enough time and effort, I said, I would earn my vanilla wedding cake, my new married name, and 1,500 words dedicated to me and my groom in the *Times*. I didn't intentionally tailor my American life to appeal specifically to the *Times* wedding section; that's too much even for me. But its qualifying criteria aligned with the trappings of an upwardly mobile queer immigrant life as dictated by the model minority myth and homonormativity. If I could tick the boxes, I figured I might as well submit.

———

WHEN I GOT into Vassar—the historically all-women counterpart to the men-only Yale—a small part of me, that little Filipino boy from Las Vegas who devoured the *Times* at his local Borders, was glad that coverage of my grand love came closer within reach. On campus, my WASP drag became a running joke, a semi-ironic reverence for the white upper class and its stuffy customs we proclaimed to disdain.

How convenient, I said archly to my fellow Vassar Girls, that Yale insisted on bussing men to our school, their choirs of boys already tuxedoed and bow-tied. I might yet find a husband before commencement, I joked, hoping in my heart of hearts that I would.

I didn't have to look far from my own dormitory to find Adam. He lived down the hall from Noah and Vincent, my erstwhile competitors for Adam's capricious attention.

In the end, Adam chose none of us, met another man who would become his on-again-off-again boyfriend for at least four years, and only kissed me when they were broken up or on a break.

His boyfriend and I never considered each other rivals. We were compatriots who shared his ID to bypass bouncers and guards, two brown immigrants who loved a white man who loved us both. He and I respected each other, without resentment, and so developed a strange camaraderie. The only person who could fully understand why I adored Adam was, in theory, another who adored him too. We both stood by this man we knew could never stand still.

But if Adam was fickle in romance, he was constant in his charms. He was learnèd enough to drink white wine with fish, handsome as a leather club chair (in that his face was a nice place to sit), and, like me, irrepressibly ambitious. He and I were both children of working single mothers who ensured our happiness before theirs. We were devoted to them in return. In order to give our mothers their second homes on the beach or in the forest, we were determined to live up to our potential.

He had known me at my most unsure and vulnerable, seen me stripped of my armor, yet still thought me brilliant and brave. I loved him too—his care, his cleverness, his laughter I wished to bottle—even on the days when he was not his best self. In my fantasies, however, I turned Adam into an accessory, a means to a goal. In the future I dreamt for us, I would join him in a sacred marriage and, like

Psyche, be subsumed by a husband. Vows would announce how I had dropped Ortile and taken Adam's surname, a readable one evoking lumber and moss.

Stephen fulfilled the same requirements in my fantasies. He was my first boyfriend in New York, with a name luminous as his smile, as the sun, and he was the center of my solar system for longer than was healthy. I envied him, an all-American boy, down to the stars and stripes around his shoulders at his family's farm for the Fourth of July. I met him two days upon moving to the city, was enchanted by his good morning texts, how his body fit against mine, and the way he moved through the world, with careless grace and mom-and-dad's credit card.

At the Pride March that year, I blacked out before sunset and woke up after dark in the twin bed in his Williamsburg bedroom. By the amber glow of the streetlights outside, I found him sleeping on the couch, learned that I'd left my bag at a restaurant in the West Village and that he'd gone back to get it after tucking me in. I pulled him into his bed and, with my sunburnt arms around him, kissed the nape of his neck. I'd been in distress, and how lucky was I, to have my very nice prince.

I thought Stephen was my fairy-tale ending, thought I would never again find a man this chivalrous and this good-looking and this into me—until I saw less of his kindness, less of his pretty face, less of him at all. He could be unreadable, inflexible, so aloof he bordered on cold. In response, I was paranoid and vicious and incredibly me: One night, I stole his phone, read his texts, and asked him, "Are you dating someone else?" Stephen paused, tightened my duvet around himself. "You're not lying to me in my bed."

My boyfriend said, "I'm not *dating* anyone." The next morning, we woke up with our backs to each other.

To celebrate one of our month-aversaries, we broke up. We'd been making each other miserable. I demanded too much of Stephen: twice-a-week dates, the dissolution of boundaries, and the constant assurance I was desired and therefore invincible. I yearned for his name and his weight on me, his white body as coverture. That would make me safe, I thought, protected by someone in possession of what I lacked. Not money or success but simply his mass or his matter. A boy like him matters more, according to the physics of our world, gets to take up more space than I do.

Nate certainly did, magnetic as he was, whether online or in real life. Gay Twitter seemed to fawn over him—industrious and intelligent, a toothsome data wonk—and I wanted that validation by extension, to move up in court by becoming his favorite. Though Nate was tough to pin down, I clung to the evidence that he was the one to DM me first, believed that meant he wanted me. It would've made for a great column in Vows; our twenty-first-century meet-cute ticked the "unique meeting story" box on the editors' checklist. The headline: "Direct Messages Directly to the Heart."

I dreamt of a future that revolved around Nate—or someone who resembled him, who fit into homely visions of a "normal" American life. Green and uncooked as I was, I had yet to internalize Vincent's advice to decenter white men like Nate (and Adam, and Stephen, and even Christian—someone who didn't submit to, as Vincent put it, the violence of monogamy mythology). Like the more traditional wives in Vows might, I still wanted to take my husband's name.

"I'd change my name," Nate said on our first date. His was an immigrant name as well, a Slavic toponymic with a suffix denoting nobility. Perhaps he thought it was not refined enough, not WASPy enough, too strange or too foreign compared to those of our pedigreed peers. When I said that I found no fault in his name, he challenged me to say it.

At my perfect pronunciation of the title I hoped to take, Nate scoffed. "You're just good with names."

There were other men, too, other names more unique and intriguing than "Jones." There was a lovely pianist with a chalet in the Swiss Alps and a Germanic name to match. There was that strapping MFA grad with sturdy biceps, a formidable novel, and a venerable Jewish patronymic. There were those baptized with the names of Catholic saints and those named in various languages with words meaning "peace" or "good man" or "hero" or "love letter." But none snared my fantasies the way that a Hughes or a Ford did— simple names, common in this country, yet imbued with connotations of industry and wealth, of legacies and roots, of eternal, inarguable Americana.

My delusions of salvation via marriage were persistent, allowed for a rotating cast of men to take a role opposite me. The lion's share of my romantic life was spent pursuing men who might be my rescuers, royal princes representing unimaginative ideals: good-looking and white, with an expensive haircut and a passing fancy for me. Though they varied in style and speech, careers and levels of commitment, I expected from them something they could never give me—deliverance from being Other.

It's no surprise that, of all the men I met in the steam room, I chose to go home with Theo. He was older, wealthy, white. He welcomed me into his apartment, arranged like a gallery of beautiful objects. Theo stood among them, sculpted like the Laocoön, though without any sons and tied up only when he wished. I was still tied up in colonial imaginations—others' and mine. I couldn't help but see Theo as a white savior, a masculine white man with an "Island Boy" he might be paying for.

I spent a night with Theo in the week my roommates asked me to move out. Without a security deposit or savings to fund another move in New York, I weighed my options over breakfast in Theo's stainless-steel kitchen: I could move into his guest room, ask to borrow the money from him, or ask him for cash outright. Theo had just spent thousands of dollars on a pair of accent tables from Sotheby's, so he had the pennies to spare. Or he could be my guarantor, sign my lease in his name, which meant "beautiful fortress."

Before the solution came in a wire transfer from my parents, I had enough sense to at least rule out marriage with Theo. A growing part of me began to resent the idea of being saved, to consider the possibility that I might not need saving at all. (Besides, imagine our Vows headline: "In Chelsea, He Kept a Kept Man.") Still, my first instinct was an old one: I wanted a man to give me a home.

Choose me, I once beseeched, and toast to me and my grand love in 1,500 gushing words. I dreamt of the tuxedoed choir and the procession, the matching suits and the rings in gold triplicate. I wanted love and to live the American Dream, a love deserving of glory. I was willing to make the Vows, to marry into whiteness. I was willing to love and so become a Mr. Hughes, a Mr. Ford, a Mr. Jones. To those who might welcome me into their homes, their lives, their America, I delivered my old plea: Grant me your name and give me your roots. Love only me and let me be fixed.

―――――――

A YEAR INTO my life in New York, I got to choose my name.

I had been musing aloud on Twitter about shortening my handle to just @ortile. There's a certain mystique to being a one-name entity, in the way there's only one Cher or Madonna, one @jack, @millie, or @krutika. People tweeted at me, replying that I could just change it myself. But any alteration to my handle unauthorized by the platform would have cost me my blue checkmark, my verification as @MattOrtile. (A petty concern and perk of working at a website that capitalized off not just what we created but who we were.)

The social media editor at work read my tweets and sent me a message. He could have my name changed via his connections at Twitter, he said. He just had to confirm: *u sure u wanna be @ortile?*

I thought about grabbing @matt, but it was already taken by a white Brit who works in radio. Just as well; there are already too many Matts online. But according to the genealogy portal Forebears.io, I was the sole Ortile in all of New York state, certainly the only one within our insular media industry. People at the office were already calling me by my last name, proud that they knew how to say it, once they got to know me and I added the phonetic pronunciation to my Twitter bio (Or-TEE-lay).

yes please, let's go with @ortile!! I typed, before second-guessing myself. I deleted the second exclamation point and hit send.

My name changed within twenty-four hours. The social media editor reminded me that if I altered the handle myself, I would lose the verification badge. For now, he said, it's stuck as @ortile. That's fine, I replied. I had no plans to become anyone else.

This was in the spring of 2015—a year after graduation, a year after I first moved to Manhattan, alone and lost. I felt untethered, aching for a home, removed as I was from my culture and my people. The antidote, I had thought in my youth, was to let go of my birth country entirely. It's the immigrant's paradox: I hoped that forgetting what I missed would relieve me of something to miss at all, that nicer things, stateside things, might take their place, that I might assimilate into this American life and call this land home instead. Surrendering my Filipinoness, wishing to surrender my name—these survival tactics did not heal but rather deepened the wounds of severance, the cuts and lacerations of the immigrant experience, which, in turn, increased my desperation to be cured, to be fixed.

My name was an obstacle to that, reeking too much of Otherness. In the face of violence, I'd be protected, I thought, by changing my name to one more legible, clear, white. But Ortile carries a strange history and, in fact, was used as a tool by the Philippines' first colonizers. It comes from the *Catálogo alfabético de apellidos*, the compendium of Catholic names the Spanish brought to Las Islas Filipinas. To abolish a native name and make their subjects more legible, more firmly ensconced in their new positions as the subjects of Mother Spain, a bunch of white people named an old Filipino family Ortile.

As a word, Ortile is likely imported from the Italian "cortile." It refers to a courtyard, an outdoor space surrounded on all sides but open to the sky, a staple of Italian architecture, as seen in palazzos like the Pitti and Medici-Riccardi. Cortile means "little court," a diminutive of the Italian "corte." In Spanish, the feminine "la corte" is also a court. But the masculine "el corte" means "cut," a cutting—"el corte de una flor." I prefer the idea of a courtyard, with space for air or a fountain or maybe even a garden. I'd rather not know more of being severed.

Colonization works by cutting off peoples from their own heritage—be it traditions or languages, orthographies or names. Spain supplanted the animist faiths of our precolonial ancestors with Roman Catholicism. They gave us new names, destroyed documents written in our native scripts and replaced them with the Latin alphabet, punished us for communicating in our own words. They taught us Spanish for the same reason Americans taught us English: to homogenize colonial subjects under one tongue, one fist. ("You're in America," we're told—not only as immigrants to the US but as erstwhile property of this American empire. "Speak English.")

From the moment the United States purchased the Philippines from Spain, white Americans relied on cultural propaganda and counted on their Filipino subjects to internalize their supposed inferiority. My colonial inheritance gave me away when I dreamed of white flowers, white linens, and a white husband. I didn't think twice when I picked those images to represent my happily wedded bliss, accepting whiteness as the default, the peak of beauty. I hoped the glorious spectacle of sacred marriage would save me from my feelings of severance, my distance from the Philippines, by heralding my full acceptance into America.

To be fixed in this country, I believed I had to surrender my name.

I have surrendered enough. I have changed who I am, modeled the ideal brown brother for too long. Even with Americana as armor, the poison in this land maims me, rejects me, tells me to go back to where I came from. Even at my most polished, respectable, and eloquent, worthy of basic citizenship, I am held at arm's length in the framework of white supremacy, commended and marginalized at once, patronized for how beautifully I speak a language that their empire has beaten into my tongue.

Despite this, I occupy a relatively privileged position in American society. By buying into the model minority myth, I've been able to assimilate in certain ways, seen as "acceptable" up to a point. I cannot stand idly by, rest on my laurels, and leave my privilege unutilized when it could be leveraged in the name of those who face oppression, regardless of similarity or disparity to me. I should not maintain the status quo and continue assimilating as a model minority. I refuse to accept my fate as a doomed crab in a bucket, nor climb up its sides without bringing others with me.

Solidarity means choosing to topple the bucket altogether—together. Because no amount of submitting and assimilating, merits or decorations of steel, will put an end to oppression. Because no matter what we do, there is an America that will never count us among their lot, never believe we are like them. Because this is true. We are not just like them. We have paid too much in the currency of our bodies, our emotional labor and fucksweat, to persist in appealing to an America that rejects us, that tells us to retreat.

For me, part of standing my ground is the retention of my name, of all that makes me Other. That I became @ortile as I approached one of the more difficult and testing periods of my life can't have been a coincidence. My gut told me to stand by this name, to reclaim it as mine, as a source of power and faith in myself, ingrained as it was with my personal trauma and a colonial history. I was beginning to unlearn—even to unspool completely, emboldened by rage and prosecco at a holiday party—and to think for myself.

Every day, I choose the name Ortile as a promise, a vow, a commitment to resist further assimilation, to who I am and what I am fighting for. Just as my mother foretold, I am glad I kept my name.

———————

THERE'S A BLOG post on Oprah.com, dated 2009, where a woman recalls writing to Vows and mentioning to the *Times* that she would not be changing her name—and neither would her fiancé: "The groom is keeping his name." The paper of record did not publish that sentence in the announcement. ("They probably thought it was a typo," she says.) At the top of the second paragraph, however, the editors were sure to note that the bride would keep her name.

This prevailing expectation of a woman taking her husband's name can be traced to marriage's origins as a business transaction. Since antiquity, marriage has been, first and foremost, a consolidation of assets. In taking his name, she becomes his family, as well as his property. Jane Jones marries John Smith and so becomes Jane Smith, who is addressed as "Mrs. John Smith" and defers to John in all financial matters, as only he can own land or take out a bank loan. Laws viewed a wedded couple as one person—because, apparently, only the husband was a full person. In this way, my younger self had the right idea about marriage: At a wedding, two become one.

In 2015, the *Times* analyzed the number of brides in Vows who keep their maiden names. They reported that 29.5 percent kept their names in 2014—up from 26 percent in 2000 and 16.2 percent in 1990. This is a very selective sample, of course, but the pattern held when the *Times* pulled data from sources beyond the paper. The trend began in the 1970s, at the height of second-wave feminism, when state laws still required that a married woman use her husband's name to apply for a passport and even to vote. To keep one's name in marriage, then, was to resist the patriarchy implicit in the matrimonial institution and society broadly.

But since the 2000s, according to the sociologists interviewed, the choice to retain one's unmarried name has become less of a political act of feminism than a matter of practicality. More people are marrying at later ages and so enter marriages with established careers attached to their unmarried name; it might be in the best interests of writers, for example, to keep their connections to old bylines. A newlywed interviewed in the *Times* article said she kept her surname because it's been hers for thirty-three years. "Plus, I'm Asian and he's not," she added, "so it's less confusing for me to not have a white name."

My mother kept her name because of all the paperwork. Her three weddings to my stepfather dealt with matters of divorce and annulment, citizenship and the church, so consistently keeping her maiden name helped make things less difficult. For a while, when we were living in Las Vegas, it did mean that she, my stepfather, and I all had different surnames. When I pointed this out to her, she replied, "That doesn't make us any less of a family."

The consistency and convenience of sharing one name together is a common incentive for families straight and queer alike. For some queer marriages, there's an added element of validation. In 2013, *The Atlantic* spoke to married gay and lesbian couples who believed sharing a name would make it easier to be taken seriously as life partners, as growing families. As we live in a world built on heteronormative foundations, we sometimes make allowances in the name of survival. One of the women interviewed said, "I have friends who are radical, separatist, lesbian feminists and nobody blinked when I changed my name. People understood the desire for safety we were feeling and you can't argue with safety."

That safety must have been what Noah saw as the value in marriage too—"pragmatism," he called it. When we first met at school, Noah and I differed in that he never felt the need to marry in order to be personally fulfilled. Then he met Evan. "If marriage is important to the man I love," Noah said, "then it is important to me." Their wedding in San Francisco wasn't transformative, as I had imagined my dream nuptials would be. Instead, it was an affirmation of their commitment to each other—before a spectating crowd, within a legal framework—and of the terms of their relationship, of who and how they love.

Mia and Sarah filed for a domestic partnership in the winter of 2015. When I saw on Instagram that they'd sneaked off to city hall, marriage was on my mind and I texted them heart emojis and question marks in our trio's group chat named "Family."

Sarah replied with a kissing emoji: *relax! we wouldn't have gotten married without you*

It was pragmatism again: *LOL we got DP'ed*, they said, for the health insurance and hospital visitation rights. A week later, when they had me over for cake and bubbly, they came to see it as a way to deepen their commitment and to honor the family they were building.

Obergefell v. Hodges had been decided that summer. Marriage was incontestably available to us as queer people in the United States, but domestic partnership was the right step at the right time for my sisters. Now, given the freedom to choose, many people of all genders and sexualities forgo marriage altogether. They find that their personal commitments need no legal recognition.

"If people can love together happily, what's the point of having a nice pretty paper?" Vincent's partner said to him recently, winning a smile from the Frenchman. "Benefits aside, it's pointless. I won't love you less or more after we get married." In a time where we are making more room for evolving definitions of love, friendship, and fidelity, it's a worthy question: Why go through the trouble of marrying at all?

"I want the trouble," Mia told me. "I want the ring and the honeymoon, the dress and the officiant, and I want my Filipino family to attend and take this choice I made with Catholic gravity."

Marriage still carries weight in the communities to which we belong. There's an appeal to publicly declaring and celebrating queer love before those who have historically rejected queerness. For Mia and me, as queer brown immigrants, to have a same-sex wedding would be an impactful gesture with respect to our Catholic Filipino culture. It's less a pious choice than it is punk, to leverage sacred marriage against the systems that have marginalized us for so long.

But Mia writes off marriages for vanity: where a person only discovers self-worth in marriage, where one dominates another, where there is more to be gained from the grand wedding than the partnership of consenting individuals. ("Drag me," I said.)

Above all, Sarah reminded me, being married is not a cure for loneliness. "Honestly, we've seen too many marriages crash and burn," she said over brunch, "to continue deluding ourselves that it's a silver bullet to all our problems." Marriage is not necessarily a happy ending. "If we're lucky," Sarah said, splitting a strip of bacon with me, "it won't be an ending at all."

When my mother returned to Manila full-time in 2013, to start again in her home country, she hyphenated my stepfather's surname onto hers, into a heptasyllabic double-barrel. She said it was again a matter of documentation: passports, medical forms, deeds, wills. On a personal level, she considered it another sign of their connection, one they had worked so hard to ratify in the eyes of various global authorities. It was also a public show of their commitment—especially significant in the Philippines, where it's relatively unusual to keep a maiden name.

While Filipino law does not require cognominality in marriage, it's a social expectation: Are you really his wife if you don't take his name? Is he really your husband if he doesn't wear his wedding ring? My mother wanted fewer questions, less needling. If names would effectively signal their marriage, then so be it. It matters little to their mutual promises of love, friendship, and fidelity. They have made these vows every day of their lives together—with or without wedding rings.

This is what I admire most in my mother's relationship with my stepfather—as in Mia and Sarah's partnership, as in Noah's commitment to Evan: that mutual support, the commitment to caring for one another, for a chosen family, and to accepting their care in return.

Natakot ako para sa'yo, said my mother when I first came out. She feared that I'd face hate on all sides for being different. That I'd hate myself for being Other, that I'd internalize shame so deeply I'd become unable to love for the right reasons. Sure enough, that happened, though not because I was gay. Then again, she could have anticipated, as an immigrant mother in America raising a gay son, how white men would fuck me up.

My colonial mentality snuck up on me, nearly choked me in its coils. What loosened its grip and reminds me to actively decolonize my mind and my body has been communing with people doing the same work. We build our relationships—and sustain them—with love, friendship, and fidelity.

In fact, allow me to make that promise right now, an oath of allegiance to my people and the communities we build. Let me commit this in writing here, to hold me accountable, to hold this fast: I vow to love myself with grace and have love, in turn, to share.

That's the wedding I'd like one day: a celebration of the family we've created, of the sanctuary we find in those we love. Make it a marriage of equals, a resilient romance that could cross continents and oceans, differences and divides.

Let us ready a feast and eat joy together, ensure we have enough to go around.

With that in mind, should I ever make Vows, here's a heads-up for the lucky *Times* reporter: The event will be in a garden or at city hall, in a backyard or at Vassar (without the tapestries of Cupid and Psyche, please). All my family will be there—chosen and otherwise. All three of my parents too; there's a fantasy for you. We'll nix the choir of gay men; the attendees will do. We'll keep the Judy hologram and add Lea singing live. She'll reprise her role as the goddess of love in Ahrens and Flaherty's *Once on This Island*, singing her ballad of "The Human Heart," of courage and foolishness, of a love that lives forever.

She'll sing during the procession, as we walk down the aisle. My groom will wear what he wants; it'll be his wedding too. As for me, I'll wear a barong Tagalog—with tailored linen trousers and a flowing piña cape. At the reception, there will be bottles of Veuve Clicquot and San Miguel and Manille Liqueur de Calamansi. For the cake, the frosting will be French vanilla and the sponge Filipino ube, the batter enriched with purple yam. Do take photos of our families laughing, open-mouthed and purple-tongued. Hear my mother's toast as she fears for me no more. Let the paper of record show: The groom will keep his name.

My name is Matthew Manahan Ortile. It's there on my Vassar card and my New York ID, my expired learner's permit and my two passports, blue and brown. In accordance with Filipino custom, my middle name is my mother's maiden name, meaning "inheritance." My surname is my father's and makes space for a garden, something like a sanctuary. They indicate my descent, where I come from and my roots. This name—a mouthful and all mine—I choose to keep, even when it's my turn to wear white.

ACKNOWLEDGMENTS

THANK YOU TO Remy Cawley and Ed Maxwell, my editor and my agent, both champions of my work ever since I first wrote about love and decided to call it discourse. To everyone at Bold Type Books, Type Media Center, and Hachette—particularly Brooke Parsons and Katy O'Donnell—your support has been dreamy. To my colleagues at Catapult, I'm the writer I am today because I'm the editor you've helped me become. To Nicole Chung, my boss and mentor and friend, you are a blessing and I am grateful. Thank you to my editors at BuzzFeed, past and present, for their trust—especially Isaac Fitzgerald and Kat Stoeffel, who edited two previously published essays that inspired two chapters in this book. To Ashley Ford, who has believed in me since day one, it's because of you I am here.

This book needed space and cold brew to grow, so thanks to every bar and café that let me camp for entire afternoons, even though I only bought one chocolate croissant. Shoutouts to my neighborhood mainstays Edie Jo's, Bonafini,

Parkside Creamery, and Brooklyn Perk. (Support your local small businesses!) Also, thank you to the MacDowell Colony for giving me yet another place to call home. And to Monique in Guérande: Merci pour votre générosité. La prochaine fois je reviendrai pour de vraies vacances.

Heaps of thanks to my chosen families too: Communion, my pride of Vassar Boys, and ThriveOps. Some of the aforementioned appear in these pages, and I thank them immensely for their collective memory, for sharing their lives with me, for their endless love. To my sisters, Mia and Sarah, I feel lucky to love and be loved by you. To Krutika, make this the thirty-second time.

My deepest gratitude to everyone who has read my writing over the years. Your comments and tweets and DMs are saved in my archives in a folder called "Keep Going." Thank you so much. Maraming salamat po. This is for us. Para sa atin ito.

Thank you to my parents—all three of them. To my mother, especially. I hope I have made you proud.

And to all the men I've loved before: I'm glad we made the most of the night.

Photo credit: Mia Fermindoza

Matt Ortile (or-TEE-lay) is the managing editor of *Catapult* magazine. Previously, he was the founding editor of BuzzFeed Philippines and the global publishing lead for BuzzFeed International. He is a Mac-Dowell Colony Fellow and his work has appeared in BuzzFeed News, *Self*, *Out*, and *Into*, among others. He graduated from Vassar College, which means he now lives in Brooklyn.